Published by CelebrityPress®, Orlando, FL

CelebrityPress® is a registered trademark.

Printed in the United States of America.

ISBN: 9780990706489
LCCN: 2015931045

This publication is designed to provide accurate and authoritative information with regard to the subject matter covered. It is sold with the understanding that the publisher is not engaged in rendering legal, accounting, or other professional advice. If legal advice or other expert assistance is required, the services of a competent professional should be sought. The opinions expressed by the authors in this book are not endorsed by Celebrity Press® and are the sole responsibility of the author rendering the opinion.

Most CelebrityPress® titles are available at special quantity discounts for bulk purchases for sales promotions, premiums, fundraising, and educational use. Special versions or book excerpts can also be created to fit specific needs.

For more information, please write:
CelebrityPress®
520 N. Orlando Ave, #2
Winter Park, FL 32789
or call 1.877.261.4930

Visit us online at: www.CelebrityPressPublishing.com

CELEBRITY PRESS®
Winter Park, Florida

CONTENTS

CHAPTER 37

OPPORTUNITIES EXIST IN ALL ECONOMIES — SIX STEPS TO TAKE ADVANTAGE OF THEM

CHAPTER 1

MENTAL CROSS TRAINING

BY BRIAN TRACY

We are living in the Information Age. Today, the major source of value in our society is knowledge and ideas, combined with the ability to put them into action in a speedy and efficient way. The movement from the industrial age to the service age to the information age has been so fast that most people have missed it completely. In fact, our school system is still turning out people to work at relatively unskilled jobs requiring limited education. But those jobs are all gone.

The rule today is that "the more you learn, the more you earn." The future belongs to those few men and women who continually work on themselves to upgrade their knowledge and skill in a balanced way so that they are capable of taking advantage of the opportunities that come along from day to day.

The expression "cross training" comes from athletics. World class athletes have known for many years that the only way that they can perform at their very peak is by developing all of their various muscles and abilities in a balanced way. In its simplest form, physical cross training requires that you work on endurance, strength and flexibility in a rotating format. When I was lifting weights as a young man, it was quite standard for us to work on the muscle groups that were less developed to keep them growing in balance with those muscle groups that were further ahead.

In mental cross training, you must do the same thing with your repertoire of knowledge and skills. Many economists have stated in recent years that the average income in America has not gone up since 1979. However, this is both true and false. It is true in that the average income has not gone up because there are now so many single parent homes earning lower incomes. It is false in that the income of the top 20%, those men and women like yourself who are continually learning and growing, has gone up steadily over time. You cannot do much to affect those who are missing the boat in the information age and allowing their knowledge to become obsolete. But you can help yourself by getting onto the fast track and developing a wide range of skills that enables you to perform at your very best in your field.

Don't be afraid to read outside your field. Attend an occasional seminar or lecture on a subject that may be new to you. Associate with people socially who have different interests than you and ask them about their various interests. Ask for recommendations about books to read, things to do and even places to go. Resist the temptation to get into a rut with your existing knowledge and skills, and instead, force yourself to expand your horizons by involving yourself in different mental activities.

One of the things we know is that your knowledge and skill, in any field, is becoming obsolete at a more rapid rate today than ever before. Knowledge in your field is probably doubling every two to three years. This means that your knowledge must double every two to three years as well just for you to stay even. If you want to make any progress, you have to be learning more and faster than ever before.

With mental cross training you need first of all to determine the subjects that you have to be good at in order to be in the top 10 or 20% in your field. Your job is to make the decision, right now, to go all the way to the top. And the fortunate thing is that, if anyone else has done it, you can do it as well. You simply need to follow in their tracks.

Harvard Business Review did a study some years ago on a subject that they called, "Critical Success Factors." The idea of critical success factors revolved around the discovery that in any field of endeavor there are seldom more than five to seven skill areas that you absolutely, positively have to be good at to dominate your field. There may be a hundred or a thousand things that you have to do, but there are only basically five to seven areas where you need to commit yourself to excellent performance in order to move way ahead of the rest of the field.

These critical success factors are where you begin your program of mental cross training. If you are in sales, for example, your seven critical success factors may be prospecting, getting appointments, establishing a relationship with the client, identifying the problem that the client has that your product or service will solve, presenting your product or service as the solution, closing the sale, and personal management. You will have to be absolutely, positively excellent in every one of these areas for you to be a great success in selling any product or service in any market. And here's one of the most important discoveries about mental cross training. If you are weak in any one critical area, that one area will set the height at which you use all your other skills. It will be the chief factor that determines your income and your level of success in your field. If you are absolutely excellent in six out of seven critical success factors but you are terrible in the seventh, you will be held back from ever realizing your full potential in whatever it is you do.

Let me give you an example. Let us say that you are absolutely excellent in every single part of selling except prospecting. Because of fear or negativity or competition in the marketplace, you are poor at getting appointments with new prospects who can and will buy your product or service. You may be outstanding at everything else but if you can't get in front of people, you will ultimately fail and have to leave the field.

In another example, let's say you are good at prospecting and getting appointments and establishing rapport, but when it comes to actually getting the client to take action or closing the sale, you tense up, you are unable to do it, and you leave empty handed. Again, you could be outstanding at everything except closing the sale and that alone will sabotage your entire career.

If you are in sales, or in any other field, the first thing you need to do is to identify your critical success factors, the key areas in which you must be excellent if you want to be successful. You then give yourself a score from one to ten with one being the lowest and ten being the highest in each area. You will find that wherever you have given yourself a low score, that is the area of performance that causes you the most problems. It is your primary area of stress, frustration, anxiety and underachievement in whatever it is you are doing. You need to have a score above seven in every area for you to perform excellently in a well-balanced way.

It is essential that you be perfectly honest with yourself. It will do you no good to pretend that you are good at something when in reality it is interfering with your success in your career.

Once you have worked out your critical success factors and you have given yourself a score in each of the five to seven areas, take your score to someone who knows you and who will help you by scoring you themselves. The best person for this is your boss, but if you have a friendly customer, go to your friendly customer and ask him or her if he or she will give you a score as well.

If you are in management, there will probably be seven critical success factors that determine your level of achievement in your position. They could be a variety of things but the most common, what I call the "big seven" are planning, organizing, staffing, delegating, supervising, innovating and reporting. If you are poor in any one of these seven areas, that could be sufficient, in itself, to hold you back from using all your other talents.

For example, let's say that you are excellent at planning, organizing, staffing, supervising, innovating and reporting your results to your superiors. You just have one problem. You are terrible at delegating. By the way, this is quite a common weakness in management.

If you were poor at delegating, and good at everything else, you would never achieve your full potential as a manager. You would always either delegate poorly or not at all. You may delegate to the wrong people, or you may delegate in the wrong way at the wrong time. You may delegate in such a way that nobody knows for sure exactly what it is you expect of them, and in what quantity and quality. The inability to delegate is a major reason for failure when a person becomes a supervisor or manager.

Fortunately, if you feel that you are not particularly good in a critical success factor area, like delegating, you can read books, listen to tapes and take courses, thereby bringing up your skills above seven out of ten so that this area is no longer a problem for you.

It is always easy to tell where you need to go to work on yourself in mental cross training. The areas where you are weak are the sources of your major problems in your career. They are the areas that preoccupy you and concern you the most. And, they are often the activity areas where you get the worst results. Sometimes you are fearful in those areas and become anxious when it comes to performing those activities. If you are not careful, you will have a tendency to avoid performing in those areas, or even go one step further and convince yourself that you are already quite good in those areas. This is why it is so important that you ask other people around you to evaluate you in an objective way and tell you how well they think you are doing.

There is a new management technique that is becoming quite popular throughout the country. It is called the "360 degree method." In this managerial method, managers and subordinates are evaluated by all the people who work around them. Questionnaires are sent out to everyone within an organization and each person is asked to evaluate their superiors and their subordinates. These questionnaires are then collected and analyzed for presentation at a meeting where each person sits in the middle of a 360 degree circle and is critiqued and evaluated by all the people with whom he or she works.

If this is done properly, it is extremely helpful to people. It comes as a great shock to most people that in areas where they think they are quite good, their co-workers and subordinates think they are quite poor.

In psychology there is a word called "Scotoma." This refers to a blind spot. What psychologists have found is that most of us have blind spots with regard to certain areas of our lives. We have blind spots with regard to certain qualities and characteristics that we either have or don't have. And what I have discovered in my consulting career is that people are blind in the areas where they are the very weakest.

For example, I had an executive working for me some years ago who felt that he was absolutely excellent at hiring people. He would not take any advice or input from anyone. He made his hires from the seat of his pants. And every single person that he hired turned out to be a disaster. Eventually, his right and authority to hire people had to be removed completely. This inability of his to learn how to properly interview and select the right people eventually proved to be fatal in his career. He had to go back to working as a salesman and an individual entrepreneur because he was simply incapable of picking people to work with him, no matter what position he had.

So here's the question. What are your scotomas? What are the areas where you are weak? What are the areas you need to work on to bring yourself up to a high level of performance? If you are not sure, have the courage and the honesty to go to other people and ask for their feedback. Remember, feedback is the breakfast of champions. You can't get better unless someone else is willing to give you an honest critique and help you see yourself as you really are.

If you are in sales, it is absolutely essential that you get your sales manager or someone else to go out with you at least once per month for an entire day to evaluate your sales performance. When this person comes out, he or she should sit there quietly and say nothing, and just watch the way you interact with the customer. Afterwards this person should tell you exactly what they saw, both the good and the bad. Unless you have this kind of honest feedback, it is impossible for you to improve. But once you get this feedback, instead of becoming defensive, make a decision to go to work on yourself and bring up that skill area so that it is no longer a limitation on your performance.

The final point that I need to make on mental cross training is that whatever knowledge and skill you have today, it is not sufficient for the future. One educational journal recently said that fully 99% of what you know today will be irrelevant 10 years from now. Knowledge in your area is doubling every two to three years. This means that your knowledge must be doubling as well. Wayne Gretsky is famous for saying that the reason that he plays hockey so well is because while most people are going to where the puck is, he goes to where the puck is going to be.

Your question must be, "Where is your puck going to be?" What knowledge and skills will you have to have three to five years from today in order to continue earning an excellent living in your particular field. What talents and abilities are you going to have to develop that may be brand new? Are you already excellent with a computer? Can you function well in terms of communication skills? Are you excellent at every part of your job today? Whatever it is, and wherever you are, make a decision to identify your weakest areas and then go to work on yourself. Make a decision to learn what you need to learn so that you can accomplish what you need to accomplish.

There are three rules that I want to leave you with regard to mental cross training. First, it doesn't matter where you are coming from. All that matters is where you are going. The future is more important than the past. You can't change the past, but you can change your future by changing what you do today.

The second rule is that, for your life to get better, you must get better. If you want to earn more, you must learn more. Knowledge is the chief source of value today. If you want to improve the quality of your life, you must improve the quality of your knowledge and skills.

Third, you can learn anything that you need to learn to become any person that you want to become and to achieve any goal that you can possibly set for yourself. There are no limits except the limits that you set on your own mind.

Mental cross training is a discipline that you can use all the days of your life. Make a decision, right now, to bring up your skill levels in the critical success factors of your career to the point where you are one of the best people doing what you do. Then, expand your thinking and your learning outward and begin to take in new subjects. Dedicate yourself to lifelong learning. Remember, your mind is like a muscle. If you don't use it, you lose it, but if you continue reading, listening to tapes, taking additional courses and working on the development of your knowledge and skills, your future will be unlimited.

By developing the habit of regular mental cross training you can become one of the most competent, confident and capable people in your field. You can fulfill all your dreams and achieve all your ambitions. You can push to the front and lead the field.

From this day forward, resolve to become a "do-it-to-yourself project." Begin and continue the lifelong process of continually getting better in all the areas that are important to you. Just as a champion athlete develops all of his or her muscles symmetrically and in balance, you must develop your mental muscles in a balanced way as well. Mental cross training is the key to making yourself a master of the information age and putting you in complete control of your future destiny. Go for it!

About Brian

Brian Tracy is Chairman and CEO of Brian Tracy International, a company specializing in the training and development of individuals and organizations. Brian's goal is to help people achieve their personal and business goals faster and easier than they ever imagined.

Brian Tracy has consulted for more than 1,000 companies and addressed more than 5,000,000 people in 5,000 talks and seminars throughout the US, Canada and 55 other countries worldwide. As a Keynote speaker and seminar leader, he addresses more than 250,000 people each year.

For more information on Brian Tracy programs, go to: www.briantracy.com

CHAPTER 2

FINANCIAL ADVICE IS WORTH A FORTUNE

BY BRIAN FARKAS

When I was ten, my mother was an office manager in Farmingdale, N.Y where we lived. There was a man who came in monthly to her job and he was their CPA. My mother knew I loved cars so she would have my father who was a night worker bring me over when the CPA would show up because he had a Rolls Royce and a Jaguar XKE. It was then I thought that he must make a lot of money to be able to afford these cars and so I decided I would become a CPA.

Well, life changed for us on September 17, 1971 when my father died. It was a strange morning I'll never forget. I heard noises coming from my room at about 4:40 am and went out to see what was going on. My mother and sister were crying. So I asked what was wrong and was told, "Daddy didn't make it." I said Daddy didn't make it where and was told that Daddy died. I don't know to this day why I asked these questions, but I did: Could we afford to live in this house?...and could we afford to eat?...to which my mother answered that she didn't know. I said at 16 to my mother, "Don't worry, I'll take care of it."

In April of 1971, my father who knew he was dying brought me into the NY Times to work as a Junior Pressman. I started shaping up – which meant I traveled an hour to NYC and would wait to see if they needed me to work and if they did, I worked and got paid and if they didn't, I went home without getting paid.

After my fathers' passing, I sat down with my mother and started going over the bills and income. Her income, the social security that we would receive and what the shortage was. We had a mortgage on the house, a car payment on a 1970 Pontiac and credit card debt. I also found out we had no money. No savings. They didn't have IRA's back then. No life insurance. What were we to do?

In reviewing things, I took a look at everything and made a budget to pay off the highest interest accounts first, and within a year all of the credit cards were paid off and we started to save money. The only thing was where to put the money so it would earn the most. It was then that I started studying about investments, and the nights I worked, I read the NY Times from cover to cover. It was only 2 years after my fathers' passing that we had money in the bank, money in a Dreyfus account, and because her car was a lemon, we got her a new car. Upon all of her friends seeing her new car, people started asking where she got the money from and her answer was to talk to me…as she had more money now than when there were 2 incomes. So before I knew it, I was helping her friends who were widows and divorcees with their money issues. It was then I decided I should become a Financial Advisor and not a CPA.

In college, I started learning about stocks, bonds, mutual funds, options etc. I started asking my professors about stocks as they knew my family's situation. So I bought stocks. I would take the dividends to help pay the bills. I also worked hard, especially when school was out. Then I would shape up whenever school was out the next day. And if I couldn't work at the NY Times, I would run cross town and shape up the NY Daily News, in NYC, Brooklyn or Long Island City. As I would get more money, I would buy more stocks.

I also took on other jobs as I could. I ran a disco. I tried working for First Investors, an investment company that I answered an ad for and attended a free seminar on how to become a stockbroker. In 1979, I went to work for my friends' father, Hank, who owned a Coin and Gold store in Bellmore, and before I knew it, I was trading coins, gold, silver and jewelry. After a robbery shootout, where Hank got shot, he shot one robber, shot and killed another robber, and tried to shoot the third robber. He and his son escaped and I came driving down the road, seeing Hank and Henry running west and another man (the third robber) running east. A month later, after another customer who was selling us lots of stuff had come in with the police, because the stuff he was selling us was "hot," Hank decided Henry and I should find a business and he would put up the money. That night I got a call from my sister that my Uncle was dying and did I know anyone who wanted to buy his business, *Manhattan Pennysaver*. I said we would, Henry and I. But Henry didn't want to leave his father at that point, so I did it myself.

On 12/17/79, my 25th birthday, I went to a Manhattan hospital where my uncle was and gave him a $5000 deposit. And on January 1, 1980 I took over *Manhattan Pennysaver*, the smallest of five advertising publications in NYC. I started a Printing Company called F.U. Printing and sold out everything on 12/31/1986, when it was the largest of three.

I then went interviewing at some of the big wire firms, like Merrill Lynch and Shearson Lehman, only to find out that because I wasn't right out of school and didn't already have a book of business, they wouldn't hire me. My answer to that was that I have a wife and a mortgage, but that wasn't good enough. So I went to work for different companies that were in the investment business until I joined Chemical Bank, then Chase Manhattan investment programs, and in 1996 started my own Financial Planning firm called Barons Financial Strategies, Inc.

One of the things I realized from the very beginning was that people needed more advice than they realized. Many don't have the basics like savings accounts, wills and trusts, powers of attorney, etc. I also find that a lot of people spend more than they make and don't know how to change those bad habits. That's where I come in.

I believe that everyone has an area of expertise, I use a CPA to do my taxes, I go to a doctor when I'm sick, I use an attorney to prepare all of my legal papers, and take my cars to the dealerships where I got them. Like them, I eat, sleep and breathe what I do for two reasons:

1) Because I love what I do and...

2) Because the more I know, the better I can help my clients.

For instance, when a client told me they were selling a Rental property, I suggested a 1031 exchange, whereby they could flip what they have, get the same income with the same amount of risk, but avoid giving up 20% for capital gains taxes. Another time, I had a client who was leaving his company. But instead of telling them to roll over his investment, he asked for a lump sum distribution. Upon finding out, I called their old employer, had them re-fax the paperwork to me, had the check rolled over and saved them over $100,000 in taxes. They're both still clients. There is no assurance your experience will be similar or suitable.

When I sit down with a new client, the first step is to put together a Financial Profile – getting all of their particulars. This is where I find out their income, their expenses and their assets. In looking at all of this, the first item is to find out if all of their legal papers are in order. If they have any non-deductible debt, car loans, credit card debt, I try to encourage them to pay those off before they ever invest any money...especially if that credit card has double-digit interest rates. I find out if they have retirement plans such as 401(k)'s, IRA's etc., and how they're invested.

What we learned after 2008 was to determine how much money (percentage) is needed if there's a loss. Let's discuss the years 2000-2002 when the S&P lost 42% as per NYU Business School. So let's assume (hypothetically) on 1/1/2000 you had $100,000 in an S&P 500 Index, you would have lost $42,000 leaving you $58,000 In order to get back to even, you need to get 72.4% on your investment. How one figures this one out, is that you divide the amount you lost by the amount that's left. You divide the $42,000 by the $58,000.

The years following 2002, 2003-2007, the S&P gained 65% as per NYU Business School and yet I said you would need 72%. Now 2008 comes and the S&P loses about 37% as per NYU Business School and again, assuming (hypothetically) you had $100,000 on 1/1/2008 and you lost 37%, you would need 58% just to get back to the $100,000 you had. Remember if you needed 58% and were strictly invested in the S&P index, you wouldn't have gotten back to even until almost the end of 2012.

What are some ways to deal with this? For one thing, after 2008 I started thinking we needed to do a better job for our clients as many of them are retired and they don't have the time and are not working to make it up. What I found was a money manager that is tactical, and in 2008 his balanced portfolio was actually up and his growth model was down a little over 2.8% net of fees.

Many people ask me about things like mortgages, credit card debt, refinancing their debts, reverse mortgages, buying and or leasing cars. Mortgages are tax deductible loans on real estate. They are typically lower interest rates than on a personal loan or on a credit card. They are paid monthly or bi-monthly. Many also use credit cards like cash, but they are not, they're another loan with much higher rates that accrue daily and I don't recommend them.

Back in 2011, one of my clients called that he and his wife needed to speak with me. Sometimes they would come to the office and sometimes I would go to their home. This time they came to the office and they were upset. They found it difficult to afford their home and they were thinking of selling it. I was shocked because when they bought this particular house, they said they wanted to die there. Upon going over their finances, I could see where the problem was, they had an adjustable rate mortgage that was moving up even though interest rates were down. Their minimum payments were getting out of hand. Their older son and daughter lived in the same town and their younger son lived about 8 miles west of them. They babysit two grandchildren a couple of days per week. So I asked them if money wasn't an object, would they stay in their house and their response was YES. So I told them to invite their three children over. I gave them three choices, one was to sell the house and move, one was to have their children help them with their monthly bills, and the third option was a Reverse Mortgage. The children couldn't help and they didn't want them to move, so they did a Reverse Mortgage. (There is no assurance your experience will be similar or suitable.) They still live in their home.

One of the things people always call me about is cars. I have taught many people about Swap-a-lease.com and Cars.com. Many ask if they should lease a car. My first question was how many miles per year will they drive? Many leases come with 10-12K miles per year. Now if you only do 3k miles per year, you're paying for miles you're not using and won't get a refund, however, if you exceed the mileage allowed, they'll penalize you at 25 cents per mile. Now for cars.com, the place I found my last three and my current two.

If we get back to Swap-A-Lease, that's something I started doing in 2003 when I did my first one. I remember when in 1980 I had leased a brand new Riviera at a monthly cost of $456 a month. After 3 months, I called the leasing company to find out how to end the lease. Imagine my surprise when I was told that if I wanted to terminate the lease, it would cost me 60% of what I owed or $9,028.80. I typically get people who are desperate and get them to pay me between 20-30%. My best story was a client/accountant that I work with who was looking for a Cadillac Escalade. We found one in Washington DC from a diplomat who was going back to his country and he needed to get rid of it. I told him I was doing this for a client and I needed 30% or $5K and he agreed, and she paid $500 a month less than getting it from a dealership.

Being an Investment Adviser Representative at American Portfolio Adviser, Inc. an SEC Registered Investment Advisor which is not affiliated with Baron's Financial Strategies, Inc. or any other named business entity, is fun when the markets are going up, and a drag when markets are going down. 2008 was brutal for the markets and for me. So many people were calling out as the markets were tumbling. Not only were my clients calling and we were trying as best as possible to explain what was going on, but other peoples clients who were not getting return phone calls from their brokers were calling me. What I found amazing were the meetings I was attending from representatives of mutual fund companies and insurance companies telling us to stay the course. My answer to that was we did that from 2000-2002 and the world didn't seem anywhere as bad as 2008 and we moved a lot of clients monies into money markets.

Being an Investment Adviser Representative is such a rewarding job. Besides making people money, you're their adviser and confidante. They come to me with their marriage problems, their legal problems, their tax problems and even what to do about their children. I remember a client calling me about her husband who was mad at her for spending money to see her pregnant daughter in Germany. I told her to tell him that she called me and that she had already made more money this year than she was taking out, he shouldn't make her feel guilty.

Then I had another client that calls me up and tells me he needs a million dollars right away and what ideas did I have. Because I had his money in brokerage accounts we used those accounts as collateral like those old passbook accounts. We were able to get him his million dollars within a week without an income or credit check. There is no assurance your experience will be similar or suitable.

If you ever came to my office, you'd be surprised at the THANK YOU cards I have on the fireplace and on my desk. My clients have thanked me for helping them get homes, putting their children through college, helping them to retire and have even gotten people out of debt.

About Brian

Brian Farkas started working for the *New York Times* in 1971, and then the *New York Daily News* in 1972. He graduated High School in 1972 and went to Nassau Community College, followed by SUNY at Farmingdale, graduating with an Associate's degree in Business Administration. Brian then attended one semester at Hofstra University, but quit after the first semester, as his job made it difficult for him to continue. In 1978, while still working for the *New York Times*, he was asked by two pressmen from the *New York Daily News* if he would take a look at their Disco. After he did, he took on the challenge of running it and turned it around from a losing business to a profitable business.

In 1979, while working part time for Collector's Corner, his friend's father's gold, silver and jewelry store, he was told that the *Manhattan Pennysaver* was for sale, and he bought it for his 25th birthday. After converting that from the smallest of five local weekly publications into the largest of three, Brian decided to sell out and went into Financial Planning.

Brian worked at a small bond brokerage firm, and after a year he joined a wire house called Thomson McKinnon Securities which was bought in 1989 by Prudential Bache. That wasn't the right fit for him, so he joined a small broker-dealer as a partner and trader, where he sat on the desk and placed orders for other brokers. Brian was only there a year when he started receiving phone calls to join Invest with Chemical Bank's Investment Services. Brian eventually said 'YES' and the next five years he accomplished becoming #1 at Chemical in 1992, #1 for Invest in 1992 and #1 in the country for Putnam Investments in the Banking Division. Brian maintained his #1 position for Putnam for three years in a row, 1992-1994, a country record.

It was in 1995 that Chemical and Chase Banks merged, and he was asked to help with the merger on the Investment side. He went to Chase as a VP in charge of High Net Worth clients in all of Suffolk County, New York. A year and a half later, he started Barons Financial Strategies, Inc. where he could help everyone.

The rest, as they say . . . is History.

CHAPTER 3

"WELL, THAT DIDN'T WORK… NOW WHAT?"

BY CHRIS DUNCAN, NCTM

Does your business have DOWN TIME that is not bringing in revenue? Wouldn't it be great to take advantage of that time by generating income and delivering excellence?

Challenges and creative solutions come with the territory when you're a business owner. You want to keep your inspirations and visions alive while actually operating in the positive. That's where the challenge comes in; especially if your business has limited service delivery hours like ours did. Your expenses run 24/7, but revenue can only be possible for about half of that time. That was our situation with our business, Frisco School of Music (booking weekly music lessons for children and adults), and my business partner Steve and I set out on a quest to find a way to make more out of what we were already paying. There was one catch, however, it had to still be aligned with the passion and purpose of the business we already had.

Knowing we had a concern and needed a solution led to a mission. We began exploring the best ways to effectively utilize the 'real estate' we were already paying for during the mornings and early afternoons.

TURNING IDEAS INTO ACTION

Setting the parameters to ensure we were focusing on the right solutions for maximizing our real estate—all 7,000 square feet of it—was an important first step. An idea can be great, but if it doesn't fit your business model it may not turn out to be as great as you'd envisioned. The two criteria that we decided were important for us in our pursuit of sound ideas were:

1. We must offer a daytime service that people wanted.

2. The service we offered needed to engage the whole family to enhance enrollment in our after school programs.

We began brainstorming and researching, investigating any and all ideas that we thought might work until we decided on which ones we were going to invest in. A few that fit our criteria included: 1) "Mommy and Me Classes" using a published curriculum for 12-15 week sessions; 2) morning music lessons targeted for adult students; and 3) classes for home-schoolers available in the mornings. People enrolled, and of course that was exciting. The students came and had a great time, really enjoying what they were doing. We were thinking, "This is great! We found it." But…that was not so for long.

When it came time to sign up for the next session, the predicament we discovered was that although everyone enjoyed the classes quite a bit, families were already on to the next thing for their children or themselves (wanting to "try it all" instead of committing to one ongoing activity.) They'd go with art lessons instead or maybe a dance class, just to try it and expose their child to many different activities. It was only a matter of time before we'd gone through our target audience and were left in the same predicament as when we started. It was time to go back to the drawing board!

There was one concept that a few other similar businesses were trying in other parts of the country that we had heard about, where families stayed for several years without looking elsewhere for more activities. They were opening up structured preschool options for children during the day with arts-based programs. It was an interesting concept but one that we really had to analyze deeply and contemplate thoroughly. After all, preschools and daycares are on every corner in our community when you drive around a town or down a residential street. Was there a market for one more? And, if so, what would set our school apart?

Feeling that we had a unique concept down that focused on our interest in performing arts and academic excellence, we took the plunge, put our own unique "spin" on the concept, and committed to starting a PRIVATE DAY SCHOOL for ages 3 through Kindergarten. It was a huge risk due to the cost related to licensing by the city and state, equipment and materials costs, employee costs, and insurance liabilities, but we felt that what we had to offer *definitely set us apart* from other options that parents had to choose from. We opened the MUSICAL ARTS SCHOOLHOUSE.

EIGHT IMPORTANT STRATEGIES THAT HELPED TAP OUR POTENTIAL

There's a widely-known concept in the performing arts world that was a huge motivator for us as we embarked on organizing our new business endeavor. That is:

Children who participate in deep academic learning through a performing arts environment with small class size become the leaders in their next school experience.

Our new business, The Musical Arts Schoolhouse opened in 2009. It was exciting, a concept that kept us energized. For our program, children rotate through music, art, dance, theatre, Spanish, and core-academics classes <u>each day</u>, focusing on a deep learning of academics in each of these artistic disciplines. We offer a half-day Private School with options for extended activities through 3:45 p.m. In order to ensure that our concept blossomed into the potential we saw, we knew we had to keep a few important elements in mind.

1. Never give up!
Even the best of ideas can have some bumps and bruises along the way. There was more than one day when I mumbled to my business partner, "Let's forget it. I'll just go back to teaching piano and be done with it." However, surrendering wasn't an option that was seriously considered despite those occasional thoughts.

Best idea – having neither partner wanting to give up <u>on the same day</u>!

The most favorable time to open a school in our area of the country is August when the other schools in the area are beginning their year. However, because of delays in getting state and city approval, we were forced to open the second week in September, well after the prime registration season for families. Even then it was touch and go, the final approval was a vote from city council, and if any citizen objected ... ANOTHER MONTH DELAY!

So there we were on a Thursday evening at the City Council Meeting, our docket number comes up, the City Clerk asks for any objections, no one in the audience stands up...the gavel goes down... APPROVED! Then we breathed.

We were ready, thriving on optimism. The next day the advertising went out, it had been printed and waiting, but if there was a delay in approval it would have had the wrong date on it and needed to be reprinted. The school opened the following Monday. It took us two years to get to that point and we had $50K invested (HUGE for a Private Music School), and 10 teachers hired – and only ONE BRAVE STUDENT had enrolled!

Over the next week the one student turned into two, then into six, as word started getting out (rainmakers) and within three months we were featured on Good Morning Texas (local ABC Affiliate,) had a multi-page write up in a local, high-end, full color magazine, and had a full school!

2. Continue to evaluate.
We kept looking for new ways to generate new business and ensure we were offering more families options with our school. This included trying an afternoon academic program. After all, many communities offer an afternoon Kindergarten option so it wasn't a far-fetched idea or foreign concept. Despite seeming logical, it didn't work for us. A three-step evaluation process came into play.

- *Accept the reality quickly:* Despite advertising and word of mouth, the afternoon preschool program was a flop. We knew that we would fulfill our obligation for that year, but it wouldn't be offered again when next year's enrollments came around.

- *Keep your commitments:* Since credibility and reputation are everything with a business that relies on word of mouth and referrals, we kept our obligation and delivered above and beyond despite the program not being a success in our business model.

- *Continue to make decisions:* Even though this one idea didn't work out for us, we knew we had to keep thinking of ideas and not be hesitant to implement them. If we did, the winning idea might be the one we passed by. We learned our lessons and a bit more about our market and moved on.

3. Celebrate when you hit the jackpot.

Our experiences showed us what did not work, and when we discovered *what WAS working* we decided to maximize those opportunities and focus on improving them, further creating our distinction. It was so exciting for Steve and I to realize that we'd found the formula that had a great chance for success.

4. Find or create a rainmaker.

This is so important. A rainmaker is someone who loves what you offer and becomes your walking, talking PR person. They love sharing what you do and how it has benefited their lives. Hands down, this is one of the most effective testimonials you can have. There's life to it, not just words on a page. For Musical Arts Schoolhouse, the parents of the kids who benefit from our program are our rainmakers and we are so grateful for them. They talk and they share, letting our community know more about us.

We create rainmakers by:

- Staying in touch with parents even after the students are graduated from our school (first grade and beyond).

- Delivering a quality, educational experience that gives them a solid foundation for their next step in education.

- Keeping parents involved throughout the school year. One example: we added Fall Parent Conferences, along with the end-of-year assessment conferences, with our panel of Lead Teachers. Parents LOVED this, being able to have the chance to discuss their personal goals for their child and visit with the Teaching Team early in the year made a big difference in our families feeling comfortable telling all of their friends and neighbors about this amazing school their child attends.

Every business has the ability to create rainmakers!

5. Deliver more than you promise.

This may seem like a rather cliché statement because it's definitely overused. The beautiful thing about truly delivering more than you promise is that you don't have to tell people you're doing it. They know through their experiences with you. It isn't always realized immediately, either. Quite often we hear parents tell us that they didn't realize just how much our Private Day School was providing their children academically until they went on to their next stage of school, where parents found out how academically advanced their children were compared to others. Occasionally parents would come back to tell us how their child had advanced to the NEXT grade level. Comments like that are music to our ears and reinforce why we are committed to helping each child reach excellence through small class sizes and ensuring every child in our classrooms reaches their full personal potential.

6. Engage the whole family.

Not every small business requires a family engagement philosophy, but for Musical Arts Schoolhouse it is a must. One way we do this is by holding five student performances per year for our families, each focusing on different elements of our curriculum. The students sing, dance, and perform on stage. This past year they even sang a song at graduation that listed every President of the United States—in order. How many adults can do that, with or without music?

We are also aware of how hectic many family's work schedules are and that there are many parents that have to travel during the week that may miss the performances we offer. Not all family lives close by, either. That doesn't mean they have to miss out, though! We take engaging the whole family a step further by coordinating a way for anyone to view the performances live on the internet from anywhere in the world. It's been a highly effective way to help us stand apart from what other child centers can offer.

7. Repeat numbers 4, 5, and 6!

Nothing is "one and done" when you're in a business that continues to cater to new students each and every year. That means you cannot take for granted that everyone will remember you if you don't remember them. That's why we always continue to:

- Create new rainmakers and keep the ones we have earned.

- Deliver more than we promise through action, not telling.

- Engage the whole family in the unique experiences we are offering.

8. Find a system that works and work the system.

Don't be afraid to let the world know about your success when you find it. It's exciting and it's the ultimate compliment of your hard work. Does it mean you stop trying new things? No way, unless you want to remain where you're at and not continue to improve. With Musical Arts Schoolhouse's formula, we embrace and reiterate that:

- Our classes are small—fifteen students maximum.

- Our program produces high-academic achievers, the *Talented and Gifted* of Day School Programs.

- Parents are choosing us because their children have an interest in what we offer.

- We have a unique program that is not being replicated in our area.

LIVING UNLIMITED

Our business has come so far! As it continues to grow and be nurtured, we continue to learn and implement new ideas that fit our business criteria. We keep up with the high standards the children with us deserve, and their parents expect. This has led to waiting lists for our school and more referrals than we can take on.

It's created a new goal. We are now able to expand our business, adding a sister school: Frisco School of Performing Arts, right next door to our current location, which will provide space for more group teaching and performance areas, too. Great things are on the horizon and for us, and just like all businesses, this wouldn't be possible without hard work, laughter, and some tears along the way, plus the dedication to keep the vision moving forward. I love thinking about how it all started, with a realization that we could do more and be more if we chose to explore and pursue the right opportunities.

About Chris

Chris Duncan, NCTM has loved playing the piano on the very first day her fingers first touched those ivory keys, and she knew that she wanted to be a teacher and help others embrace exploring their gifts through learning. Piano and education were a natural fit and one that inspired her to obtain her B.A. degree in Piano Pedagogy and Music Theory from Michigan State University in 1978. In 1997 she also obtained the highest level of certification that can be achieved with the Early Childhood Music and Movement Association.

It was through some ups and downs with her own children that Chris realized how different all children are with their motivation to learn to play the piano and other types of music. It led to some innovative thinking on how to inspire them and develop their skills and interests. This was the foundation for her thinking when she opened up the Frisco School of Music in 2000, offering group and private music lessons for many instruments and to children of all ages and levels. She also offered Rock Band School and pre-ballet dance classes.

In 2009, Chris and her business partner Steve South, founded Musical Arts Schoolhouse. This program has really become the foundation and signature of all Chris's achievements in the performing arts and her natural love of everything associated with it. What makes this school unique is that it teaches high academics through the performing arts to children ages 3 through 6 for Preschool and Kindergarten.

Frisco School of Music and Musical Arts Schoolhouse have over 45 teachers, dedicated administration support staff, and over 950 students. The blueprint that Chris and Steve have created is one that continues to be improved upon, giving quality education and performing arts options to the many students who are enrolled.

Chris believes strongly in family involvement in continued learning and always brings enthusiasm, energy, and a joyful love of teaching to everything she is involved in. Today, Chris lives in Little Elm, TX and has two grown sons, one of whom is a jazz pianist.

Notable Awards and Accomplishments:

- Licensed Preschool Director, Texas Department of Family and Protective Services

- NCTM; Nationally Certified Teacher of Music, Permanent Certificate, Music Teachers National Association – Piano, Theory
- Founding, Charter Member of the Carrollton Music Teachers Association
- Member, Texas State Music Teachers Association
- Member, Music Teachers National Association
- Member, Texas Licensed Childcare Association
- Early Childhood Music & Movement Association, National Board Member 1995-1997

CHAPTER 4

THE UNCOMMON REAL ESTATE INVESTOR

BY CHRIS GOFF

We've all done it.

At some point, we've driven by the house with the general abandoned vibe and thought, "Man, somebody should buy that and turn it into a (insert… restaurant, boutique, salon, office or remodel, here) ."

Some of us have even wished we could, or momentarily considered doing it ourselves. That's the voice of our inner real estate investor talking. Everyone has it in them; some voices are just louder than others.

Most people continue on down the road and go about their daily lives, but a few special people will choose to listen to that voice and attempt to take action.

How do we make this dream a reality? The common route that most real estate investors take is to either empty out their savings or apply for a loan at the local bank. But what happens when you don't have adequate savings or credit for bank loans? Do you just bow your head and walk away from what could potentially be a very good real estate deal, leaving it for someone else to come along and profit from? The **UNcommon** entrepreneur won't let less than ideal circumstances stand in the way of achieving his goals. We've heard cliché's like 'where there's a will, there's a way' all our lives, but what does it mean to actually live by this code? How far would we be able to go if we did?

With the new real estate climate and barrage of reality 'Fix and Flip' real estate investing shows, more and more budding entrepreneurs are looking at investing in real estate as a viable way to expand financial portfolios and satisfy their dream of becoming the boss.

If you're considering taking advantage of the wealth of opportunities to be found in every town across the country, there is no shortage of education available to help you get started on the road to real estate investing. Almost every method of delivery is available on the subject— from books and digital media to live seminars and one-on-one coaching. The large majority of these tend to focus on teaching one or two strategies, however, and leave large gaps in a prospective real estate investor's training. This can cause major frustration and even some serious problems.

Outdated information can lead to legal difficulties and cost thousands of dollars in 'learning curve' losses; while not knowing all of the available strategies and how to properly execute them will let deal after deal slip through your fingers. Unfortunately, this is enough to make many investors throw in the towel before they have the opportunity to reap the rewards that a successful career in real estate investing can bring.

There's a lot to be said for unwavering determination; diligently working one or two investing strategies will definitely pay your bills, but it won't make you rich. Unfortunately, this is the common route that most would-be investors take when seeking to learn how to navigate the world of real estate. They think that if they can just learn one way, one niche strategy, they will be able to become successful. These people rarely make it to success, though. This is because there is no one-size-fits-all strategy. Every situation is different, but here are five basic strategies. These are:

1. Wholesaling
2. Lease Options
3. Retailing
4. Owner Financing
5. Straight Options

If you have a clear understanding about how they work, you will be able to tackle any situation that you come across.

It's the **UNcommon**, out-of-the-box thinking of the savvy real estate investor who can understand and adapt to each unique situation that closes the most deals and consistently deposits the most money in the bank every month.

Let's take a look at an example of the **UNcommon** approach that I'm referring to:

Mary Smith bought her home two years ago for $215k.

The company that Mary works for closed its doors last month and she finds herself out of a job, with no prospects in sight. With her savings depleted, she is no longer able to afford the payments on her home, and needs to sell, quickly. She now owes $195k, but with the recent plant closings and general economic downturn, Mary finds that her home is only worth $200k. This leaves her unable to employ the assistance of a real estate agent to sell it, and the average real estate investor won't touch it because of the narrow profit margin.

Mary has two obvious options: she can either rent it out or let it go back to the bank through foreclosure.

While Mary doesn't have the desire, money, or knowledge to deal with the headaches of being a landlord, she doesn't want to ruin the good credit score that she has worked so hard to build.

Many people find themselves in similar situations all across the country EVERY DAY, but who helps people like Mary Smith?

How CAN she be helped?

A savvy real estate investor knows all five strategies and how to make them work out for a win-win-win situation when the average investor would just walk away.

Mary is researching her options online and comes across a website that catches her eye on a search engine. A lady by the name of Laura Phillips has a website and claims to be able to help people in Mary's situation. The content on the site is professional and relevant to what she is dealing with, so she decides to give Laura a call.

After meeting with Mary and evaluating the home, Laura presents her with two separate offers. Mary chooses to accept Laura's Lease Option offer of $195k with zero down and $1400/month for a 1-year term. Laura agrees to be responsible for maintenance costs and repairs during the option period. Mary is able to move on without the worry of covering her mortgage payments or being a landlord.

Since Laura doesn't plan to occupy the home, where does she have room to profit in this deal? How does she do it?

Laura has a pool of potential buyers and sends the house info out to a few she thinks might be interested.

Jack and Lois Lehman fall in love with the home and settle on terms with Laura of a $200k purchase price with $5k down and $1600/month for a term of 1 year. They agree to be responsible for maintenance costs and repairs, and there is no early cash-out penalty.

This works perfectly for them, as Jack just got a job transfer from their hometown 2 hours away to the local hospital. Lois and the children can move to the new house with Jack immediately while they wait for their old house to sell and don't have to worry about short-term renting or long commutes for Jack. Once the sale of their old home is complete, they are able to qualify for a bank loan on the new house and close well before the 1-year term is over.

WIN-WIN-WIN:

- Mary received a fair price for her home and doesn't have to deal with landlord headaches or foreclosure.
- Laura receives $5k on a down payment and $200/month in positive cash flow.
- The Lehman family moves into their new home on terms that give them time to get things in order for a bank loan and cash Mary out.

Of course, I'm giving you a simple, straightforward scenario, but the concept is the same for virtually any set of circumstances.

It's important to know how to properly execute all five strategies and how to decide which are right for each situation, instead of just focusing on one technique. Without this knowledge, you are letting the bulk of opportunities pass you by, and relegating what could be a rewarding career to the equivalent of a hobby.

Don't settle for taking the common path. Decide to think outside the box and the next time you drive by that abandoned property, listen to your inner real estate investor. Go for it and make it happen!

About Chris

Chris Goff:
- Successful Real Estate Investor since 1999
- Specializing in Creative Real Estate Investing
- Author, Coach and Mentor
- Real Estate Marketing Expert

Chris Goff resides in Houston, TX and is a husband and father of three. Chris grew up in Northern VA where he started his real estate investing career.

Chris Goff started Real Estate Investing in 1999. Chris didn't have any money to work with, so he was interested in learning 'no money down' strategies. He absorbed any and every bit of information he could find on the subject, and started on his first deal. Chris was lucky enough to break even on the deal, and quickly learned that not all information is good information.

Chris continued, learning as he went from his mistakes, and began to see some pretty amazing results. Chris took what he learned from others and combined it with what he had learned by trial and error, to develop a system for investing that would produce as much income as possible, without many of the pitfalls that can be found in RE Investing. In his first 20 months, Chris Goff did 46 deals with NO money down. It didn't take long for those around him to figure out that Chris was onto something good, and they began to ask him how he was doing it. Chris explained his system to one person; one led to two, two led to four, four led to 40, and working for Donald Trump, writing books, programs, and teaching materials for his Real Estate Education company. Chris learned a valuable lesson while with Trump. Anyone can DO Real Estate, many can SPEAK about it, but not everyone can TEACH it to others. In this, Chris Goff has a genuine gift.

During his time with Donald Trump Education Companies, Chris mentored hundreds of budding Real Estate Investors. The impressive level of success that his students were able to achieve, and the perfect satisfaction ratings that Chris received, led to an invitation to head up Trump's in-field training program, training the other mentors in his unique teaching style and writing the *Apprenticeship Program, Fast Track to Foreclosures, Real Estate Blueprint, In-field Training Program,* and the *Quick-Start Program.* In two years, Chris helped develop over 70 Real Estate Investment companies, as well.

In January 2012, Chris was nominated as one of the Top 30 Entrepreneurs in America. Chris is also a Best-Selling Author and was a featured guest expert on the Brian Tracy

Show that aired on ABC, CBS, NBC and FOX affiliates across the country.

Chris Goff never stops to rest on his laurels, however. Chris and his team are constantly searching for ways to improve their Real Estate Investing approach as well as teaching technique, doing what so many people fail to achieve – keeping on top of a constantly fluctuating Market. To contact Chris, visit him and the REI&ME team at: www.REIANDME.com or call them at: 1.877.781.7379!

CHAPTER 5

FIVE CRUCIAL MISTAKES MOST PEOPLE MAKE TRYING TO BUILD AN ONLINE BRAND

BY BO MANRY

You have put together your website and are now ready to conquer the world. You have spent countless hours getting prepared for success and have ensured that your website will outperform the competition. You are going to dominate the online world and you know it. Finally, your website goes live and you kick back on the sofa just waiting for your phone to ring off the hook, which translates to you counting the dollar bills rolling in.

After days, weeks, or even months, you just don't understand what could possibly be wrong. You have done everything right. You have built the best website out there. You have built a great logo, a brand, and a website to help launch your business. What could possibly be wrong?

Whether you already have a brick-and-mortar store and want to build an online brand for your product or service, or you have come up with the next big idea for a business online, building an online brand takes work. Hopefully, I didn't just lose half of my readers now because I stated that it takes work to build a great brand online. But as with most things in life, they don't come free and building an online brand is no different. We are going to explore why most people simply give up on creating an awesome brand and instead they settle for a mediocre online presence.

49

MISTAKE #1 – NOT MARKETING YOUR WEBSITE

We have all seen the movie Field of Dreams where an Iowa corn famer hears a voice telling him: "If you build it, he will come." That might have worked in the movie where after the corn farmer built a baseball diamond and Shoeless Joe Jackson and other dead baseball players emerge from the cornfields to play ball, but it will not work for you in building an online brand.

No matter what line of business you are in, failure to market your product or service is the number one mistake that most people make. If you think about it – every one of us – we are constantly marketing. We market ourselves to potential customers or clients by how we act, the way we carry ourselves, and the way we interact with people in general. We are all on display every day. So why would someone not market their website to help build their online brand? I don't know either. Maybe it is because they think it is not necessary and their website will magically bring in customers. Or, perhaps they just don't know how. Or, maybe they don't have the money to spend on marketing. This line of thinking is a mistake and there are things that can be done to market your business online that are free.

When you first get your website up and running, no one will know about it immediately; including Google and other search engines. It takes time for search engines to index your site so that people can find you. You may ask yourself, then, what can I do to market my business online? There are paid versions of marketing and there are free versions as well. I cannot possibly go into detail about each in this chapter but here is a list of some options you have.

Pay Per Click (PPC) – Pay per click or PPC as it is known in the industry is one of the best ways to get immediate visitors to your website. Simply put, you write an ad about your product or service and people that are interested in your ad click on it. When they click on your ad, they are directed to your website, where it is then up to your website to convert them into customers. This type of marketing is great as you only pay for visitors who click on your ad that are interested in your product or service.

Social Media – Facebook, Google+, Twitter, Pinterest, Instagram, Foursquare, Snapchat, LinkedIn, and the list goes on and on. While most of these social media platforms have some form of PPC, they are free to setup an account. In fact, not having a social media presence is another mistake we will discuss next. For now, just know that it can be a very effective way of marketing your product or service virtually free.

MISTAKE #2 – NOT HAVING A SOCIAL MEDIA STRATEGY

In Mistake #1, I mentioned that Social Media is a platform by which you can advertise your product or service both via paid methods and free methods. More importantly, having a social media presence helps to build your brand. I cannot emphasize enough the power of friends recommending your product or service to their friends. More and more people are relying on reviews and friend recommendations when making purchasing decisions. If you offer a great product or service at a fair price, and your customers love it, they are willing to share their experience with others. All you have to do is ask them to do so.

There are so many social media sites available that you may be wondering which ones to focus your efforts on. That is a fair question and it depends on your target audience. For example, if your product or service caters to young adults between the age of 18 and 29, then choose a social media outlet that has a high percentage of young adults. To date, Facebook is still one of the largest social media sites worldwide. But, other social sites are also rising in popularity simply due to the fact that social media as a whole is constantly growing in popularity among all age groups. Knowing which sites to use to reach your target audience is key to spending your marketing dollars effectively.

MISTAKE #3 – NOT PAYING ATTENTION TO SEO

SEO? What the heck is SEO? My point exactly. Search Engine Optimization, or SEO is the process of affecting how search engines show your website or webpages in their natural or un-paid results. In theory, the higher your page is displayed on the search results, the more visitors your website will get. While this sounds simple enough, it is quite complex. In fact, Google and other search engines are constantly "changing the rules" and a great website is also constantly working to improve their search engine rankings.

Entire books are written on this topic with all the do's and do not's about SEO. Since we cannot delve that deeply into the subject of SEO in this space, a future book will contain all the gory details of SEO. But, I can guide you on the basics of what you need to be aware of. The number one rule for all SEO is content. I cannot stress enough what the simple word content means to SEO. Search engines love great content. But, the content must also be original. Search engines do not like content that has been copied from other sites or even other pages within your own site. Each and every webpage on your site needs good original content.

The title tag is the next item on the list of importance. This title tells the search engine what the webpage is about. It gives a "hint" to the search engine on what to expect in the content on the webpage. These two items, title tag and content, make up the basis for a great webpage.

Obviously, there are many other factors that go into how search engines rank a webpage, but without these two concepts, the rest do not matter. Focus on these two aspects of SEO and you are well on your way.

MISTAKE #4 – NOT ANALYZING YOUR WEBSITE TRAFFIC

I constantly ask people if they know who is visiting their website, what age group are they in, what gender are they, and what pages on their website get the most traffic. Over 95% of the time I get a blank stare with no response. As a business owner, it is crucial for you to know who your target audience is and if you are reaching them. Using analytics software like Google Analytics can help answer these questions. Not only can you see what age group and gender your visitors are, but you can also tell how they got to your website and geographically where they live. Knowing this type of information can help you make decisions on where to spend your marketing dollars both online and offline.

For example, if you are reviewing your website traffic and notice that 40% of the visitors on your website are coming from Facebook, it might prove beneficial to spend some marketing dollars on PPC for Facebook. Or, maybe you have a large number of visitors coming from various blog sites. Could you reach out to the blog owners and offer a coupon or discount code for their customers to purchase one of your products or services?

In Mistake #2, we discussed engaging with potential customers on social media outlets. As an example, I recommended choosing a social media platform that had a high percentage of users 18-29 if your product or service caters to young adults. Now that you have setup a social media platform to target that specific audience, you can use analytics software to determine if people are coming from those social sites. If they are, and these visitors are becoming customers, then your marketing dollars are being spent wisely. Do you see the connection?

Knowing the answer to these types of questions allows you, the business owner, to make good financial decisions on how to improve your website and where to use your marketing dollars in the most effective way.

MISTAKE #5 – NOT FOLLOWING UP WITH CUSTOMERS

After all the hard work and marketing from PPC, Social Media, SEO and analyzing your website traffic, you finally reach your audience and convert them into customers. It is an awesome feeling to wake up in the morning and see new customers or orders on your website. But the connection you have made with your new customer shouldn't stop after they purchase your product or service. You should at the very least send a Thank You email for their business and explain how customers like them make a difference.

If you really want to complete the circle, ask your new customers, or old customers for that matter, to review your product or service. You can also ask them to like you on Facebook or other social media platforms that you now have in place. Ask them to share their experience with their friends about your company, product or service. Consider giving them a coupon code for a discount on future orders to encourage repeat business.

What I am trying to say is that the overall perception and customer experience doesn't stop after the order is placed. In many cases, it is the after care and customer service that keeps the user engaged with your business. Don't fail to make them feel special. If you roll out the red carpet for your customers, they will be loyal to you and share their experience with friends and family.

Building an online brand for your company takes time, effort and persistence if you want be great instead of mediocre. I have outlined five (5) mistakes that I see most business owners make when building their website and online brand. Most of these mistakes are easily avoidable and many do not cost a single penny to implement.

It starts with writing great content for your website so that others see your website and therefore your product or service as useful and compelling. Focusing on great content also sets your website apart from the rest which allows search engines to index your quality content and therefore show your business higher in the search engine results. This ultimately leads to free advertising for potential customers. Marketing your website with PPC and Social Media will bring immediate traffic that will help turn visitors into customers. After all the above efforts, analyze your website traffic to make sure you are spending your marketing dollars effectively. Above all else, treat each customer as if they are the single most important part of your business. Proper follow-up with every customer and asking them to share their experience is worth all the effort.

About Bo

Bo Manry graduated in 1997 with a degree in Electrical & Computer Engineering. Since that time, he has worked with many companies including government agencies to develop computerized-based systems and automation.

Bo is also a successful entrepreneur and business owner. Over the past two decades, he has started and sold multiple businesses. With his degree in Electrical & Computer Engineering, he has been able to master the art of delivering systems that sell. Currently, he owns several companies and all but his real estate investment company are 100% online businesses.

Utilizing proper marketing and social media strategies, Bo Manry's companies generate millions of dollars each year in revenue. One of Bo's latest projects is REIPro (www.myreipro.com), a multi-million dollar company providing a software system for real estate investors.

Bo Manry is a national speaker, mentor, and coach, where he teaches people how to be successful in today's digital world and provides tools to make it easier. He enjoys travel, his large lap dog and spending time with his busy family activities. As often as possible, you can find Bo hanging out around the local golf course, always trying to master the game.

To learn more about Bo Manry, visit: www.bomanry.com.

CHAPTER 6

THE BIG SIX — MAXIMS BY WHICH I LIVE MY LIFE

BY CLAYTON HART, CEO,
Diverse Technology Solutions, Inc.

More than 20 years after starting my information technology career at IBM, I am still learning from my colleagues, employees and clients. I have surrounded myself with successful people who have inspired me while the experiences of others serve as cautionary tales. These lessons, seeming at first to be just plain common sense, have far deeper meanings that have been effective strategies for great success in my business and my life:

1. "THE CUSTOMER IS ALWAYS RIGHT!"

As a young, still green to the corporate world, field service engineer at IBM, I occasionally got myself into trouble. I would say the wrong thing to a client or rub someone the wrong way. Fortunately I had a great manager whose guidance has remained invaluable throughout my career. I'll never forget that day he called me into his office to give me some sage advice that has proven time and again to deliver great results for my business and me personally.

His first comment was, "The customer is always right, even when you know they are wrong." Before he could even finish his sentence I attempted to interject but was abruptly hushed. He continued to explain in detail that customer service means everything in business. If you service the client at the highest level, even your legitimate mistakes can be more easily forgiven. But if your customer service is poor, any slight inaction can exacerbate even a trivial issue, potentially putting your client relationship in jeopardy.

2. "WALK THE WALK AND TALK THE TALK."

My manager continued, "If you want to be successful, the way you present yourself should emulate the position to which you aspire, not the position you are in today. Your presentation is 70% of the game and your technical skills are the other 30%." While the exact proportion for your particular field may be debated, it is undeniable that the way you present yourself has a disproportionate impact on how the rest of the world perceives you.

If you enter any business situation speaking well, listening even better, dressed to impress and treating everyone with the utmost respect, you will reach a higher level of success no matter what your field or profession. Most successful people have exceptional presentation skills; it is difficult to become and remain successful without them. The question is . . . are you passing those skills on to your staff for their benefit and for the benefit of the business? It's the ability to embed great presentation and customer service into the very fabric of your business culture that makes a great manager and becomes the foundation of a great company.

3. "DON'T PUT ALL YOUR EGGS IN ONE BASKET."

Early in my IT career I took a huge risk. I quit full time employment to found an IT Consultant business in the mid 1990's. Soon after I started my business, I met with a business owner who happened to be my largest client and later became a trusted friend. This CEO was the most insane guy I ever met. He was arrogant and brutally frank, but fiercely intelligent. He worked seemingly endless hours and was completely dedicated to advancing his business to successively higher levels. I didn't know it at the time, but he was working so hard because he was in the midst of selling his business. Eventually he sold it, started a second company and then invested in a third. He is a truly brilliant serial entrepreneur that understands the complexities of increasing the value of a business to attract investors who will pay top dollar in an eventual sale.

One day he called me into his office and started asking intimate questions about my business. I can't be exactly sure, but in retrospect it appeared he was sizing up my company, perhaps to see if it was something he wanted to invest in. "What are your revenues?" he asked. "Over one million in sales year to date." I exclaimed proudly. "How much of your income is recurring?" "Huh?" I replied. "How much of your income is from recurring contracts with your clients?" he asked. "I don't have any contracts with my clients," I said. He completed his interrogation by asking this enlightening question: "How much do you think your business is worth?" I replied, "I don't know, maybe a million?" He shook his head and held up his thumb and index finger, your typical "ok" sign and replied "ZERO! Your company is worth exactly zero," he said. My face turned red with embarrassment. "What do you mean?" I asked. He then went on to explain the enormous benefits of creating value within your business by developing a recurring revenue business model.

"Which has a more stable stream of income, a good hair dresser or a tee shirt shop? Which business has the better chance of longevity: a landscaper or a restaurant?" he asked. His point was made. I acted quickly on this advice being that it came from such a trusted source. I immediately started to change my business model from IT Consulting to Managed IT Services, which was driven by long-term support contracts and a recurring revenue model. Years later, I took it a step further, reinventing my business a second time, adding cloud computing services to our portfolio of already successful IT solutions. I realized not only the value of the recurring revenue formula, but of having multiple recurring revenue streams from different products and services. Thus I don't have all my eggs in one basket. I've developed over a dozen different services into a recurring revenue model and have become an expert in how to package and market them. I'm still waiting for my friend to ask me that question again: "How much do you think your business is worth?" My answer today would be quite different.

4. "WORK LIKE A DOG, PLAY LIKE A DOG."

Tenacity and an amazing work ethic are undoubtedly two defining characteristics of successful people. I have always worked like a dog. I had two jobs at 13 years of age. I mowed lawns throughout my neighborhood and held several other part-time jobs in pizza places and a donut shop throughout high school. Early in my IT career, I can remember sleeping overnight on desks at client sites to get the job done. That work ethic isn't something I was taught; I just did it!

I once had a meeting with a new customer who was a colorful character with a ton of energy. After a short discussion on our services, he ended our meeting with this comment, "I may not be the smartest guy in the world, but I'll outwork my competition every time to get to the top." He explained how he works until 2:00 am, goes home and is back at the office at 5:00 am. While his sleep schedule may have been untenable to most people, I left that meeting reinvigorated and excited to get back to my own work.

You absolutely can outwork your competition. The nature of most people is to attain success and then become complacent. There is no way I could have brought my business to its current level of success without outworking my competition – which I still do. Recently I worked an 18-hour day followed by a 13-hour day and said to myself, "Gee, some people probably don't work that many hours in a week!"

However, learning how to master and best manage your time is the biggest challenge to finding balance and happiness for even the most dedicated business leaders. Over the years, I have found that in order to work like a dog, sometimes you have to play like a dog. I've built the luxury of flexibility into my schedule. I might work 31 hours in two days, but if the sun is out on a random Tuesday and my workload permits, I will take off at noon and go to the beach with my family. Tenacity and an amazing work ethic are essential to success. Achieving the quality of life to which you aspire, the right balance between work and personal life in my case, should be the ultimate result of your work ethic.

5. "DISCRETION IS THE GREATER PART OF VALOR."

I have one ultimate goal in life. It is to retire as soon as I can, working thereafter only for the sheer enjoyment of it with the financial security to provide a very nice life for my family without having to worry if I ever work again. What is your ultimate goal in life? Do you allow disruptions to consume you, forcing your attention away from your ultimate goal?

I knew a great businessman and client that experienced an all too familiar story. He and his long-time business partner of 20 years had a falling out. I watched his company of 80 employees disintegrate in a matter of months down to 20 employees, and then eventually zero. My friend took a strong stance, "lawyered up" and engaged in an epic legal battle against his ex-partner that lasted for over five years. He may someday win a judgment but his life has been financially ruined in the process. He lost his million-dollar home. He lost his business and career. At the age of 45, he moved to another state, having to start a whole new life with his wife and two children. The experience was brutal to watch. Even if he eventually wins a judgment, he likely will never collect a dime from his ex-partner who is also broke.

Another colleague of mine once had a new customer that was referred to him. His company did the agreed-upon work and the client defaulted on payment for products and services. He could have spent endless hours building a case with his lawyers, with countless emails and phone calls, and finally court appearances. In pursuing legal recourse, he would be lucky to break even after expenses, if he ever recovered anything. He chose to walk away, preventing the negativity from affecting his psyche and focused 100% of his energy to replace that lost income.

It is inevitable that people will intentionally or unintentionally financially harm you throughout your life, causing significant distraction from your long-term goals. There will always be someone who resents you, who may want to cause you emotional or financial harm. Whether that ends up being a business partner, a friend, a rogue employee, a jealous ex-wife, the contractor who steals your deposit, your competition, or even a bad client, there is no doubt you are likely to face at least one of these situations. Heck let's face it; your competition is out there trying to steal your customers at this very moment!

It's easy for your ego to cloud your judgment and obscure the path to the best, most cost-effective resolution to these situations. You can let these events consume you with grief and aggravate yourself to the detriment of your mental health or, you can put your emotions aside and take a more methodical approach. Don't waste any more time than you have to, and determine the best way to reach the fastest return on investment. That's right, I said, ROI! I look at negative situations in life the same way I look at a new investment. What is the fastest return on investment of my time and money?

I have trained my mind and ego to spot these situations approaching a mile down the road. When confronted by a distraction in business, I attempt to mitigate it quickly. I try to reduce the time consumption, which allows me to continue focusing only on my ultimate goal. If you can discipline yourself to think and act this way you can save a fortune in time and money. I can't help but remember my colleague who lost his business and think to myself, "Gee, when the two partners had their falling out, what if they had split the business, income and employee-base in half? What if they had sold the business and split the proceeds? What if they hadn't turned to their lawyers and instead cut their losses and went their separate ways?" I believe their ego and hatred toward each other prevented them from seeing the best ROI for both of them. It's not always so simple but I always look for the ROI that allows me to get back to focusing on my ultimate goals in life as quickly as possible.

6. "ALL GOOD THINGS MUST COME TO AN END."

I have a very successful colleague who decided to sell his company. Annual revenues had reached $500 million; we're not talking about a hot dog stand here. His largest client was a big box store that comprised 30% of his overall revenue. As the deal to sell the business was reaching its final stages, this client canceled their contract. 30% of his business valuation disappeared overnight and there wasn't anything he could do to quickly replace it. That loss significantly devalued his business at the worst possible time.

I have faced similar challenges in my company's exponential growth. There was a time that I had one client that comprised 20% of our revenue. When a much larger company acquired that client, there was a regime change that quickly resulted in the early termination of our service contact. It didn't matter how stellar the service we provided was, or how we had supported the client's worldwide IT operations for over a decade, there was nothing we could do to stop the inevitable income loss.

I bowed out gracefully and quickly negotiated a fair exit deal. It was a difficult financial time for our company and I wasn't even sure I could keep my staff intact. But I didn't rush to make any dramatic changes. Instead we focused all our attention on new client acquisitions to keep focused on the ultimate goal I set for my business and myself. Working tirelessly with great tenacity, it took a mere ten months to replace that lost revenue and float expenses without having to lay off a single person.

So today, no single client makes up more than 2% of our revenue and that number shrinks every year inversely proportional to massive growth. Never let any single entity account be greater than 3% of your revenue. That's not to say that if you encounter a whale of a prospect you should reject their business. But if you can ensure that your business does not depend on one whale after another, you'll create a more financially stable and higher value business, which leads to a less stressful life. Never get complacent riding a whale's tail and never forget that all good things must come to an end.

About Clayton

As CEO of Diverse Technology Solutions, Clayton Hart keeps his clients at the very pinnacle of the Information Technology age. Founded in 1998, Diverse Technology Solutions Inc. is one of North America's fastest-growing Private Cloud Hosting providers. Clay has been instrumental in accurately forecasting emerging trends in IT and implementing services to provide dramatic return on investment for his clients. Clay and DTS bring a strategic partnership to their client relationships by aligning Information Technology as the epicenter of business profitability.

Clay's career in IT and expertise in fiscal management spans more than twenty years and has afforded him in-depth knowledge of the highest level IT decision-making processes in thousands of businesses. Clay spent the genesis of his career in network engineering, implementing complex IT projects for prestigious organizations including St John's University, Sotheby's, Credit Lyonnais and IBM. His subsequent success in financial management and business workflow expertise has given Clay a unique perspective on how to leverage technology to position a company for financial growth.

A national speaker, Clay has shared the stage with some of the world's top business leaders, delivering keynote presentations and CPE accredited continuing educational seminars to Fortune 1000 C-level executives. His speaking engagements include topics covering aligning Information Technology with business financial goals, using IT as profit generator, business workflow, IT security and Cloud Computing.

Clayton Hart has lent his business and information technology advice to over a dozen major publications and has been seen in *Forbes Magazine, Yahoo finance, marketwatch.com*, and various other media outlets. As author of the DTS blog, Clay strives to bring education, advice, tools and resources to help business owners make more fiscally responsible decisions on the appropriate direction of their Information Technology and business practices.

You can connect with Clay at: Clay@DTSTech.net
www.Diverse-Technology.com

CHAPTER 7

TAX-ADVANTAGED INCOME AND RETIREMENT...IT'S YOURS FOR THE TAKING

BY DOUG CHAPMAN

Everyone can have tax advantaged income in retirement. Yes, you read that correctly. It takes an uncommon approach to one of people's greatest concerns and problems—retirement. Retirement income takes into account two variables that we can control: assets and lifestyle management. It also takes into account several things we cannot control, such as: inflation, interest rates, and tax rates. Some people will argue that you cannot control taxes and I counter with, *"Yes, you can work to control taxes* and in many cases, **you can take them down.**"

This is true and it is something that doesn't work for only the super wealthy. Your average middle class American can also take advantage of these techniques to help work to eliminate taxes, which can help create a more stable retirement income. We all realize that we should start to save money for retirement. That message has been effectively relayed to most people. There are still a high number of people that feel it's too early to start saving. This is definitely not true! Regardless of your age, you should start saving and working toward retirement income that is tax advantaged. Why?

Saving money for a tax advantaged retirement is just as easy as saving money for a taxable retirement.

BREAKING IT DOWN TO BASICS

Admittedly, most people are not passionate about the topic of taxes, unless you're a guy like me—someone who gets so excited to help people's lives be better by not running from taxes, but accepting them for what they are. Here's a great example of how paying taxes upfront, instead of down the road, could be beneficial:

> There is this hard-working farmer. He doesn't make a lot of money and definitely has to make sure he knows where all of it is going, and why. Great news arrives one day. He has the option to pay taxes on the seeds he purchases upfront and then he will not have to pay a dime when he sells the crops. To him, this is a huge advantage because a single kernel of corn can be the start of growing acre upon acre of corn—none of which the farmer would ever have to pay taxes on when harvest time came.

Theoretically speaking, I believe people want that deal that the farmer in my example had. I bet you do, and you can have it. There are strategies and common sense solutions to unpredictable tax burdens, and it's what I know best. I want all of you to understand this message:

> *You cannot control tax fluctuations, but you can control how they impact you!*

THREE WAYS YOU CAN WORK TOWARDS TAX-ADVANTAGED RETIREMENT INCOME

Money. The word naturally evokes emotions. Add it into a question, such as, "How will I know that I have enough money to live out the remainder of my days?" and wow, it can make your heart start racing. This is the biggest fear that many people have when they approach retirement. Suddenly, they doubt how prepared they were. Some will just hope for the best and others will finally reach out to someone like me—a person who is a retirement income and estate planning specialist.

If you have never had your retirement strategy evaluated by someone who specializes in this area, **it should be considered**. You do not know what you are missing, and this type of expertise and the possible tax advantages that you may experience are numerous. Also, they are not saved for an elite group. They are for every person who is or has worked hard in life and is interested in having stability in their retirement.

There are three main scenarios that will show you the advantages of investing tax-advantaged dollars whenever possible. These scenarios help lessen the gamble on what we cannot control—(1) tax rates, (2) inflation, and (3) interest rates.

CONTROL BY DESIGN...this is important!

NOTE: We are not going to give any specific dollar amounts for the following strategies. Depending on adjustments to tax codes and contribution limits, these things can change frequently, but the underlying principles that make Roth IRAs, Roth 401(k)s, and Permanent Life Insurance great options, are easy to understand. These ideas are options to consider and it is not possible to say if any of these choices are better than the others for your situation. No comparison is being made between the options, rather an explanation of options. Only after meeting with a qualified specialist in this area, can a determination of the proper strategy for you be made.

Traditional IRA versus Roth IRA

A person's retirement income, and a family's long-term savings are impacted by the choices made when organizing their Individual Retirement Account (IRA). Traditional IRA contributions are typically tax deductible for both state and federal tax returns for the year you make the contribution. Eventually, withdrawals will be taxed at ordinary income tax rates. This is not how a Roth IRA works. With a Roth IRA, you will receive no tax break when you make a contribution, but earnings and withdrawals are generally[1] tax-free.

The distinction: With a traditional IRA, you are avoiding paying taxes when you invest the money, and with a Roth IRA you are avoiding paying taxes when you take it out in retirement. The result is a more stable retirement income—one with no tax surprises. This is why Roth IRAs have gained in popularity since their inception in 1997 under the Tax Payer Relief Act.

---

[1] For a Roth IRA, earnings withdrawn prior to reaching age 59½ and/or not meeting the five-year holding period may be subject to a 10 percent penalty in addition to income tax. After-tax contribution amounts are generally returned income tax free; however, for Roth conversions, if converted amounts are not held for the five-year period, distributions may be subject to a 10 percent penalty.

Additional benefits of a Roth IRA:

- Withdrawals are not mandated. If you don't need the money it can keep accumulating value and you don't have to withdraw it. Mandatory withdrawals are required after the age of 70½ on a traditional IRA.

- You don't have to factor in tax predictions into your retirement planning. Sound financial and retirement strategies are challenging enough without having to guess what tax rates may be.

- Tax laws currently offer ways to withdraw Roth IRSs penalty-free and before the age of 59½. This is not guaranteed, but it has a history of being one of the benefits since its inception.

Considerations of a Roth IRA:

- It is possible that an investor may be in a significantly lower tax bracket in retirement than during their working years, and in such a case a traditional IRA may prove to be a better tax selection.

Traditional 401(k) versus Roth 401(k)

I think you're starting to understand why the word Roth in front of any retirement investment is something to learn about. To help illustrate some of the differences between a traditional 401(k) and a Roth 401(k), take this hypothetical example:

Samantha and Benjamin are both 40 years old and contribute $10,000 per year to their respective 401(k)s. Both receive a hypothetical 7%[2] investment return and both plan on taking withdrawals of approximately 5% from their 401(k) starting at the age of 65. Everything is in place, only they have each decided on a different retirement route to take. Samantha has gone with a Roth 401(k), contributing after-tax monies to her account while Benjamin decides on a traditional 401(k). Samantha has decided that she will most likely be in a similar tax bracket during retirement, not a significantly lower bracket, and thus uses the Roth option. What could their accounts look like?

---

[2] This is a hypothetical rate of return solely for illustrative purposes.

Both Samantha and Benjamin have $632,000[3] in their accounts at age 65. However, Samantha's Roth 401(k) owes nothing further in terms of taxes. She paid the $2,000 of taxes out of her pocket each year so she still contributed the entire $10,000 to her plan. Benjamin's traditional 401(k) still owes taxes. Assuming a tax rate of 20%, any amount that Benjamin decided to withdraw would be taxed at that rate. If he was to take the entire amount that would be $126,400 In order for Benjamin to end up with the same amount of after tax money, he would have to accumulate over $780,000 in his 401(k).

When both have turned 65, Samantha would have paid $50,000 of income tax on the amount she has contributed with no future income tax liability. Benjamin now has to start to pay income tax on every dollar he takes out of his plan. If they both took 5% and the plan continued to perform at 7% growth with taxes remaining at 20%, after retirement, Benjamin would only be ahead of Samantha for 8 years or until age 73. Beyond that, Benjamin will have paid more in income taxes than Samantha. If both live until age 80, Samantha would still have only paid $50,000 in income taxes while Benjamin would be up to $118,553. If both live until age 85, $50,000 would be paid by Samantha and $163,000 would be paid by Benjamin. In this case, at age 85, it would have been a $100,000 mistake by Benjamin. Futhermore, when each one passes away, Samantha's beneficiary owes no income taxes and can do whatever desired with the total amount inherited. Benjamin's beneficiary will not only inherit the money but an income tax liability as well.

In the first year of retirement both withdrew 5% for income, Samantha would get to use all $31,150 while Benjamin would only be able to use $24,920 because he would have to pay income taxes (20% in this example) on his withdrawal.

Uncommon use of Permanent Life Insurance
Permanent life insurance's primary purpose is to offer death benefit protection. There is one other benefit, and it can prove beneficial come retirement. A Permanent life insurance policy also offers the ability to accumulate tax-deferred cash value that can be accessed during your

---

[3] These values assume that the currently assumed hypothetical elements will continue unchanged for all years shown. This is not likely to occur and actual results may be more or less favorable than those shown.

lifetime, through policy loans and/or withdrawals[4], supplemental retirement income that you may be able to use not subject to taxes. That's why purchasing a permanent life insurance policy, not only for the important death benefit protection it provides your loved ones, but also the living benefits it provides has become an increasingly popular option for individuals . These benefits are all subject to the underwriting of the insured and the offerings of the insurance carrier.

To reiterate the *Primary Reason* to purchase life insurance:

- It is self completing, which means that if someone dies prematurely, the income tax-free death benefit will help fund a spouse's retirement goals.

Additional features:

- Protection in the event of disability may be available on many policies or for an additional premium and possibly subject to restrictions. This means that if you become disabled you can obtain a Waiver of Premium rider, which will continue to pay premiums if you cannot.

- Option to have access to funds in case of illness. You may be able to access all or part of your death benefits to help cover costs associated with critical, chronic, or terminal illnesses.

Some important considerations:

Life insurance products contain fees, such as mortality and expense charges, and may contain restrictions, such as surrender periods.

Imagine if you could...

1. Have income tax-free death benefits in place for those who depend on you.

---

[4] Policy loans and withdrawals may create an adverse tax result in the event of a lapse or policy surrender, and will reduce both the cash value and death benefit.

2. Possibly access cash using income tax-advantaged loans or withdrawals.[5]

3. Defer taxes for accumulated cash values.

WHAT ABOUT SELF-EMPLOYED INDIVIDUALS?

Self-employed people do have to do more of their ground work right off the bat to find the right retirement funding opportunities. There is no company meeting where HR or an advisor comes in and explains the process a bit, offers a few options, you sign up and then you are set—for the time being, anyway.

The main action a self-employed individual can take is to open up a solo 401(k) with a Roth Provision in it. This type of 401(k) is strictly for a sole proprietor—someone with no employees. However, spouses can contribute if they earn an income from the business. The Roth version involves putting in after-tax dollars and the traditional version is pre-taxed. Another interesting feature of them is that you are allowed to borrow against your savings. This is a unique benefit reserved for a sole proprietor.

ALSO, contributions are split between the employee and employer.

You know you need to revamp your strategy. What next?

Retirement planning is next to impossible to do all on your own. You may want to find someone you can trust and work with, a dedicated professional that can give you the guidance that you may benefit from in order to make smart choices that lead to a tax-advantaged retirement. It really is the only way to go.

---

[5] Administrative and insurance charges are deducted every month regardless of whether premium outlays are made. Depending upon actual policy experience, the Owner may need to increase premium payments. Any policy loans and partial surrenders will affect policy values and may require additional premiums to avoid policy termination.

IN CONCLUSION

When I started Wealth Management Group, I had one mission in mind when it came to retirement:

To help people establish comprehensive tax sensitive retirement plans.

There were also two criteria that every one of our experts would adhere to: expert knowledge and dedication to proven strategies. Your retirement money is not meant to be gambled with. With knowledgeable professionals and staff, we are able to help maximize the resources that will offer you the tools, services and resources to meet your financial needs.

Every client is different, coming to us with different expectations, needs, and starting points. Our approach to your success is as individual as your situation. We welcome you to expect this from the professionals you rely on, and we encourage you to take steps to make sure you are lessening the risks associated with retirement income that will adjust with factors that are beyond your control.

Common sense ideas are behind everything we offer and available for everyone to take. What is uncommon is people taking advantage of preparing for retirement that works to minimize taxes. Remember, tax-advantaged income in retirement is yours for the taking. No one ever lost out because they considered all their options. What is your next move?

About Doug

Douglas Chapman is the Co-Founder and Managing Member of Wealth Management Group, LLC.

With nearly 25 years of proven experience in helping individuals and families grow and maintain their wealth, Douglas Chapman co-founded Wealth Management Group, LLC, and has the role of Senior Partner. He is the lead person in the retirement and estate planning division of Wealth Management Group. Previously, he was with Langdon Ford Financial Group, which is now known as Allied Wealth Partners, a relationship he values greatly to this day.

With a specific focus on risk management, Douglas has helped a wide variety of clients with smart financial services, including: professional musicians, television actors, investment bankers, business owners, corporate executives, and retirees. In addition to this, he serves in an advisory and consultant capacity regarding risk management issues for hedge fund and private equity firms.

Douglas is a sought-out speaker for television and radio on various aspects of financial services. He has appeared on: CNBC Television regarding Estate Tax, and Retirement and Investment Strategies; Bloomberg Information Radio; *Investors' Business Daily; Smart Money Magazine*; and *Readers Digest Magazine*. He also hosts a weekly radio talk show, *Your Financial Future*, which has been on the airwaves for 19 years and is on three stations weekly: WMTR 1250 AM on Saturday from 8:00 to 9:00 a.m.; 1410 AM from 9:00 to 10:00 a.m. on Saturday; and WJRZ 100.1 FM on Sunday mornings from 7:00 to 8:00 a.m. Furthermore, Douglas is an endless advocate of continuing education and often makes presentations to attorneys and CPAs on various aspects of finance.

Awards of Excellence and acknowledgement from industry-leading financial service professionals are two things that Douglas is appreciative of; it's an acknowledgement of his excellence and commitment to sound financial strategies. These achievements include:

- Since 1998, Douglas has been a member of the Court of the Table, part of the Million Dollar Round Table. This prestigious award places him in the top 2/3 of 1% of all financial services professionals in the world.

- Langdon Ford Financial Recognitions:

    o Awards of Excellence in 1999 and then again in 2004—an unprecedented accomplishment.

o Top Producing Strategist in 1995.

o Associate of the year in 1994.

o New Associate of the year in 1993.

Community and family are two things that are equally as important to Douglas as financial services. He is an active community and civic volunteer, who can regularly be found helping feed the needy, raising money for handicapped citizens, and even coaching PAL football. He and his wife, Michele, also volunteer for various animal rescue organizations in the community. One organization that Douglas is particularly proud to be associated with is CASA of Union County, a non-profit organization that advocates for children's rights in the foster care system. He is currently serving as President of this organization. Douglas believes that with a genuine interest in your community, you can build stronger personal and professional relationships.

Doug Chapman is a Registered Representative and IAR of Securian Financial Services, Inc. Member FINRA/SIPC. A securities dealer and registered investment advisor. Wealth Management Group is independently owned and operated. 1199 Raritan Road, Clark, New Jersey 07066. Tel: 732-340-1410.

Tracking:1062043 DOFU: 11/2014

CHAPTER 8

THE 1/10ᵀᴴ OF 1% RULE AND INTERGRATED WEALTH PLANNING

BY EDWARD STORER,
Certified Tax Coach, Financial Wealth Strategist and Advocate

99.9% of all financial planning is done right. Unfortunately, once the planning is done, most people *assume* they are done and forget about the 1/10th of 1% Rule. What is the 1/10th of 1% Rule? It is a rule that, if not paid attention to, will cause horrific financial disaster for you and your family.

Let me share a story with you, please. Most of us who are old enough, will recall what we were doing on January 28, 1986 at 11:30 a.m. EST. It was the day that the Space Shuttle Challenger was lifting off for its tenth space flight. It was an exciting time, because for the first time, a civilian – Christa McAuliffe, a teacher – would go into space.

With nine proven successful trips, there was little to be worried about. All systems had been checked by the world's best—yes, the world's best scientists and engineers had given the go ahead for the Shuttle to take-off. Even though there were major warning signs, *NASA assumed that it would be safe.*

The countdown began…3, 2, 1, liftoff! It was so exciting to watch the Challenger rise up into the heavens. Can you imagine how excited everyone felt? Then in 73 seconds everything changed. The Shuttle exploded, killing all seven crew members. What caused that catastrophe? Not what anyone would have guessed. It was an O-ring. A gasket! In the scheme of things, this was a small, inexpensive part—1/10th of 1% of the entire makeup of the Space Shuttle Challenger.

If 1/10th of 1% can destroy the Space Shuttle, imagine what can happen to your financial plan if you assume it is correct. It could create a disaster for you and your family.

Let me explain it in this way: My mother, rest her soul, was a wise individual. One day she said to me, "Have you ever heard of anyone dying from an elephant bite?" I answered, "No." Then she asked, "Have you ever heard of anyone dying from a mosquito bite?" I answered, "Yes." She said, "Good. Why?" I knew I was being tested about something. I thought about it briefly and said, "When you see an elephant coming you get out of the way, but a mosquito is so tiny that it can sneak up on you. So you don't see it until it's too late." It's the little things, not the big things, which can cause problems or even death.

So the 1/10th of 1% Rule is assuming 100% of everything has been done right, and not paying attention to the little things. However this disaster can be avoided.

TIIE IT TOGETHER!

I love being a Tax and Wealth Coach. I love helping people create and maintain a custom designed Integrated Wealth Plan, engineered to *TIIE* the four areas of financial planning areas together:

1. **T**axes and tax planning

2. **I**nvestments and investment planning

3. **I**nsurance and insurance planning

4. **E**state planning, including trusts, wills and powers of attorney

Everyone needs a plan that *TIIEs* everything together. YES, EVERYONE! It's the only way to ensure you are addressing the 1/10th of 1% Rule. Usually, when I introduce this to our potential Wealth Coaching Members, I hear, "I have different people working for me on all those things. Why do I have to *TIIE* them all together?" It's a great question. Here's the answer:

> *Financial professionals should be working for you to create and maintain a custom engineered, Integrated Wealth Plan. It must be designed to **Shield, Protect, and Grow** your wealth. In order to do this, your tax professional, investment professional, insurance professional, and your estate planning attorney must meet on a regular basis and focus on the betterment of you and your family. Also, each individual should be an independent fiduciary.*

This is a highly <u>*Unusual Concept*</u> and it's why I was asked to co-author a chapter in this book. People need to know this information! *A fiduciary is someone that has a legal obligation to act in the best interest of another.* Would you rather have a fiduciary on your side or someone who wants to sell you something?

It's not a matter of intelligence; it's a matter of insight. Doing your research and hoping and believing you have a financial plan in place is good, but it isn't a guarantee that nothing will go wrong. I want to share a case study with you about Mike and Mary.

I met Mike and Mary through a referral by another couple, Todd and Sarah, who are our Wealth Members. Todd and Sarah invited the couple to come to a class I was teaching, called *Shielding, Protecting, & Growing Your Wealth in an Unusual World and Economy.* Mike and Mary are very private people and were reluctant to go at first. However, Todd and Sarah promised them there would be no sales pitch, just a fun time and education. Todd and Sarah also told Mike and Mary if they didn't like it, dinner was on them that night.

A little about Mike and Mary:

Mike is an Engineer and Mary is a Doctor. They are busy, successful, and embrace life to its fullest. They are conservative and private by nature. In order to make sure they were on top of everything, Mike and Mary hired a Certified Financial Planner to assist them in planning and preparation for retirement. They had a CPA, but Mike kept noticing mistakes, so he decided to start preparing his taxes himself. Smart, right? They have a broker helping them with their 401(k)s and other investments. Mary has also opened online accounts for Mike and herself to buy low-cost index mutual funds. They also have an insurance agent to handle their insurance needs, as well as an attorney that created a Trust for them. To them, it's a complete picture. A full 100% plan. They have addressed the important issues and assume everything is done right with their taxes, investments, insurance, and estate planning. They know they are blessed and believe they are prepared. But are they?

Night of the Class:

I met Mike and Mary just before the class started. During the class we talked about today's uncertain political environment, economic conditions, as well as tax ramifications for the U.S. and the world. The big question was "How will these issues affect your Wealth?" Mike and Mary were used to an investment person telling them, "Everything is great." "Everything will rebound." But the real shock came to them when they heard:

> *The first thing a business owner, pre-retiree, or retiree should do is shield and protect the wealth that has already been accumulated. At the same time, create a guaranteed income plan for you and your spouse. The income plan must be ever-increasing and able to grow ahead of taxes, inflation, and unforeseen medical expenses.*

"I've never heard this before," Mike whispered to Todd. "The people we have always want me to stick my money in the stock market."

"What kind of plan do you have in place for when the market crashes?" Todd asked Mike.

"I don't. I actually asked that question of my CFP and broker last week."

"What did he say, Mike?" Todd asked.

"Hang in there. It always comes back."

By the way, does anyone really find that advice comforting? Or, is it something that you just become accustomed to hearing? Mike started to feel that his investment people may not be as invested in him as he had been led to believe. Both Mike and Mary started looking uneasy. This is the defining difference between a broker/sales person and a Fiduciary. You see, when you work with a Fiduciary, they are going to share with you the truth—whether you like it or not.

Next, the class was asked, "What is the slogan for BMW cars?" Everyone shouted out, "The Ultimate Driving Machine!" Then, everyone was asked to close their eyes and reach out in front of them to grab a hold of the steering wheel of their pretend brand-new BMW. It didn't take long for all these adults to start having fun, driving their imaginary cars down the road at 90 miles per hour.

I shouted, "BAM! Your steering wheel is gone." Mary's eyes flew open. "What would happen?" I asked.

Todd yelled out, "You'd crash!"

"You're right. We'd better put the steering wheel back on." I went on asking questions such as, "What would happen if the tires fell off, or the transmission was gone?" Everyone agreed that they would end up having a lot of pieces from an automobile that was impressive as a whole, but not so much in small parts. My final question was, "How many of you have your taxes, investments, insurance, and estate planning, TIIEd together to create an Integrated Wealth Plan? A plan designed to Shield, Protect, and Grow your wealth?"

Mike and Mary saw only a few hands go up around them, including Todd and Sarah's. It was a wake-up call. Mike and Mary decided to schedule a financial checkup with our Fiduciary Team. Then Mike walked over to Todd and said, "Let Mary and I buy Sarah and you dinner tonight."

THE CHECKUP WITH THE FIDUCIARY TEAM.

Mike and Mary are the type of people that we see and help every day at *Edward Storer & Associates, Integrated Wealth Management and the Wealth Training Academy*. During their checkup we found the following:

TAXES: SEVEN (7) PROBLEMS

1. They never had a tax planner – they had a tax preparer previously, and were presently using tax preparation software. They had no ongoing tax reduction plan in place for today or the future.

2. They were missing out on $12,014 in current year (and beyond) tax savings strategies

3. They were missing out on conversion opportunities to move from a traditional IRA to a Roth IRA, and pay little to no tax on

conversions (as of the time of writing this chapter).

4. They were not taking advantage of catch-up opportunities inside their retirement accounts.

5. They did not realize that they had a cost basis in their IRAs, which meant:

   a. They would pay double tax on a portion of the retirement account.

   b. They did not know that some IRAs have a cost basis.

6. They were going to pay unnecessary tax on their Social Security.

7. They were unaware of the advantages of Medical Savings Accounts.

INVESTMENTS: ELEVEN (11) PROBLEMS

1. There was no guaranteed income plan other than Social Security.

2. They had no knowledge of Social Security maximizing strategies.

3. No written Investment Policy Statement.

4. They did not know the *actual rate of return necessary to maintain their lifestyle regardless of tax rates, inflation, and unforeseen medical expenses.*

5. They did not realize there is a way to have effective asset withdrawal—knowing which account is best to spend first.

6. They did not understand *proper asset allocation.*

7. They did not know how to measure portfolio diversification and risk.

8. They were not aware of the costs they were paying to invest, including those so-called low-expense indexed mutual funds, hidden fees, and commissions—even inside their 401(k)s. *Remember: insurance agents and brokers are salespeople.*

9. They did not understand the difference between a ***Fiduciary***

__Responsibility Coach/Partner__ versus a *__Suitability, which is a salesperson, financial advisor, insurance agent, or broker.__*

10. *They were not aware of the risks they were taking* in regards to: income, markets, interest rate, liquidity, inflation, and timing. NOTE: Remember, Mike and Mary told us they were conservative people!

11. They did not have a cohesively Integrated Wealth Plan. Instead, they had a bunch of investment products that had been sold to them. No Wealth Machine!

INSURANCE: NINE (9) PROBLEMS
Property-Casualty Insurance

Home Owner & Car Insurance – 7 Problems

1. No language included for their Trust.

2. Not enough coverage to replace home, based on new building costs.

3. No protection against law suits.

4. Titling on insurance was wrong.

5. Cars were placed in the Trust.

6. No Umbrella Liability Coverage.

7. Inadequate protection against Identity Theft.

Life Insurance and Long Term Care

Life Insurance – 2 Problems

8. Inadequate beneficiary language.

9. Outdated policies. There are new policies that cover both life insurance and long-term care. One premium, one policy, and it covers your needs. It's cheaper than having two individual policies. NOTE: *These policies are available for individuals with pre-existing conditions!*

ESTATE PLANNING: FOURTEEN (14) PROBLEMS

Power of Attorney Documents – 4 Problems

1. 6 years old.

2. Inadequate gifting language.

3. Did not allow power to fund other investment plans.

4. Made the children potentially liable for laws suits.

Incorrect Titling on Assets and Accounts – 4 Problems

5. Subjecting them to unnecessary probate time and cost.

6. Subjecting them to unnecessary potential lawsuits.

7. Subjecting them to inability to access assets in case of an emergency.

8. Subjecting them to the inability to liquidate assets if necessary.

Trusts & Wills– 6 Problems

9. No Survivors Guide in place.

10. No Living Will in place.

11. There was no Quality of Life Directive in place, which is different than a Living Will.

12. They unintentionally disinherited their grandkids.

13. Beneficiary language was not up to date.

14. The Trust was structured to cause 30% to 50% more taxes on retirement accounts due to state and federal taxes.

Every asset Mike and Mary owned was at risk. Does that sound conservative? They believed that they'd conducted good research and had done an effective job of protecting what they worked so hard to earn. Mike and Mary's names are fictitious; *but their situation, issues and concerns are real!*!!

PROTECT AND PREPARE

Every day my team, the Fiduciary Wealth Team, visits with business owners, pre-retirees, and retirees that only have 99.9% of their financial world right. After reading this chapter you don't need to be one of them. By understanding the 1/10th of 1% Rule and creating a *custom engineered, Integrated Wealth Plan, that is designed to TIIE it all together, you will:*

SHIELD, PROTECT, AND GROW YOUR WEALTH.

About Edward

Edward J. Storer is a **Financial Wealth Strategist and Advocate,** an independent fiduciary, Certified Tax Coach, Investment and Insurance Advisor, as well as a Retirement and Estate Planning Specialist. For over 25 years, Ed has been assisting business owners and families plan "to and through" retirement.

Ed is the founder, owner, and president of *Edward Storer & Associates, Integrated Wealth Management*, an independent Wealth Planning firm in Greenville, SC. He is also the founder of the **Wealth Training Academy**. The Wealth Training Academy is a place designed to coach, teach, train, and educate those who are ready to understand and take control of their Wealth. According to Ed, "My goal in creating *Edward Storer & Associates, Integrated Wealth Management*, and the **Wealth Training Academy**, was to gather experts in each of the four areas of financial planning: Taxes, Investments, Insurances, and Estate Planning, and put them under one roof to create an integrated team approach in planning that must **"TIIE"** together for proper wealth management. *This is the only way to Shield, Protect, and Grow your wealth."*

This innovative approach to financial coaching is Ed's specialty. He works with people of all income brackets to educate them in effective strategies to save them money and set up protection for them with taxes, investments, insurance, and estate planning. Ed has saved his Wealth Members millions of dollars from losses in the market, as well as overpayments to the IRS. For this original concept, he has been quoted in various industry publications and financial articles, as well as authored chapters for books. Ed enjoys sharing his expertise and has also been a keynote speaker at various industry events.

Ed loves life and enjoys it to the fullest with his wife Jeannine, and his two children, Brooke and Brittney. They live in the Greenville, SC area where Ed and Jeannine are very active in various community events.

Ed can be reached by calling the office and scheduling a phone appointment at: 864-297-6125 or on line at: www.EdwardStorer.com.

CHAPTER 9

THE PROSPEROUS LIFE FORMULA

BY JAKE SCOTT, MBA, PMP

It would be great if our lives provided us with an "aha" moment. You know, the moment of truth where we undoubtedly realize what the secret to a truly abundant life is—it is as an individual definition. Well, as life would have it, many of us miss the clues which can lead us to the information we need to experience this. We may be so busy we do not even notice our moment is presenting itself, or we are so tired from trying to find it we mentally fall asleep and miss the opportunity to take action. How do we make sure we do not miss out? It is a balance of three important factors, which will make for one complete, passion-filled individual; a balance of **family, financial health and fitness**, or **F3**.

I will always recall an experience I had as a younger man. It changed my life, and more so, it changed my perspective. I was married and in the military and had received orders to report to a base in South Korea for the upcoming year. I was worried about missing my wife, which is common for anyone in the service, but she delivered me some amazing news. She was pregnant with our first child. Of course I was excited, but three short days later I had to go. Wow, it was a hard year, but being an organized guy, I bought a ticket and arranged to have leave so I could be home for the birth of my child and for a few weeks after. It was perfectly planned, but alas, life is not always in agreement with our greatest of plans.

One day, while working near the flightline I received word my wife called. This was highly unusual. I quickly made my way to a phone. She was in labor. My heart sunk; I was halfway around the world in South Korea. There was no way I could get back home to be there for my first child's birth, much less do what I was so excited to do—cut the umbilical cord. This experience cemented one thing in me: *I was not going to be the guy who was unavailable and missing out on the most important moments in my family's life.*

How was I going to have a successful career—something else I was devoted to achieving—and not miss these moments? There was only one solution for me. I needed to find balance between my personal life and professional aspirations. Plus, I needed to give both of these things ample amounts of energy and devotion. I understood how this could only be achieved if family, financial health, and fitness all existed in my life. They complemented each other and the quality of life I wanted to live.

GET IT DONE! DO IT RIGHT!

This is a motto I use in all areas of my life. It is based on the motto of my first Civil Engineer unit in the Air Force, which was: _Do it right, not twice_. This was one of the most important lessons I learned in the military and I learned it the hard way. Like many people who enlist, I did not get to pick my career field as "Air Force needs come first." To my surprise, I was to be a Structural Specialist—aka: carpenter/welder. I initially had zero interest in it, but it was my place to be and I would make the best of it.

Just eighteen years old, working in facility maintenance at my first duty location, I had a job to build a wall in one of the dormitories. I used the wrong thickness drywall and my work didn't meet the local fire code. Somehow my shop superintendent got word of what I had done. It surely was not me who told him. He came up to me and asked, "How did you approach this?" He pointed to the wall. I responded, "Well, I did this and this…" He walked over there to inspect it and I stood there, nervous as could be, and heard exactly what I did not want to hear—I had to do it again and do it right.

The shortcuts I had taken for convenience's sake had not saved me time, they had cost me time. If I had done it right the first time, I would have been finished with the project after the first attempt. This lesson transcends into so many things in life. Learning this has helped me to:

- Solidify my formal education while simultaneously working full time and raising a family with four children.

- Realize how much my time matters so I can balance family, financial health and fitness. Wasting time avoiding doing something today means it will have to be done tomorrow.

- Become a business owner with a solid plan, knowing my dedication and experience will shore up my success.

It is absolutely essential to acknowledge that we must do it right the first time. Wasted energy leads to failure. I know I am not alone in this belief. Success is considerably more pleasant than knowing we have not done what we were capable of doing in life. **Get it done! Do it right!**

THE PROSPEROUS LIFE FORMULA

There are some people who feel there is just not enough time in a day to do everything they want to do. We have all experienced being this person at one time or another. Truthfully, thoughts and feelings such as those are an excuse for the person that does not have a plan; a plan for Family, Financial health and Fitness – **F3**. Let me explain:

- The core of most people's happiness is their family and friends, the people they surround themselves outside the work environment. They are the reason we do what we do. I want to be present for these people, which means I take care of business when appropriate. I do not procrastinate and I give great effort in my work life, which means my family deserves the same. We all win!

  Every day I prioritize my tasks. Each task is given an *A, B, C,* or *D.* "A" tasks must be accomplished today, they are important. "B" tasks need to be done soon. "C" tasks can wait but have the potential to become "B" tasks. "D" tasks can be delegated. Writing them down solidifies my daily planning process. Also, understand time urgency is often orthogonal to importance. A work task may be urgent, but your family is more important.

- When we are not financially healthy, it impacts our own happiness and our family lives, too. Worries and stress invade us, reducing the quality of our time with those we love. Plus, stress and worry make us less likely to workout, which is disappointing because exercise is what our bodies need to recharge, to come up with those "aha" ideas and the energy we need to be successful in our professional and personal relationships.

Do not get me wrong, money does not buy happiness. However, according to Pew Research, economic growth helps improve feelings of well-being. I find this to be true. If I am able to take care of the basic essentials in life then the moments I have with my family are more meaningful. This allows for more quality and quantity of family time activities. These activities do not have to cost money, but eliminating financial stress enhances amazing moments.

Take the time to invest in yourself. Spend about 3% of your annual income to grow your knowledge. This could include formal training, seminars, or even books. Your personal growth is the key to your individual financial success.

- Choosing a sustainable fitness routine is one of the best ways to kickstart a success- filled life! We are the only person who will take the best care of ourselves. I do not mean having a model body or whatever your "ideal" body may be; I am referring to making sure our body, which is our vessel and something we rely on to get through life, 24/7, is operating at peak efficiency.

According to Dr. Rick Kattouf II, a fitness and nutrition expert, quoting Henry Ford, "Whether you think you can or whether you think you cannot...you are right!" In order to take care of others in our lives we must take care of ourselves first. Making fitness and nutrition changes is not always easy, but you will never regret working out or eating a macronutrient-balanced meal. A fit body will lead to a focused mind, which in turn shores up a successful business and family life. Finding the motivational support of a certified fitness and nutrition coach can help ensure success.

We are all busy people because we want great things for our lives. Through experiencing life and having the right mindset for what it entails, I have been given opportunities to lay out a path to success. Taking advantage of life's opportunities is exciting, and the focus of everything I do lies around a balance of **F3**. Do you want to have time for Family, Financial health and Fitness? I believe you do. It is time to find out how you can achieve it.

F3 IN ACTION

Diligence is a word you must embrace and pursue with every bit of gusto and enthusiasm you have. Pursue persistent exertion of both mind and body. Develop a plan and execute to success while understanding your risks. With diligence, you can:

- Have success in your career

- Enjoy a fulfilling family life

- Participate in the activities that bring joy

When you diligently pursue the things you want in life with a plan, you are more likely to accomplish your goals. Write your goals down and post them on your bathroom mirror and then tell your family and friends what you want to accomplish. Once your goals are internalized and given life through your actions, they soon will be realized.

During my time in the Air Force, I transitioned from my enlisted career to being an officer working with space systems. I was afforded the opportunities to travel the world – from the Great Pyramids of Giza to the busy streets of Manila – all while working with some of the smartest people on the planet! I loved my time in the military, but eventually it was time to retire and make my way into civilian life. So, at the age of 37, I retired as a Major.

Transitioning to the next chapter of my life was amazing. I had fitness to keep me focused and family to keep me grounded. At the same time, I was able to find opportunities because of my success in the military. I found steady work, but felt there was more I could do to help me find the perfect combination for true fulfillment. I decided:

- To become an expert public speaker.

- To become a project management SME.

- To open my own business. (This was something I had always aspired to do.)

Working full-time and operating a full-time business takes coordination and focused effort. It takes planning. If I was going to do it, I was not about to fail. Eventually, I decided to open a kickboxing fitness gym.

I approached my new gym like I would any of my major projects and developed a solid business plan. It led to my doing what is often considered impossible after just one month—I was breaking even. This was huge! It took only eight months for me to start turning a profit and defying the odds of a heavily-saturated fitness market. This did not happen by good luck and chance. It happened because of careful planning and a "bucket-load" of energy and enthusiasm.

When we realize that everything we choose to do—or not to do—has meaning, we can act accordingly and create milestones and markers to show we are doing what is meant to be done. Instead of watching a television show, read a book to help you learn something new and advance your goals. I recommend you start with *The Power of Self-Discipline* by Brian Tracy. If you do not have time to read, get the audio book. Have enough energy to play with your kids, hang out with your friends, or go on an adventure. The one thing I really love about fitness is how it is a family activity if we want it to be, or it can be an activity we do alone. You can hit the gym, go on a hike, or briskly walk around the park. Just remember to make the most out of your day; be diligent in pursuing the things you desire and aspire to become – whether you want to be a better spouse, parent, entrepreneur, or employee.

KEEP THE PURSUIT OF EXCELLENCE ALIVE—PEP

Every step we take to have a better life and achieve wonderful things is a step we should look forward to taking. If it is hard work, so be it. Some things are hard, but they are also worth it. However, it is important to work smarter, not harder:

- Passion

- Energy

- Personality

These three things are all must-haves for success, PEP for short. Love what you do and do it with compelling **Passion**. People will be drawn to your success. Positive **Energy** will support your efforts to reach your goals. You know this type of person when they are around you; you can feel it in the air. **Personality** goes without saying. We want to be around vibrant people who are likeable, trustworthy, and dedicated to what they are doing. They are natural leaders who let us know if there is a will, there is a way!

TAKE A CHALLENGE TO LIVE A PROSPEROUS LIFE

Life can be complicated, but to live it in a meaningful, fulfilled way is simple. Enjoy what you are doing because in life we often do not get a do-over. Have fun every moment and realize that knowing how fortunate you are to know what drives you . . . is wonderful. Realizing how to have a balance between **financial health, family** and **fitness** is essential. Embrace your **passion, energy** and **personality** to create paths which will lead you to success. You know exactly where you are going when you are the captain of your ship. It is time for action! What is your passion? **Get it done! Do it right!**

About Jake

Jake Scott, MBA, PMP is driven to help others succeed in business and life. Understanding the pleasure that comes from living out your passions is the core belief behind how he approaches life each and every day. As a small to medium business expert, Jake understands all areas of a person's life can be amazing when a person is living out their passions. Jake exemplifies this in his career and his personal life. Presently, he is the co-owner of a successful fitness gym, where he helps others achieve their fitness goals. He is also a Project Manager and System Engineer, focusing on being agile and objective in the deployment of technology and helping others reach their lifelong business goals. It's a unique combination of careers at first glance, but Jake has found these professional avenues complement each other in a special way. They work together to develop focus and a positive mindset that are needed to offer true solutions and ideas, which are an essential part of being successful in life.

Twenty years of service in the Air Force provided Jake invaluable opportunities to work at various locations around the world. He developed skills that lent to his personal philosophies that include embracing family, finance health and fitness. To further enhance these valuable philosophies, Jake earned his BS in Business Administration and an MBA with an emphasis in Project Management. His collective set of experiences give him a unique insight into career and business.

Jake has a natural tendency to pursue success through personal excellence and is a natural inspiration to those around him. Through his actions and commitment to living a more inspired life, Jake has begun reaching out to others to share the powerful motivators that can lead to greater joy and balance in their personal and professional lives. His experiences offer great insight and show that when people apply themselves and use their strengths to achieve better results, amazing results can follow. Every day he is committed to "learning and growing" with new information and ideas, bringing value to projects in which he is involved. This carries over to a natural leadership style that is encouraging, supportive and inspirational to others.

Despite a busy schedule, Jake never forgets the greatest gifts of his life—his family. He takes great joy in those special moments with his wife, whether it be working out together at their gym, or going to cheer their four children on at one of their sporting events or band activities. He is committed to making their time together meaningful. For "wind–down" time, Jake enjoys photography, music, science and travel.

Are you ready to bring your life to the next level? Visit: www.teamjakescott.com

CHAPTER 10

CREATING YOUR TRUST-BASED MEDIA PLATFORM

BY GREG ROLLETT

I had met Mel Taylor a few times before. She was quite possibly the biggest supporter of local Orlando music, spending her Friday and Saturday nights at the bars. She popped in and out of shows ranging from the funky sounds of *Beyond The Sun* and *The Aristocracy* to the hard rock tunes of *Atomic Tangerine* and *Social Ghost*. These were all bands on the rise, playing for their fans and friends, completely accessible and selling $5 CD's and $10 t-shirts to cover their bar tab.

It was also the heyday of Myspace.com, the once all-mighty giant in the social networking space. Our favorite piece of the entire Myspace system was their bulletins. In one self-promotional post, we could share a flyer for our upcoming event, solicit RSVP's and tell everyone in our network about the things we had going on. This was best used to promote tour dates and local events, but also served us well when releasing a new song on the platform, or even posting pictures from the previous night's show so fans could see if they were included in the photos somewhere.

These bulletins were the first real platform I ever had to share a message with hundreds of thousands of people. Think about the power in that. Every day we could send a message that had the potential to be seen by a few hundred thousands fans of our band. These were not strangers, or people who might like our music.

As powerful as the Myspace platform was, we thought the platform that

Mel Taylor controlled would make Myspace as little as a minnow in the Atlantic Ocean. You see, Mel Taylor controlled the local night on Real Rock 101.1's radio station. They were the goliath in rock radio, and still are in Central Florida. And once a week, on Sunday nights at 11pm, they gave the controls to Mel and welcomed in a band of the week. These bands would be interviewed about their start, their mission and their ideals. They would play a few songs live in the studio and have a song or two played from their album on the air.

Every week, rising star after rising star would have their opportunity to shine. Week after week the bands featured would be taken from mere local band to "The Next Big Thing."

And one fateful week back in 2007, we were next. Mel had seen us perform at a local establishment we would frequently sell out, the AKA Lounge, off Pine and Magnolia in Downtown Orlando. We would pack in 200 or so college kids, a few high school seniors who had fake ID's and were raving fans, mixed with friends we had collected along the way.

Each time we played, the room was electric. When Mel saw us perform, the crowd was especially magical, shouting the words to our closing track, *Car Crash*, a song about a girl who sent her boyfriend's world crashing down. Mel instantly wanted us to get into the studio and talk about our band and play some tracks live.

We got to the station early, around 10:30pm, not wanting to be late for our spotlight on the radio. We were led down a long hallway that opened up to a small studio, maybe 10 feet by 10 feet. To say we were tightly crammed in like sardines in a can would be an understatement. We sat on bar stools and raggedy chairs that should have been tossed away months prior to our arrival. It was hardly the red carpet treatment we had billed up in our heads.

The actual interview and live performance went smooth as ever. You can actually watch the performance today on YouTube with a little bit of researching and searching.

What I am about to share to you about this story is the real power of a platform. That evening's audience wasn't the biggest the show had ever had, but people did listen.

We expected our sales to climb off the charts and for folks to be calling us in to headline their venues and shower us with caviar and champagne as they courted us to join their record labels.

This was a fantasy. A big mirage.

The disappointment of the radio platform didn't discourage us however. Instead, we leveraged the station's platform to have our music and our story heard by influential booking agents, club owners, record label executives and music store owners. We took the interview and show recording and sent it to other stations and mailed it to everyone we wanted to hear it. We leveraged our relationship with Mel to keep playing *Car Crash* week after week, continuing to leverage the radio to build our fan base and collect more friends on Myspace – who would in turn see our bulletins and come to our shows.

Put another way, we used the mass media to fuel our internal media, our platform. It wasn't the audience on the radio that continued to build our band and our business. It was sending the listeners a message from a media that the market trusts, and directed it to the media that we control. The larger the group of fans that we had control over - how and when they received communication from us, from our voice, with our calls-to-action – that was the power in the platform.

I've previously talked about the power of celebrity and mainstream media in building trust. Getting on the radio allowed us to develop trust in the market. It gave us instant trust with new fans who had never previously heard of us. Fans who wouldn't think twice if they saw us on the street, but who are now raving about us because they discovered us on the radio.

That is Step 1. Step 2 is now bringing them over to a platform that you control.

THE POWER OF HAVING YOUR OWN PLATFORM

In order to establish yourself in this trusted advisor role and become that celebrity in the minds of your targeted affluent group of prospects, you must create and leverage media platforms that have proven to build trust. You must use media that gives you a place to deliver your state of the union, reinstate your battle cry and motivate the troops that you wish to take into battle.

It is not a place to regurgitate facts, to deliver another Top 10 list, or sell your wares as any other sales person would do. It is a place to integrate personality. To inject emotion. To build and tell your legend.

These media platforms need to come from many angles to give you the appearance of being seen everywhere, like a celebrity, another Trust Trigger. I think you are starting to see many of these Trust Triggers working together and in concert with each other.

It's why Oprah controls you on TV, on the web and with her own magazine. Notice that she has her own magazine and didn't rely on publicists or PR agents to get her cover articles. She put herself on the cover of a magazine she controlled and has continued to put herself on the cover each and every month since April of 2000.

Knowing the value of projecting to your market who you are seen with, Oprah has only shared the cover of her own magazine twice - once with Michelle Obama and once with Ellen DeGeneres.

Working in multiple channels and formats is no stranger to possibly the hardest working man in Hollywood, someone I look up to and attempt to model in my own, small world, Ryan Seacrest. 5 days a week, 4 hours per day on the radio to more than 150 markets, add in a weekend gig hosting the Top 40 Countdown Show, hosting American Idol on FOX, producing hit reality shows like the Kardashians. Add in specials like New Years Rocking Eve, contributing to the Today Show, the Olympics and more.

This is a guy that knows how to be seen and be seen in all the right places for his market.

When you look at Ryan's body of work, he could easily stop showing up to radio, 4 hours a day, 5 days a week. What you might not understand is that radio is Ryan's platform. It is his email list. It is his newsletter. He hosts the guests he wants, gets to talk about what he wants and pushes it out to his legion of fans on the radio, on demand through iHeartRadio and then repurposes the content on another platform he controls, ryanseacrest.com.

Which begs the question, what is your platform? What is the media that you control that has direct access to your clients, your customers, your prospects and people in your tribe and community?

Having a platform isn't just about showing up. It's not about going through the motions. Oprah doesn't go through the motions on her TV shows, in her interviews and writing columns for her magazine.

Ryan Seacrest doesn't go through the motions when posting on social media, chatting with guests on the radio and when posting messages online that drive more page views and sponsor money back into his universe.

On your own platform, you must show up as an ambassador. . . As a resource. As someone who understands the needs and desires of the community you are aiming to serve. That is how you develop trust with an audience. Not by creating more noise and adding to the daily commotion and clutter that fills up our inbox, our mailbox and our voicemail.

In his brilliant book, *Platform*, Michael Hyatt says,

> *"Without a platform - something that enables you to get seen and heard - you don't have a chance. Having an awesome product, an outstanding service, or a compelling cause is no longer enough.*
>
> *A platform is your tribe. People who share your passion and want to hear from like-minded people. A platform enables you to cut through the noise and deliver your message or product right into the heart of your best prospects."*

It's time to create your platform.

THE FORMATION OF YOUR PLATFORM

You probably already have a platform in your business that you are not taking full advantage of. An email list that has been neglected. A client or customer list you haven't send a print newsletter to or mailed anything to in ages. Maybe it's a Facebook page that isn't getting the likes, comments and shares you thought it would get. It might even be your blog or website that Google stopped indexing or you stopped posting on.

You might not have anything resembling a platform. I've worked with business owners and entrepreneurs who keep their client list on an Excel Spreadsheet and think loading them into an email service or writing them a warm letter in a newsletter is like conducting brain surgery.

No matter the level you are at right now, it's time to focus on developing a platform. A place where you can communicate with your prospects and customers at will, on a media that you control, with communications and messages they actually welcome into their lives. They read, they watch, they listen and respond. They hang on every word. They share the messages with their social circle.

Where do you start?

You start by having a message worth sharing. You start by forming your own ideals and opinions. You start by having a mission that has to be told. A mission that can be bolted up no longer.

Without a clear message to shout, no media, no tool, no platform will grow, expand or collect legions of fans and followers.

Let's analyze Glen Beck as an example. He has a very clear message and obsession. That message has very devout followers. He talks about "the right to life, freedom of religion, limited government, and family as the cornerstone of society."

If Glen Beck was wishy-washy, flip-flopping on issues like gun control, abortion and his thoughts on governmental decisions, he would not have the audience he has today.

These opinions, for Glen Beck, are very polarizing. They make the left side go absolutely crazy. They make half the right side go crazy. His conversations get heated. His callers are emotional. Hi audience lives and breathes for everything he does. They hang on every word for 3 hours a day, 5 days a week.

Glen can put that message on nearly any platform and it will work. And it does. His radio show is constantly among the top-rated syndicated talk radio shows in the country. His books become instant Best-Sellers, in fact six of them have hit the New York Times Best-Sellers List.

Take away Glen's very strong opinions and no platform or fancy tool will put him on the Best-Seller list or give him the audience and legion of fans he has today.

You must declare the things you stand for. The things you believe in when it comes to how you help your audience and community. This could be the way you show homes, or the process you have for listing homes if you are a realtor. This may be your investing philosophy if you are a financial advisor. It may be the way you feel about the current justice system as a trial lawyer. It may be your perspective on marketing or advertising.

No matter your business model, the amount of regulations your industry has and the social norms you think your industry has, you must stand for something. This something should not be the same "something" that everyone else stands for. Trust isn't created by sounding like everyone else. Trust occurs when someone falls in love with you and your opinions. How are you blazing your own trail? What are you doing to set yourself apart and place yourself alone, in a sea of "me-too" competitors?

I consult with and work for a large number of financial advisors, more specifically who work with retirees and pre-retirees to help them distribute their assets and create enough income to live during their retirement.

They work in a sea of competitors who offer similar services, with similar brochures, similar sales pitches, similar products and similar returns.

What makes them stand apart? Their values. Their personality. Their spin on it. Their story. Injecting this into your platform will get you herd. It will make you stand apart. It will make someone pay attention.

This is the start of the creation of your platform. The place where you control the message, the media and the market. Once you do so, you can have complete control over your business. Time to go create your platform, isn't it?

About Greg

Greg Rollett, @gregrollett, is a Best-Selling Author and Marketing Expert who works with experts, authors and entrepreneurs all over the world. He utilizes the power of new media, direct response and personality-driven marketing to attract more clients and to create more freedom in the businesses and lives of his clients.

After creating a successful string of his own educational products and businesses, Greg began helping others in the production and marketing of their own products and services. He now helps his clients through 2 distinct companies, Celebrity Expert Marketing and the ProductPros.

Greg has written for *Mashable, Fast Company, Inc.com, The Huffington Post*, AOL, AMEX's Open Forum and others, and continues to share his message helping experts and entrepreneurs grow their business through marketing.

Greg's client list includes Michael Gerber, Brian Tracy, Tom Hopkins, Coca-Cola, Miller Lite and Warner Brothers, along with thousands of entrepreneurs and small-business owners across the world. Greg's work has been featured on FOX News, ABC, NBC, CBS, CNN, *USA Today, Inc Magazine, The Wall Street Journal*, the *Daily Buzz* and more.

Greg loves to challenge the current business environment that constrains people to working 12-hour days during the best portions of their lives. By teaching them to leverage marketing and the power of information, Greg loves to help others create freedom in their businesses that allow them to generate income, make the world a better place, and live a radically-ambitious lifestyle in the process.

A former touring musician, Greg is highly sought after as a speaker, who has spoken all over the world on the subjects of marketing and business building.

If you would like to learn more about Greg and how he can help your business, please contact him directly at: greg@dnagency.com or by calling his office at 877.897.4611.

CHAPTER 11

THE HARD WAY OF THE WOLF TO SELL MORE IN TOUGH TIMES

BY FRANK MERENDA

In order to become a successful seller, a wide range of expertise is needed. Personalities come before acquired skills, and they guide us in the right direction. Before jumping to judge me negatively based on what you are about to read, rest assured that I am being ironic, and I don't want to judge others personal attitudes or their professional or business choices. It is important, however, to debunk the myth that "Anybody can achieve anything if they work hard enough."

We are born strong in certain areas, and weaker in others, therefore our true paths mustn't be suppressed by the desires of other people. They must be chosen based on the strengths that we were born with. There's a tiny genetic difference between wolves and poodles - roughly 0.000001% - yet, this difference is huge in terms of behavior and attitude.

Poodles are accustomed to being fed by their master and lazing on the couch all day. Whereas, wolves live in the woods, and have to cope with freezing conditions. They sleep outside, and must hunt for their food. Poodles live in enclosed "kennels", whereas wolves roam *free*. Obviously, the life of a poodle is an analogy for that of many people, who want an easy life – i.e., a "safe" income. The wolf represents self-reliance, drive, and the desire to explore.

There is nothing "wrong" with having either of the two driving factors, but what is important is to recognize the "genetic stock", and follow that it is a fundamental pillar in order to reach personal fulfillment. If you have the poodle mentality, the bad and brutal world out there is not for you. The ice and snow will ruffle your delicate fur, and if you actually had to get off your ass and hunt for your food, you would most likely end up a vegan dog.

Some natural wolves accidentally find themselves in a poodle pack, but they soon develop a strong dislike for that kind of "boring" lifestyle. There is always something deep within. Jack London called it: "The Call of the Wild." Many wolves remain "trapped," buried under social pressures and the expectations of others.

A poodle really believes that on the day it was born, another person was born with the task of giving it a job. It thinks that it has the right to paid holidays, and that it can always clock off at 18:00, even if its work is not finished. This is because, in the end, the salary is always the same. A wolf knows it will have to skip lunch in order to keep its prey in sight.

A wolf that is a true entrepreneur, knows instinctively that it must regularly pay its employees by ANY means necessary. Wolves work 14 hours or more a day, non-stop, trying to get their business off the ground. On the other hand, the Poodle would never even consider giving up its weekends away in THE HAMPTONS to progress in life.

I can never bite my tongue when I encounter this type of person. Here's how it always goes; I'm invited to an event... I arrive, I sit down, I introduce myself, and then my inner brain screams:

"!!! POODLES !!!"

With very few exceptions, they are all employees of someone else. This would be commendable IF they didn't always complain about their a*****e boss because sometimes they have to sacrifice their 'after-work cocktails' in order to work late. As long as all is well, there's peace, but as soon as they receive a smaller biscuit, they become negative and unbearable. They immediately start complaining and finger pointing.

It wouldn't be so "bad" if they just left me alone, but the problem with poodles is that they have the bad taste to ask me, "What do you do?" Unfortunately, it is impossible to explain what I do to poodles. After asking the question, they glare at me and then ask: "Yeah right, but what exactly do you do?" After giving the dumbed-down version - the inevitable response is always, "Okay. Got it! You've been lucky!"

This statement automatically brings out my inner wolf. I know that I probably shouldn't be so aggressive, dismissive and unhelpful, but why stop when it's so much fun. Some people are born to fight. It has been like this forever. There's a race of warriors different from the rest. If they don't have a just battle to fight, they always end up getting into trouble. It is no coincidence that the Roman soldiers kept their minds and bodies busy during peacetime by constructing fortifications.

Not surprisingly, in every run-down neighborhood, boxing instructors are constantly transforming "street bullies," and turning them into champions in all aspects of their lives. These are examples of "wolf" kids who lacked the proper guidance.

Unfortunately, many wolves grow up in the wrong environment. They become "emasculated" and find themselves living the monotonous life of a poodle. This isn't a problem. The Poodle is HAPPY with its lifestyle, and that's fine, but a wolf who feels compelled to lead the life of a poodle inevitably ends up badly.

Many of my students who have arrived at a "difficult" stage of their lives, ask me how they can deal with it. I don't have skills to help them, but I can commit them to the "care" of those who can free them from their "poodle" lives. The wolf is in the minority and is free. The poodle will always be in the majority. I know from past experience how hard it is to resist the desire to try to please everyone, to conform, to bury dreams deep within, all in order to follow the whistles of the "Poodle pack."

I can tell you from personal experience that life is tough. No one knows how hard it will hit them. If you choose the path of the wolf, you will sometimes hit hard, and other times you'll have to take a hit. There are days when you will want to give up...when your legs scream, "Stop! I can't go on!" These are the days when you will have to bite the bullet, and remind yourself that you are a wolf who lives on the edge. You'll have to remember that those pangs of hunger make you an even better hunter.

The path of the seller...the path of the entrepreneur!

The path of the wolf...the path of the warrior!

There are archetypes written in our genetic code, and we cannot escape from them. It is up to us to live our lives as best we can.

What are the "Magic Secrets" to transform yourself from Mediocre Salesperson to Superstar? Why should I buy from you instead of from your competitors, or even choose to buy at all? Amazingly the majority of sellers don't know the answer, and this is the reason the sales sector is considered an anomaly. It is unpredictable, full of "hocus pocus," reserved for those with "the gift of the gab." . . . . . But it's not really like that.

The problem is that every business leads with things that don't mean anything to customers. For example:

- Quality

- Courtesy

- Service

- Customization

- Customer Focused

. . . and other crap from pointless Monday morning meetings.

I've seen various "sales managers," while doodling on their work pads, demand that:

- You have to be more customer focused!

- It's the only way that we can put high quality on what we sell.

- This way we can grow the business and reach our goals! And. . .

- If you don't reach them it's because you haven't enough belief!!!

The simple reality is that people buy in just two ways:

1. When they're emotionally involved (excited by a new product or service).

2. When they're not emotionally involved (they buy because they have to, or because they need the product/service).

And we can find another variant:

3. They are just not interested. There's no use talking about it. (Your boss might tell you that "You need to believe in it more." ...but it's useless.)

Who does the emotionally-involved person buy from?

Most people buy from the market leader, obviously. They do it for status and to be a sheep (because everybody buys it). If you're not the market leader, forget about these customers. You can't do anything with them. In fact, sellers do not realize that in most cases, they are just fighting over the crumbs.

In sales, the rule of 80/20 is applicable. The first two players in the market hog about 80% of it. The other players have to content themselves with the scraps that fall from the plate to the floor.

Here's an example:

Red Bull dominated the Energy Drink Market, but there are another 956 manufacturing companies in this market. Together with its closest rival, Monster, they have 78% of the market. Mathematically, the others have 0.023% of the market each.

Here's the ugly truth:

If you sell for one of the top two companies in your sector, your sales will be extremely high, and your earnings will be considerably better than those who sell for the "invisible" companies.

Said more simply, successful selling is not only what you do, or how good / determined / motivated you are. If you believed this, well then they've sold you hook, line, and sinker! The amount that you can sell and earn depends FIRST on whether your company has the capability to gain good market share, and THEN on your personal selling skills.

So, let's assume that you don't work for the market leader. Do you want to throw in the towel? NO. Do you have to be content to kill yourself with sales calls for a slice of 0.023% of your potential market? NO.

As a seller, you can make a difference. The human factor counts, but you have to play your cards right. If you work for a small company that copies follows the leader with the mantra, "We'll do what the leader does but more personalized and cheaper." – let's face it, you're f***ed. I've been in the sales business for a good while longer than you, and I can tell you that I've seen so many "die." If it had happened on a battlefield, I would be having nightmares for the rest of my life.

Do you want a reality check? Okay, go into your company's offices, and have a look around. How much does the average salesperson earn? Let's say that you are a phenomenon, and you make 30% more sales than everyone else. What now? You're moving from an old Fiat Punto to a newer one. This is the highest that you can aspire to be if you work for a small photocopying company who photocopies for the leader.

Do you want proof? As a boy I was the same as I am today. Obviously, I had less expertise, but I was basically the same person. The same, drive energy, ambition, enthusiasm, the same inability to give up. Yet I have broken my back to work for other peoples' companies, for years, until I reached the limit, and I couldn't climb the ladder anymore.

Why? Was I stupid? Was I lazy? . . . as they kept telling me to make me feel guilty.

No dear, I was a hard turbo-nuclear cock, but I made bad choices regarding the companies I worked for. Here's how they operated:

- Clones of the clones
- Zero marketing
- Made cold calls from the Yellow Pages
- "We do everything for everyone."
- "We offer better customization and offer cheaper prices than the competition."

What the f*** could I do? Could I perform miracles? Could I part the water like Moses?

I hated cold calling. They tried to make me feel guilty for a lifetime. Then I discovered that I was right all along, and that they were the a******s, not me. They didn't have the courage to admit to being failures, while I became the master of success that everyone knows.

— Did I suddenly became a genius? No.

— Was I a lucky son-of-a-bitch? No.

— Did I have "natural talent"? Not even!

I discovered that selling is an exact science of communication, and not the '"hocus pocus" that they were saying. They were talking lots of bullshit. But I won in the end.

What can you do if you're not the market leader, not selling for the market leader, or cannot copy the market leader? What else can you do rather than kill yourself by using the stupid tactics that we discussed above?

Easy. You can occupy yourself with another large slice of the market, that is, those customers who DO NOT buy from the leader because they want to be "different.".

In this case, you can swoop in and close the sale if:

1. You are able to emotionally engage the customer by working on his motives for buying.

2. The customer knows why you are the only real alternative to the market leader.

You must know how to do both together. Only one of the two is not enough. If your customers are only emotionally engaged, but your position is weak, you will push them to buy from the Leader, and it's not a good idea to do the donkeywork for your competitors.

If you engage the customers rationally with your positioning, but they haven't bought into you emotionally, they will buy, but from the company with the lowest price in the market.

This brings us to the second level: **How does someone who is not emotionally involved buy?**

Those who are not emotionally involved, but are "forced" to buy, will always choose the cheapest option. They make the salespeople parade their wares like they are on a catwalk, and then choose the cheapest option.

Try this self-analysis: Why do customers run to your competitors and you don't succeed in closing many sales?

1. Do you make a lot of appointments outside the target zone?

2. Do you know how to explain clearly that your product is very different, and it is "number one" after the market Leader?

3. Are you like a technician, who doesn't know how to stimulate customers to feel motivated to purchase?

If you have been honest with yourself in the analysis, you now have an exact map of what you need to fix, in order to begin selling more.

If you have a lot of sales meetings outside of the target zone, do your homework first and eliminate time wasters. Communicate accurately to potential customers, who might be interested in trying your product/service, and/or replacing their current one for yours.

If you have a very technical approach, I urge you to demo less, "pitch" less, and ask more questions that might trigger customers' motivations. Probe them! Be passionate about their story, about how they feel, about what more they want. Ask about their future, about what would solve their problems, and *then* things will start to flow more fluently. I guarantee it!

About Frank

Frank Merenda is a Italian serial entrepreneur, the creator of extremely successful brands like Venditore Vincente; the private mail posting franchise Posta Power; the insurance agency group Assicuratore Facile; the MMA promotion company Venator Fighting Championship, as well as other companies nationally and internationally.

Frank is the only Italian student of Al Ries, the godfather of Brand Positioning, and the only Italian in history to have been accepted into Dan Kennedy's famous Titanium Group – which is the inner circle of millionaire marketers. (You can only enter by exclusive invitation, and only when one earns a significant income – seven figures.)

Frank, along with Piernicola De Maria, co-authored *Business Caffeina*, the reputed business-training podcast in the Italian language, which is week after week number one in the download rankings on iTunes.

He was also the first specialized sales strategy trainer who created a step-by-step selling system adapted to any European culture, regardless of whether the seller has little or no experience.

CHAPTER 12

THIS IS NOT YOUR GRAND-MOTHER'S ANNUITY — SEE HOW THE MODERN ANNUITY HAS CHANGED

BY JAMES E. FOX CEP, CSA

Today's annuity options are not the same as they used to be. They have been around since the Roman days, when they were called ANNUA, but they have been revolutionized to be better for those who benefit from them. Perhaps I am biased, but I get excited about investments that offer people certain assurances that give them peace of mind as their retirement age nears, or even if they are already retired and in need of assistance. Today, an annuity is no longer associated with running out of money, and leaving you high and dry without any different avenues to rise above it.

It's true, annuities still get a bad rap. Consumers recall the old annuities— the one that their grandparents had that went away the minute their grandparents left this great earth. It was gone, just gone! The modern annuity can do so much for an investor and bring about peace of mind that is cherished by most people.

I've been a part of the stock market and witnessed the fall-out with my clients when it crashed, resulting in major losses. They were not the only ones who lost out either; I lost money, too! Guess what? I didn't care for that feeling any more than they did. My wife, who is also my business partner, and I sat down and I said, "I don't want to go down that path ever again. Let's gear up to do safe, guaranteed investments from now on." Thankfully, she agreed with my vision and *it brought about a substantial shift in my approach to helping clients experience a different relationship with their wealth advisor.* **I decided to be the guy who specialized in "sleep investments."** I cancelled my securities license, which did not give me the permission to use the golden words "safe and guaranteed." Anyone who works in the securities industry knows this.

I love the term *"sleep investment."* It's the heart of Fox Financial Group, Ltd.'s premise. When a client asks me, "What's a sleep investment, Jim?" I respond, *"It's an investment in which you can sleep at night and I can sleep at night. It's guaranteed."* I always use this phrase because I mean it! Great financial planning doesn't have to keep you awake at night, wondering what may happen to your investments at any given moment, like an unforeseen road block. Annuities are a great choice to help avoid those sleepless nights. Who would not be interested in investments that do not lead to sleepless nights staring at the ceiling, looking for pieces of your financial puzzle?

THE ANATOMY OF AN ANNUITY

Technically, an annuity is an insurance policy, but it represents so much more. It is also:

- Your savings

- A 401(k) pension rollover

- An investment in your future for your retirement

A common place that people may be approached about purchasing an annuity is at a bank. However, it is uncommon for them to realize that they actually purchased that annuity from an insurance company. It's these details that are so important for me to share with my clients. Really, what this equates to is banks are promoting life insurance companies, and that is sort of interesting, isn't it? As a broker, I represent dozens of companies.

On October 24, 2014, the United States Department of Treasury Press

Center came out with an article that promoted buying annuities that had a lifetime income guarantee. Think about it...the United States Department of Treasury is telling people to buy annuities. The article was geared toward individuals with 401(k) plans. Typically, 401(k) programs have had three investment strategies:

• Mutual funds

• Bonds

• Fixed money market accounts

Of course, there were really at least 25 options within those three strategies, but not a lot of insight on how to help you. Chaos! And risk!

Now, there is a fourth strategy: **annuities.** The world has come full circle and that is evidenced by the United States Government promoting annuities. It speaks volumes about what I do in regards to annuities and emphasizing that they provide a *lifetime income guarantee.* This is my specialty, and I am good at it. I've helped my clients invest millions of dollars in annuities for over 1,100 clients. The business keeps getting bigger. **People love safe money!**

There's a phrase out there that's coined, "The Safe Money Guy." You'll see it on billboards and in advertisements, but I have been called this by the ultimate source—clients. I have this great family for clients and have helped several of them. One day while in one of our meetings, I was explaining what I'm so passionate about and the client's son looked at me and said, "You're the safe money guy." And I said, "Well, yes I am!"

When you commit to putting your money into an annuity you will have two phases—accumulation and distribution.

Accumulation phase: This is where you are contributing and building up the account, preparing for retirement, and taking advantage of some of the benefits of no loss in the market, due to the fact gains are captured regardless of market loss.

Distribution phase: Annuities specialize in the distribution phase of your retirement planning. This is done through guaranteeing monthly lifetime income for as long as you live. That is an amazing thing!

EVERYONE BENEFITS FROM AN ANNUITY

The lifetime income guarantee is obviously the largest draw of an annuity. It is not the only benefit, though! Annuities also:

- Can give bonuses.

- Name a beneficiary.

- Are tied to the market with no losses, even if market declines.

- Are tax deferred.

- Avoid probate.

- Mean the insurance company pays 100% of the commissions, which means 100% of the deposit goes into the investor's account.

- Have no penalties at death, and only a small penalty for premature withdrawal if more than 10% withdrawal is taken in the penalty years.

- Have several liquidity options to take money out of the account without penalties.

- Have low or no fees.

- Have an annual roll-up on the income account that goes into the lifetime income; if you decide not to take the income right away, the income account grows at a certain percentage every year depending on which annuity company is being used.

- Have protection. Every state has an annuity guarantee fund (annuities version of FDIC insurance). The amount varies from state to state, and ranges between $100,000 to $300,000. It's extra assurance that if a company becomes insolvent, the consumer still has some money protected.

FINDING THE ANNUITY THAT IS RIGHT FOR YOU

I'm a broker with dozens of companies and my goal is to try and find a company that fits a particular client's needs based on what their situation is. This is done through a *financial needs analysis*. We need to find out what the *individual situation is* and *what their goals are,* for starters. From there, it gets more detailed and customized because annuities are not one size fits all. There are differences—differences that can significantly impact a client's income potential and needs.

In our industry, we cannot just sell annuities to anybody. The investment is similar to a long term CD. So, the best annuity companies will go through a *suitability questionnaire* to make sure that the product they offer is a good fit for a consumer. I love this and it is a big contributor to what keeps me being "the safe money guy." Plus, it's great protection for consumers, and agents, alike. This is what we want: **both parties agreeing that this works!**

Today, most annuities allow for a 10% annual withdrawal for any type of unforeseen emergencies that may arise. The industry's philosophy is that if 10% is not enough for an emergency, then an annuity is probably not right for you! That's why balance is important and we should never put all of our financial eggs in one basket.

The insurance product that has modernized the industry is called a **Hybrid or Indexed Annuity**. You can take parts of the three most popular annuities and roll them into one, with lifetime income. The three annuities are:

- Fixed: no adjustments and pays a flat rate return

- Immediate: can take income payments immediately for a set period of time

- Indexed: funds are associated with an interest rate tied into the S&P 500, Dow Jones Industrials, NASDAQ, and other markets

The investment goes into the plan and has a cap rate, spread rate, or participation rate. If the market goes down you cannot lose any investment dollars unless there is a rider fee or withdrawals, but if the market goes up you lock that rate for one year or more. That means that if the market goes back down you stay put—you cannot go backwards! Imagine a staircase that each time you went up a rung, you could not go backwards. It might seem complicated, but if you are working with the right planner it is easily explained.

In addition, these particular plans *offer lifetime income,* as well, so you have the *upside of the market* with all the benefits of having income every month, regardless of market fluctuation. Remember, some of these riders that offer lifetime income have fees anywhere from 0% to as high as 1.25%, depending on additional options available, like long term care and death benefit riders, caps, etc. When you calculate the fee or no-fee options, usually the lifetime income guarantee will offset the cost. This is because these plans offer a ***roll-up rate***. Each year you do not take the guaranteed income, the company will increase your income until you do start taking it. The roll-ups are anywhere from 4% with no fee and up to 14% roll-up with higher fees, approximately .95%. *Either way, you have some great options to help you sleep!*

Always Remember: If It's Good For You, It's Good for your Planner
I own several of the annuities that we offer. I'm self-employed and I use them to supplement my pension. In my position, you cannot have real credibility and earn those hard-earned referrals if you cannot **put your money where your mouth is—quite literally**. When I meet with clients, I do not hesitate to pull out my statements so clients can see what they look like and learn how to read them. It's important for them to know that as "the safe money guy," I think that annuities are safe. I also want to receive a check for as long as my wife and I live.

THE POWER OF SUCCESS

I've had so many impactful moments with clients when I've helped them sort through their finances and move monies into those sleep investments that bring peace of mind. One story, in particular, has always stood out to me. It was so poignant and powerful, a true affirmation of why I love what I do and am so passionate about it.

My clients and I were sitting at their kitchen table and I was finishing our business. I had set up an income rider for them, something that was quite typical to do. The husband started to cry. I'm used to emotional moments with clients because finances are a big deal. There was something different about this. His wife reached over and grabbed his hand, affectionately squeezing it. He looked at me and said, "Jim, how can I ever repay you?"

Repay me? I was completely awestruck. All I could say is, "Oh my God, thank you. This is what I do and I couldn't be prouder."

These words are so powerful to me because they reiterate what it is that I do for people. It's not only me, but all retirement and estate planners, that need to be more aware of how we affect people. Our business can really work if we make sure to maintain our purpose and passion, and stay educated and current. Helping others with our gifts and strengths is one of the best ways to have a happy and fulfilling career, one that you are proud to claim. I am so grateful for this business that I am in, and it's because of clients that finally feel freedom and relief from their financial concerns. They understand and they are grateful.

Talking to someone on a personal level is so interesting and when I use the term sleep investments it conjures up such a powerful image. I get to tell people that they are going to have a monthly check coming for the rest of their lives. I say, "I'm basically building a second mailbox for you, right next to the one where you get your Social Security check from every month. Now, when you go out to retrieve that check you can look for two." And you can just see them light up. They glow. I mean, it's that peace of mind of knowing you're going to have security. I'm a part of that equation and it has made all the difference. **Wow, to see how far the "UNcommon" ANNUA has come!**

[On a personal note, I would like to personally thank Brian Tracy for asking me to co-author this book, my beautiful wife, partner, and best friend, Sharon, for all her support over our 30 years together, and to all our clients, without whom our company is nothing.]

About James

There are few people that can keep up with the fast paced, ever changing Retirement and Estate Planning industry like James E. Fox CEP, CSA. With over 25 years of experience, he has seen many shifts in the industry and taken on many roles. However, year after year, there was one thing that he noticed was in need of attention—better education and options for individuals reaching their retirement years. This is the premise behind Fox Financial Group, Ltd., the company he founded, located in Burr Ridge, Illinois, a suburb of Chicago.

As a graduate of Certified Estate Planning School and Certified Senior Advisor School, Jim continues to increase his knowledge and help his clients make fundamental shifts in how they approach retirement, and structure this amazing time in life so that they will be guaranteed to have a lifetime income. His passion clearly shows through, and all his business comes from referrals from satisfied clients—1,100 strong and counting.

Jim's expertise is sought out and he has been featured in *Forbes* and *Advisor Today* magazines, and he is in the process of writing his second book, which is due out in the summer of 2015. He has spent a great deal of time talking with companies and various organizations, helping them to educate their employees about better retirement and estate planning. According to Jim, "One of the keys to my success is that I am genuinely vested in integrity, trust, and service."

Consumers' testaments to the genuine nature and integrity of Jim's business are reiterated by the best ratings (A+) at popular consumer agencies such as Better Business Bureau and *Angie's List.* Jim has received multiple Million Dollar Round Table Awards, such as the Top of the Table Award, given to the top .10% in the industry, and the Court of the Table Award, which is given to the top 1% in the world for the industry.

The passion that Jim has for his career carries over into all aspects of his personal life. He is an avid golfer and a music lover. He plays the guitar, mandolin, and harmonica, and also has two music CDs out, which he co-produced. In addition, he spent 15 years as a high school and collegiate basketball official and has appeared on television several times. Jim has also run several marathons and half marathons. Always one to have exciting goals to look forward to, Jim has begun engaging in the speaking circuit, spreading his message of safe retirement to people across the United States that he has already shared with individuals in the greater Chicago area for so long.

Jim can be reached at: 630-654-1976, or check out his website at: www. foxfinancialgroup.net for more information and educational videos.

CHAPTER 13

HEALTHY, WEALTHY, READY

BY W. ADAM CLATSOFF, CLU, CFP, ChFC, RHU
MEDICAL INSURANCE CONSULTANT

Introduction:

At 74 years old, if having learned nothing else, it's that I'd better learn to like people who disagree with me. After all, they are more interesting and there are more of them. To some people I'm a knuckle-dragging Neanderthal and to others, a source of enlightenment. Reflecting back 45 years ago as a young health insurance advisor, I can now say that what I thought was right back then was wrong, and what I thought was wrong, was right. One thing I've come to know for sure, there is no universal template that fits us all. We are all different, special and unique.

Thus any sort of boilerplate financial planning is doomed to fail—most every time.

Lessons from my Father:

My father was a Greek immigrant and true to stereotype, our family was in the restaurant business. Unlike most 12-year olds who spent their Saturdays playing sports or running around the neighborhood, mine were spent washing glasses at our restaurant. On one particular Saturday, a life insurance agent named Gib was presenting a retirement plan to my dad.

After 15 minutes or so, Dad called me over, pointed directly at me and said, "Gib, here is my retirement plan." True enough, both my

Grandparents lived in our home until the day they died. Indeed, my father was their retirement plan. Today, it saddens me to see so many people soliciting money at intersections around South Florida. Not by the signs they hold, but because they're without family willing to take them home. I cannot help but wonder what went wrong.

The Big Lie:

Humans are the only living beings that know we will die and that our time is limited. My dog's name is Cookie. For Cookie there is no yesterday or tomorrow. There is only right now. He is not making any plans or worrying over tomorrow. We deal with our special knowledge through denial. We pretend it's not going to happen. Even when we think about it, it is always in the distant future. This is the big lie. A good lie but a lie for sure. We absolutely couldn't function without it. But why is a lie so easy to believe and the truth so hard to believe? Have you ever noticed that the word "lie" is right in the middle of the word believe? We make our plans centered around the notion that we will live to a ripe old age and die quietly one night in bed. No fuss. No mess. How pleasant! Also how untrue. The reality is possibly a horribly tortuous protracted hell that leaves us with no money and few friends. Or we could live until 96, long after our health and money have run out. Either way plans should be made that are rooted in truth not denial.

Wow!

You may be thinking it's time to stop reading this. My life has been spent talking to people who want to talk to me about things they don't want to talk to me about. I get it. Reality is no fun. And yet . . . if not now, when? Doesn't it make sense to plan for the worst case scenario and hope for the best case scenario? When a couple retires at 65 its great! Everyone's healthy. We're going on cruises and going to Disney World. But by age 75, one of us may very well be in bad or declining health. We're getting tired of watching daytime television and going to funerals. And where did all that money go? Has the price of everything really doubled? Are we outliving our money? Have you ever wondered why baby diapers are named "Luvs" and "Huggies" while diapers for seniors are called "Depends"? We all love to change a baby's diaper. After all, they are so cute. But when it comes to a senior's diaper, it "depends" on who's named in the Will.

What's your point?

My point is your plan should be done now while your family can participate in some of these tough decisions. This may very well be the most important thing you ever do. Simply buying insurance, writing a Will and pretending everything's handled, is not enough. Tough questions must be asked, and if not decided, at least exposed. Often times there may not be anything you can do immediately. However, awareness can become a powerful motivator.

Some tough sample questions:

1. How will we pay for a prolonged catastrophic illness?
2. How long can our money last?
3. Should one, or both of us, be earning?
4. Where will we live?
5. Is our principal at risk?
6. Do we have any outstanding loans or leases that would be accelerated at one of our deaths?
7. What's the most important bill that we would have to pay every month if one of us became very ill? IT'S YOUR HEALTH INSURANCE PREMIUM!
8. Do we have a current notarized "Advance Directive?"
9. Do we have a trusted health insurance advisor who knows what he, or she, is talking about?
10. What's the real deal on reverse mortgages? Gold? Silver?

The number 1 reason people fail:

No, it's not medical expenses or market losses... it is procrastination. You don't have to do it all now, but you do have to start now. The hardest part is getting started. Go slow. Trust your instincts and, most of all, stay the course. Don't let anyone convince you they're the expert and you're not. If it doesn't feel good to you, then don't do it.

Remember, the reason the grass is greener somewhere else is because it may be growing over a septic tank!

Take this to the bank:

The only constant in life is that everything is always changing. I have a close friend and throughout his life we have made several five-year plans. Not one of them turned out as planned. As they say, "men plan and God laughs." The new Affordable Care Act has changed all of our plans now, and will continue to do so going forward. We all need to revisit existing plans and test them against a whole new way of protecting ourselves from the inevitable. We all know something bad will happen, without knowing what or when. Whatever your politics or feelings about the ACA, it's a sure bet premiums will continue to go up and healthcare will consume more and more of our treasure. You can count on this.

A classy problem:

At age 65, you could have another 20 or 30 years to go and may likely do so in better health than your parents. However, the cost of health care could easily become one of the biggest items in your budget . . . AND . . . that's if you're healthy!

The three-legged stool:

Years and years ago when studying for my financial degrees, conventional wisdom dictated our plans should be built like a three-legged stool. The three "legs" on which we could rely to build our financial futures were our government, our employers and ourselves. Remove any leg and the stool falls. I ask you . . . will our government be doing more or less? How about our employers? In this game of false promises, high hopes and musical claims, who are the winners, and who are the losers? Can we find a way to not outlive our money?

What's the major reason that we fail

1). Investment losses

2). Inflation

3). Probate

4). Medical Expenses

5). None of the above

If you answered "none of the above" you are correct. As stated earlier the answer most often is . . . procrastination. Take a look now at where you are. Do you have a way to increase your personal net worth? Are your assets protected? Are wills and trusts current? Are your parents, children and grandchildren provided for? What are your options? You can shrink your dreams or change your thinking. That's all folks. One or two, that's it.

Obamatunity

Millions of people are looking to make changes to their health insurance and they will need help. Most obvious and often overlooked, health insurance has to be the foundation to any retirement and legacy planning. However, Medical Insurance Consultants are in short supply just at a time when the Affordable Care Act has created millions of possible clients that need you now. This is possibly the greatest shift of income in the history of the world. This is your opportunity to start a consulting business with no big start-up costs, no franchise fees, no job risk, and no product inventory. America needs low-pressure articulate caring and informed Medical Insurance Consultants now. Could this be you?

How long will this last?

Longer than you. In the next 15 years, the number of seniors in America is expected to double. Do the math.

Retired or rehired?

The choice is yours. Your life experience is needed. What you know is marketable. You want to work but who will hire you? Will you make a difference? Actually, you have but the following four choices:

1). Employee – someone else is in charge

2). Self-employed – you are in charge

3). Business owner – you need capital

4). Investor – you need lots of money

Your rules and a tax shelter too:

If you are self-employed in your own home-based business, you get to exchange living by someone else's rules and living by yours. You become part of the solution and not part of the problem. For you it could be the perfect financial plan. Would you enjoy giving people advice? There is a critical need for common sense financial advice. A home-based business is a great tax shelter. Ask your accountant how your business could deduct home expenses such as rent, utilities, phones and computers. How about your car, meals and entertainment, or income shifting?

Medical Insurance Consultant — The perfect home-based business!

Work:

> Where you want
>
> When you want
>
> How you want
>
> With whom you want

Plus:

> Acquire an insider's knowledge of financial strategies, products and services while generating both earned and passive incomes.

. . . and ITS FUN!!!

About Adam

W. Adam Clatsoff has lectured on insurance topics nationally and is a widely-accepted authority on matters related to insurance and financial planning.

In 1969, Adam founded Adcahb Medical Coverages, one of Florida's largest and leading health insurance agencies. His titles include Chartered Financial Consultant, Certified Financial Planner, Registered Health Underwriter, Chartered Life Underwriter and Long Term Care Insurance Strategist. Adam served as President of the Gold Coast Chapter of Financial Planners and is the founding President of the Sawgrass Association of Life Underwriters. However, Adam's recognition doesn't stop there.

You'll find Adam listed in the editions of "Who's Who" in the South, in the Southwest and in the Financial Industry in America. He is the recipient of many top industry awards, the United States Olympic Committee Distinguished Patron Award and in 1998, honored as Small Businessman Of The Year by the Broward County Council of Chambers. Adam's previous books include the *One Cent Solution* (published 1994 by Noble House Publishers), *101 Reasons Why You Should Eat Fast Food* (published 2008 by Star Group International), and *Health Insurance 50% Less in 2009*. In addition, Adam hosted a radio talk show on WWNN 1470 AM for over 10 years and currently produces the Steve Kane Show.

Legislators, state insurance commissioners and industry CEO's continue to look to Adam for his unique professional insights and personal advice. He currently serves as the Vice-Chair of the Florida Legislature's Insurance Advisory Board, created to study ways to substantially reduce the number of Floridians without health insurance. Likewise, Adam is also focused on America's aging population and the steps retirees and pre-retirees can take to help outlive their retirement savings.

Celebrating 47 years of marriage with his wife Carole, Adam is the father of Heather Clatsoff-Doucette and Bill Clatsoff and a proud grandfather to Nickolas and C.J. Doucette and Lexi and Adam Clatsoff.

CHAPTER 14

PLANNING A SECURE RETIREMENT

BY JOHN BENNETT

As I was growing up on a farm in the mountains of West Virginia, I thought the only way to make money was by working hard and long hours. The family moved to Maryland at my age of 14. I started working for a Supermarket at $0.50/hour. I worked every hour I could to earn money. Being from the mountains, we had nothing. Even school clothes were scarce. Later in life, I started a swimming pool & Home Improvement company.

After 20 years, I decided I wanted to start working smarter instead of harder, so I continued my education for the financial business and I started this company in 1989 by running Leads for A.F.L.A.C. (Before the duck.) It didn't take me long to realize there were a lot of ways seniors could be helped that they just plain didn't know about.

I remember a couple in Plant City, Florida where the wife was sick in bed. The husband showed me the empty refrigerator and told me that they had to make a decision that month to choose between food or medicine for the wife. **This BROKE MY HEART.** Long story short, to position myself to better serve seniors, I became a delegate for the State of Florida – Silver Hair Legislation – meeting at the state capital in Tallahassee, Florida at the House of Representatives. I also became a delegate for the National Silver Hair Congress in Washington D.C.

I have dedicated the last quarter of a Century of my life to helping retirees, post-retirees and their families protect their money to build up a *SAFE, GUARANTEED, Retirement Pension plan*. It pleases me to improve and make a difference in someone's life and protect business owners and professionals with a *TAX-FREE Retirement Income.*

My clients are very happy because when they need help, I am here for them at no charge. <u>They have never lost any money</u>. When the market goes up, their gains are locked in every year. *When the market goes down, they can never lose any of their gains.*

Now available to those who qualify are very popular benefits that can be added that will **double their income**, if needed, for in-home or nursing home care. Example: **$20,000** from the income account will double to **$40,000!** This relieves a lot of stress. "Clients loves this!"

Many of my clients have lost money in the past by taking a gamble and placing their money in the market. Since they *transferred to a fixed index annuity*, **they now <u>make money</u> when the market goes up, but <u>never lose</u> when the market goes down.** They realize their principal is 100% protected by contract to never go down, plus they can have a *Guaranteed Pay Check* for as long as they live. This makes them a very happy client, resulting in recommending my services to their friends and family. Many have told me that they wish they had met me years ago. This results in a win-win for all!

There are many benefits of fixed index annuities and life insurance that most people are unaware of. For example;

- **<u>TAXES</u>** – No one likes to pay more than their fair share of taxes. These fixed index annuities and life insurance products give you a choice of growing tax-deferred as well as take-out tax free. This gives the product's owners approximately <u>30% more income</u>. That is a wonderful thing! Are you paying unnecessary taxes on your CD's and Social Security??

- **<u>INFLATION</u>** – Some people don't give inflation a second thought although they realize how it affects them when they go to shop at the market, buy gas, etc. It now takes approximately *$6,700 to buy what $5,000* bought just 14 years ago, approximately *$8,900 to buy what $5,000* bought in 1990 and roughly <u>$30,000 to buy</u>

what $5,000 bought in 1970. We notice inflation but we don't take notice of the costly effects inflation has on our retirement income. There are Inflation (benefits) riders and cost of living adjustments on fixed index annuities that are a great way to protect your wealth.

- **LONGEVITY** – This may be a blessing for aging Americans but, it creates a crisis that we have to solve. Most Americans are unprepared for increasing longevity. People are living into their 90's now and the number one fear for seniors has changed from the fear of dying, to *the fear of running out of money! Increased longevity is a blessing, but it is an expensive one!* Note: Consumers want long-term care coverage but very few ever write a check. Why? Number one, it is very costly. Especially for husband and wife. And two, if they never use it then the money is lost. Plus, many people do not qualify because of bad health. *That's another reason we need an annuity with a **guaranteed income** that we cannot outlive!*

- **LONG-TERM CARE COSTS** – You can choose to pay out-of-pocket and spend all of your assets until Medicaid picks up the tab. Or you can purchase traditional long term care insurance if you qualify. You can link long term care benefits to life insurance by using a specially designed policy. There will be a pool of money available to pay for long term care expenses. If no long-term care is needed, a tax-free death benefit passes to your loved ones. This means the money *will not be lost* to the insurance company. You can also link long term care benefits to an *income annuity*. Some will even double your income that will increase your payout by a factor of 200% for up to five years when qualifying long term care is needed. Like the insurance, if you don't use the annuity income, the money will be passed onto your beneficiaries.

- **RISING HEALTHCARE COSTS** – About 90% of middle-income Americans don't feel prepared to handle the financial cost of critical illnesses. According to a study done by the Washington National Institute for Wellness Solutions (IWS), just 11% of respondents have enough money saved to cover family emergencies and critical illnesses. Most said they would turn to savings to cover costs their insurance wouldn't, BUT *75% have* *less than $20,000 in savings.* A quarter of them had no savings at all. Americans understand it is expensive to be sick. Nearly half of respondents said they would probably NEVER recover financially from an Alzheimer's or dementia diagnosis and 38% said the same of a cancer diagnosis. This is just another reason it is critical to have a **guaranteed income** for life that you cannot outlive.

• **MARKET RISK** – While the future may be uncertain for investors, the owner of a **Fixed Index Annuity** can rest assured that their assets are safe and secure. Because of their unique characteristics, you can truly grow your assets in a volatile market utilizing an FIA. The *"Lost Decade"* refers to a time frame where people paid a lot of fees to invest their money into the market from April of 1998 to April of 2008. It took almost a decade for the investor to get back to the initial point where they started ten years ago, not counting their fees. **Note:** *With the Fixed Index Annuity, my clients **KNOW what their retirement income will be . . . Not HOPE what it will be!***

• **SOME OF THE MANY BENEFITS OF THE FIXED INDEX ANNUITY**

a. Some offer a *10% Bonus guaranteed in your account from day one.* From the first day you earn interest on your principal, on your bonus, your gains and also on the tax money that is deferred.

b. *Accessibility* – You can get up to 10% penalty-free withdrawals after the first year. You can also receive systematic withdrawals of interest or required minimum distributions as quickly as 30 days after your contract is issued.

c. *The nursing care benefit* – offers a 100% penalty-free withdrawal after the third anniversary if confined in a qualified Nursing Care Center.

d. *The terminal illness rider* – offers a 100% penalty free withdrawal after the first anniversary if diagnosed with a terminal illness.

e. *The death benefit* – is the full value of your annuity and is paid in a lump sum with NO surrender charges to your named beneficiaries. Other income options may be available.

The annuity gives you guarantees, peace of mind, and relieves a lot of stress. <u>We call it sleep insurance because your money is safe and guaranteed</u>. Annuities also protect (insure) your life savings against any losses, just like your home or your car, etc. There is no charge for this coverage. Most people have no idea that their life savings can be protected this way. Although, wouldn't you agree that it is no less important to protect a $300,000 "IRA" than it is to protect a $300,000 "HOME?"

Because of the market decline in the past, many retirees that were living the good life before the market decline have had to go back to a much less paying job, sometimes even two jobs. This does not happen to the owners of the fixed index annuities that have the *guaranteed lifetime income* with no loss of principal.

I can show those in the "accumulation stage" of life how to create their own $1,000,000 Fund and become their own banker by following some simple rules.

1. **Pay yourself first:** In order for a nice retirement and family protection, you must make sure that the funds go in first before you go and spend it in other places.

2. **Track your daily expenses:** In doing so, you can see where you are wasting your money and how much more can actually be attributed to your future!

3. **Target your financial goals:** Prioritize what it is you would like to accomplish.

4. **Trim your living expenses:** In order to live off of less than you earn.

5. **Learn the power of compound interest:** To avoid paying unnecessary interest. Example: Credit Cards, Finance Companies, Unnecessary Car Payments, etc.

6. **Learn how to manage and protect the money you already have, or will have:** To create more money to manage!

For those that are in this stage of their lives and have concerns about their future retirement income, I can show them the benefits of being their own banker with a product that has many great advantages.

THE IRS-APPROVED TAX ADVANTAGES

Some advantages of the **Indexed Universal Life Insurance** (IUL) policy:

1. It allows you to build an emergency fund and to avoid tax problems. The taxes (are deferred) during the accumulation phase, as the cash value is building up. When you retire you can *take tax-free distributions* of the cash value. The IULs also allows a tax-free exchange to one policy without triggering income taxes. And when you pass on, the tax-free death benefit protects your loved ones against financial uncertainty!

2. **Protection against stock market volatility: An IUL** provides market-linked GAINS without market-based RISK. It is not in the stock market. Because of the IUL's principal-protection guarantee, your gains are locked in. *Yes, even if the Stock Market Crashes, you have NO LOSSES!*

3. **Flexibility and control:** Unlike an IRA or 401(k), there are No Limitations on the amount you can contribute annually to your IUL. As a result, you can build up more cash value based on what you contribute to your plan. Even better, you can have ACCESS to your cash value at any age, any time, for any reason, without Paying Taxes or Penalties. Plus you have the ability to change death benefit amounts, premium amounts and payment frequency.

IN CONCLUSION

In closing, I truly believe that everyone should be able to retire with a **GUARANTEED INCOME FOR LIFE**, so that they can enjoy their retirement years.

Wouldn't it be nice if you could have three checks as long as you live? Social security, (an annuity), IF you paid into it. Your own private pension plan (an annuity), a paycheck for life. Also a "Play" check for life is available to my clients. When people retire, every day is like a Saturday, a day to play when the living expenses are taken care of! Use this income as your play money.

Anyone that has worked and saved for 30-40 years, it is a very sad thing for them to lose 20%-40% to the market, when there are safe guaranteed products that will protect their money. To be fair, many never had a clue about these products. No one has the right to gamble with some else's money!

In my many years in this business, I have heard many heart-breaking stories. It pleases me very much when I can protect what they have left, and give them a bonus to recoup some losses. Plus see how happy they are when they are making money, and not worrying about losing any. That's why we call it "Sleep Insurance!"

I have been blessed, by treating my clients like family and putting their interest first. This is why I have "0" unhappy clients and why I love what I do!

About John

John Bennett specializes in providing his clients with the best-rated and safest companies in the United States. He is licensed, insured, and backed by the Legal Reserve System, State of Maryland, and several well-known multi-billion dollar insurance companies.

John has been protecting clients' life savings and earning their trust "since 1989." He began his career with AFLAC (before the duck), in the Medicare Supplement and Long Term Care Division. In the interim, he discovered that some seniors were on such a small fixed income that during some months, they had to decide between buying groceries or buying medicine. At the other end of the spectrum, there were seniors that had a comfortable lifestyle and lived retirement to its fullest. The major difference between these two groups is that the group living a good life were fortunate enough to protect their savings with their principal and gains guaranteed. This provided them with a much better, and enjoyable retirement.

This revelation gave John the motivation to help as many seniors as possible. It became his mission to educate seniors in ways to get the most out of their retirement savings with safety, liquidity, tax-favored status, and a better-than-average return with absolutely no market risk. John has found that what he does to help people is the most rewarding and gratifying part of his job. He loves what he does and his clients love their Contract for Income as long as they live. It allows them to receive double their income if needed for in-home care!

John is very active in his church, has been a member of Rotary for over 30 years, and is currently a member of the Dundalk Chamber of Commerce, and a member of the Better Business Bureau, earning its highest A+ accredited rating.

John and Gaynel were married in 1957 and have two sons, John Jr. (deceased) and Barry. Barry and his wife, April, have blessed them with two wonderful grandchildren. John also finds joy in helping the underprivileged, classic cars, golf, and spending time with his grandchildren and family.

John Bennett:
Over a Quarter of a Century of Education and Training
• CEO of Bennett's Senior Service, LLC
• Licensed Agent in Maryland, Pennsylvania, Florida, and West Virginia

CHAPTER 15

12 WAYS TO BECOME A RESILIENT LEADER

BY JOHN NICHOLLS

My children are amazed at how deprived my English childhood was. Back in the seventies, we only had two children's TV channels, which would broadcast kids' programmes for just two hours a day. One of the highpoints of these dark days was a programme called Crackerjack; a mad mix of badly acted dramas, party games and pop bands. A particular favourite game of mine was called "Double or Drop", where children stood on a pedestal and answered topical, general knowledge questions. For a correct answer, they received a prize, which they had to hold. For a wrong answer, they had to hold a cabbage. As the prizes and cabbages tally got higher, the children had to cling on to the growing pile of goodies. If they dropped any, they were eliminated. The final winner was the child who held on to their prizes the longest.

In my work coaching hundreds of managers to become more resilient, I often think of that game. Many leaders find themselves clutching to all the professional and personal challenges that come their way. They think they are managing to keep afloat but then an unexpected cabbage comes their way and they fall apart. Often this leads to ill health, breakdown in relationships, professional underperformance and feeling a general unhappiness with life.

I have guided many people in leadership positions to help them develop healthy habits and would like to share some great techniques to develop your resilience.

1. CONFIDENCE IN YOUR ABILITIES

After the excitement of your promotion has worn out, often another emotion takes it place. When unfamiliar situations occur, you realise that you don't really know what you are doing. You question your ability and begin to worry that others will find you out. This "Imposters" syndrome is something most people experience from time to time and can impact their performance and wellbeing.

To combat this, spend some time thinking about all your achievements. Every month, record your achievements at work and in your private life. See what impact you make on others and yourself. One colleague of mine kept a collection of scrapbooks, where she kept emails, cards and letters (she'd worked a long time!) from happy customers. Whenever she had a bad day or had doubts about her suitability as a manager, she would find a quiet space, sit down and read through all the positive things people had said about her.

2. MANAGE YOUR ENERGY, NOT YOUR TIME

There are some great books on time management. Graham Allcott's *How to be a Productivity Ninja* and David Allen's *Getting Things Done* have helped me manage my time much more effectively.

However, this is only part of the story. It is managing energy, not time, that can really help you bounce through the tough times. Look at your schedule and find the times you are expending greater amounts of energy and then carve time out to enable you to indulge in activities that will recharge your vitality.

I used to know a Director of a multi-national finance company, who managed a complex, stressful department but always managed to look fresh and relaxed. One day, I asked him his secret. Without embarrassment, he told me it was all due to model trains. In his attic, he had a working model railway, with accurately scaled scenery, people and of course, a central station. "I know people laugh at me," he said, "but I don't care. I come home from a tough day in the office, change my clothes and spend half an hour lost in my world of trains. Then I go downstairs, my day forgotten, and I can be human with my beautiful family."

3. KEEPERS AND CHUCKERS

Starting in a new management role is a great opportunity to look at your life and work out what you want to keep and what you would like to chuck. Obviously, there are things we might like to chuck, such as our mortgage or our city's bad weather, which we may have to live with, but there are many habits or work routines that we have the chance to get rid of.

Look at the activities that fill your day and decide which ones add to your values and enjoyment of life. See if the other activities still need to be done, and if not, just don't do them. Look and see which tasks can be delegated to others.

If you have been a leader for some time, this exercise can be even more helpful. Look at the tasks that fill your day. Ask yourself which tasks are valuable to you, your values and your organisation. Can some of the other tasks be addressed through better processes, systems or through more effective delegation?

4. FIND YOUR ROCK

The most resilient executives I have coached have all had a fantastic relationship that has sustained them through the difficult periods of leadership. Sometimes, they have even been their wife or husband! Those lucky enough to have a warm, loving, supportive relationship are much better equipped to handle tough times at work. However, many people don't have this but they find other people to be their rock. Perhaps a mentor from the same company, someone who shares the same interests or humour, or an old college buddy.

For some people, this relationship does not have to be tea, sympathy and tissues. I had one coaching client whose "rock" was his pool buddy. They would meet each Friday; have a couple of beers over a game of pocket billiards, insult each other's sporting prowess . . . washing the strains of the week away in the process. Find the relationships that work for you.

5. TRAIN YOURSELF TO BE OPTIMISTIC

This is harder for some than others, but the fact is optimistic people are more resilient than pessimists.

When bad things happen, tell yourself they are temporary, that they could have happened to anyone and that you have survived worse events.

When things are going well, enjoy the sunshine, tell yourself that you deserve this and that there will be many other times like this.

Keep telling yourself these things until it becomes a habit. Challenge your negative thoughts by recognising them, finding ways to intellectually dispute them and then substituting them with the suggestions above.

6. FLEXIBILITY AND LETTING GO

In 2004, a great conflict broke out in the East of England. It is known in the local history books as "The Battle of the Straight Picture Frame." For years, all the pictures have hung from my walls in an even, orderly manner. My lovely new wife moved in and her straight wasn't my straight. Each day, I would restraighten her pictures and then when I went to work, she would restraighten my restraightening! It started quite harmlessly, but over time, it became a big issue with us and led to serious arguments. Eventually, we realised that our goal was a loving, beautiful home and this focusing on a micro-issue was not helping us at all.

Now that I have a house with four children, crooked pictures are the least of my worries!

Being a leader is about achieving goals, and it helps your staff if you let go of the reins and let them find their own way (with your guidance).

Flexibility is a great skill to enhance your resilience. Since living in Hungary, I have often heard people talking about finding the *kiskapu* (translation: a little gate). Coined during the forty years of communist rule, the Hungarians have become expert in finding another way around a problem. Ignore the locked big door, find the small gate!

7. DECISION MAKING

I have been told this story many times and apparently, it has been part of an academic study on decision-making. A man visits a car showroom, falls in love with a car and then goes home to reflect on his choice. He then buys car magazines, reads the auto reviews and scours the Internet to find out the qualities of the types of car would best suit his needs. Incredibly enough, all the research he carried out leads him to the conclusion that the car he set his heart on, was the best option for him.

Sound familiar? We often make similar decisions at work and in our personal lives. Resilient leaders will find accurate data, check their assumptions and bias, use a decision making model that works for them and then find a solution. If this becomes a good habit, in times of stress, we have an established habit to use rather than make ill-formed decisions that will come back and bite us. Or perhaps, we will be paralysed with indecision, which won't help us either.

8. KINDNESS

Kindness is a powerful force. The world is so busy and people are so occupied with their lives and "to-do" lists, acts of kindness stand out like stars in a night sky.

A deliberate or random act of kindness will make your employees love you more, but the research tells us that it makes us feel better too. Regularly reaching out to others makes us happier and healthier.

So why do so many of us see the value of being kind to others but treat ourselves so harshly?

How often have you turned to a loved one and said:

"You idiot. You always mess up. How could you be so stupid?"

How often have you said something similar to yourself?

Be gentle on yourself. Treat yourself with the same respect you strive to treat others with.

Also, ask for help. Many of us like to give help and find it much harder to ask for the same. Once again, there is research that tells us that people like you more if they helped you. More so than if they have received the help from you instead.

9. YOUR VALUES AND PASSION

It is much easier to be resilient in times of difficulty if you are working to a greater goal which fits your values and passions.

Ask yourself how your work fits your closely-held values and what you would like your legacy to be.

If you have never spent time exploring your values and life-purpose, take time out to explore:

- Your childhood dreams.

- The times you felt good at work and what triggered those good feelings.

- The times people have praised you. What attributes and talents did they praise?

These should lead you to your purpose and values.

10. CONTROL

Resilient leaders focus on the things they can control and minimise the importance of the rest. Not only is this a more effective way of working, it leads to much less stress. How often have you spent a sleepless night worrying about what people might think, the future of our loved ones or just the general state of the world? All things beyond our control.

What we can influence is how we treat people, our interactions with our loved ones now, and perhaps making our small part of the world a better place.

Effective leaders look to minimise the outside influences but pour their energies into the things they can control.

11. KEEPING HEALTHY

We all know that leading a healthy life will help us deal with stress and cope with life's difficulties in a better way.

Let's just remind ourselves of the things we already know about healthy living:

- Drink lots of clean water

- Regular exercise, with appropriate rest days too

- Eat fresh food, cut down on the processed stuff

• 7 to 8 hours sleep a night

• Reduce the alcohol, say no to drugs

Which one are you going to work on first?

12. LOVING LIFE

A. The essence of resilience is to love life, embracing its challenges and looking for new opportunities to grow.

B. Find time to enjoy your cities and get out into nature. Value and feel gratitude for your relationships.

C. Take opportunities to meet people who make you laugh, watch comedy shows and find the humour in life.

D. Continue to learn new things and look for big and small adventures.

I hope that you find these twelve steps to be a valuable guide on your journey to becoming more resilient. By taking on a leadership role, you have a powerful impact on others as well as having great opportunities to develop and grow as a person. You owe it to yourself and your staff to grow strong in resilience so you can work together to create the legacy and impact you will be proud of.

About John

John Nicholls is an internationally-known trainer and coach, specialising in resilience, staff wellbeing and leadership development. His extraordinary talent for establishing rapport has helped John support thousands of teachers around the world, who value his common sense, caring guidance and good-humoured approach to their professional and personal development.

John first came to public prominence when, as a school principal facing significant budget shortfalls, he took a pay cut, worked a four-day week and saved the jobs of class assistants in his school. This considerate act was broadcast on the BBC, Sky and ITV news and widely reported in the UK newspapers. Receiving letters from around the world, he was congratulated on his actions.

This steadfast focus on supporting staff morale and his ability to create positive environments for students, parents, teachers, board members and the local community led to new opportunities. John succeeded in running the award-winning "Norfolk Wellbeing Programme", working with nearly one thousand volunteers to improve the morale and subjective wellbeing of over 28,000 employees in 400 schools. A big part of his success was due to his talent to encourage dialogue and create consensus across various interest groups.

John's professional development work with teachers crosses four continents with workshops in eighteen countries. His coaching skills training is highly regarded and his resilience and stress management work has improved the professional and personal lives of hundreds of school leaders.

The Resilient Leader Programme, developed and run by John, is a two-day training on building healthy habits to support resilience, dealing with people we find difficult, and practical problem solving. It is supported by nine confidential monthly coaching sessions.

As well as helping schools build coaching schemes and capacity in their organizations, John advises schools on staff morale and relationship issues. His TEDx Reykjavik talk on "How To Create A Fantastic Working Environment In Your School." has won him new fans around the world.

Holding a Masters degree in Coaching and Mentoring Practice, John has given coaching skills training in places as widely spread as Singapore, the United States, Slovakia, and The Netherlands.

You can connect with John at:
http://hu.linkedin.com/in/johnpatricknicholls/
www.teachersandschool.com

CHAPTER 16

CREATE UNCOMMON MARKETING – BY BECOMING *MISSION DRIVEN*

BY NICK NANTON & JW DICKS

His aunt would bake cookies for him when he was a little boy. And the cookies were awesome. So awesome that he wanted to make them even…well, …awesomer. He always wanted things to be the best they could be and the cookies were no different.

But in the poor neighborhood where he was from, you didn't make it far on cookies. He had to find another way out. He dropped out of high school to join the Air Force. He eventually got his high school equivalency diploma, and, when he was done with his military service, he went to college to learn clerical skills. That, in turn, led to a big break – he got a job as a secretary at the William Morris Agency.

There, his winning personality allowed him to work his way up the ladder, until he became the agency's first African-American talent agent. He also found a great way to attract big clients; he would send them over a batch of his special cookies, made by himself with the killer recipe he developed when he was a boy.

The homemade treats brought him some sweet deals and suddenly, he found himself representing such huge music superstars of the time as *Simon & Garfunkel* and *Diana Ross & the Supremes*. And while that was hugely exciting for someone who came from such a humble background, he still couldn't shake the thought that his magical cookies were where his real fortune lay.

So he borrowed seed money from a couple of his multi-millionaire clients, *Marvin Gaye* and *Helen Reddy*, and opened his own store in Los Angeles. It was a success. Hollywood, however, was just one market. The trick was finding a way to market his cookies to the rest of the country.

Instead of hiring an advertising agency to create an expensive campaign that he couldn't afford, the would-be cookie entrepreneur turned to a friend he had recently met who worked at a P.R. firm. That friend, in turn, introduced him to the head of the Literacy Volunteers of America – and the three of them brainstormed a national P.R. tour where the entrepreneur wouldn't sell cookies. No, he would sell *literacy*. It was a cause he passionately believed in because he came from a neighborhood where many never learned how to read and write properly.

Suddenly, his winning personality was being displayed in *People Magazine, Time Magazine*, A&E's "Biography," NBC's "Today Show," ABC's "Good Morning America," *The New York Times, The Chicago Tribune*, plus thousands of daily and weekly newspapers, food trades, and local television stations all across America. Of course, his cookies, which were popping up on supermarket shelves all across America, were mentioned in all these media appearances.

And suddenly those cookies were selling like hotcakes.

Wally "Famous" Amos had become truly famous in one of the very first instances of modern "Cause Marketing" – still used to this day as a textbook example in universities of the power that *Mission Driven* marketing can generate above and beyond conventional selling. That power led Famous Amos to sell his brand and company to the Keebler corporation in 1998, when Famous Amos Cookies had reached an estimated value of $200 million.

It's been estimated by the Literacy Volunteers of America that Wally Amos brought the problem of illiteracy to the attention of more people than anyone else in history. He didn't just sell cookies – he did a lot of good in spreading an important message.

Famous Amos is an excellent example of how being a *Mission Driven*

Company can maximize your marketing potential. Now, when we say a company is *Mission Driven,* we mean it has a strong, positive high-profile purpose beyond just selling goods and/or services. In one way or another, it adds extra value to the standard business equation.

Believe it or not, having this kind of mission in place is becoming more and more of a *requirement for* a successful business in this day and age. Here are a few statistics that more than make that case, all taken from the 2013 Cone Communications Social Impact Study:

- 93% of all U.S. consumers say that when a company supports a cause, they have a more positive image (a number that continues to trend up – it was 85% in 2010).

- 91% of global consumers are likely to switch brands in order to support one associated with a good cause.

- 90% of Americans are more likely to trust and stay loyal to Mission Driven companies.

- 82% of consumers base buying decisions and what products and services they recommend on a company's support for a cause.

Is it any wonder, with numbers like that, Mission Driven marketing is gaining an increasing edge over the competition? Or that big business is noticing that edge?

According to a Forbes study in 2011:

- 93% of 311 global executives surveyed believed their company could, "create economic value by creating societal value."[1]

- 84% agreed that, "companies need to evolve their giving programs from simply giving money to broader social innovation." [2]

No less a business legend than Richard Branson acknowledges this *Mission Driven* trend by blogging about what he sees as *"a fundamental*

---

1. Forbes Insights, Management and Business Operations, Corporate Philanthropy The New Paradigm: Volunteerism. Competence. Results. http://www.forbes.com/forbesinsights/philanthropy_csr_2011/#sthash.zKzMn9ws.dpuf

2. Ibid.

transformation taking place in our societies. This transformation is not a technological one – it might be enabled by technology, but it's driven by people and their changing attitudes to participation and change... Here at Virgin we've been using our social media channels to help mobilize support around issues like these... truly understanding what your business can do to make a difference is a critical starting point for any business that wants to thrive in the future. And to be open to how your business will need to change in this new world."[3]

THE APPLE OF THE PUBLIC'S EYE

So far in this chapter, we've been dwelling a lot on the heavily-publicized "cause marketing" aspect of a mission – pro-social and frequently charitable endeavors with which businesses align themselves, as Famous Amos did, to create a halo effect around their operation.

But, as we made clear in the first chapter, your mission doesn't have to be limited to that category. It can simply be about the way you do business – and it can still connect with the public with the same power.

Now, there have been millions of pages written over the years about the genius of Steve Jobs and Apple, but rarely within the context we're going to employ here: As an individual, he was completely *Mission Driven*. That Mission became an essential part of his personal brand and Apple's corporate brand when he was at the helm; it was the motivating factor behind all his products.

In 2011, when he introduced the iPad2, he made this statement: *"It is in Apple's DNA that technology alone is not enough - it's technology married with liberal arts, married with the humanities, that yields us the results that make our heart sing."[4]*

Now, can you imagine Bill Gates saying something like that? Or most CEOs for that matter?

---

3. Branson, Richard. "Occupy Yourself." January 22, 2014, http://www.virgin.com/richard-branson/occupy-yourself

4. Lehrer, Jonah. "Steve Jobs: "Technology Alone Is Not Enough", *The New Yorker*, October 7, 2011

Because Jobs himself stood for more than just technology, because he made Apple adhere to incredibly high goals for usability and style when it came to all of its products, he set a new standard for a *Mission Driven* business that he made sure extended to Apple's marketing.

Jobs constantly asked two questions when it came to the company's marketing:

Question #1: Who is Apple?

Question #2: What does Apple stand for and where do we fit in this world?

His answer to those questions – and, ultimately, Apple's mission: *"Apple believes that people with passion can change the world for the better. And those people that are crazy enough to think that they can, are the ones who actually do."* [5]

Now, keep those words in mind, as we present some of the copy from one of the most famous Apple ad campaigns of all time, 1997's "Think Different":

"Here's to the crazy ones. The misfits. The rebels. The troublemakers. The round pegs in the square holes.

The ones who see things differently. They're not fond of rules. And they have no respect for the status quo. You can quote them, disagree with them, glorify or vilify them.

But the only thing you can't do is ignore them. Because they change things. They invent. They imagine. They heal. They explore. They create. They inspire. They push the human race forward.

We make tools for these kinds of people.

While some see them as the crazy ones, we see genius. Because the people who are crazy enough to think they can change the world, are the ones who do."

---

5. Byerlee, Dana. "What Steve Jobs Knew About the Importance of Values to Your Company", Yahoo! Small Business Advisor, Tuesday, August 6. https://smallbusiness.yahoo.com/advisor/steve-jobs-knew-importance-values-company-235014359.html

Few can do *Mission-Driven* like Steve Jobs did. And the pay-off for how well he marketed that Mission?

- Apple has won the CMO Survey Award for Marketing Excellence (chosen by the world's top marketers) for 6 years straight.

- Apple was voted the most Powerful Brand in the World in 2012 in a Forbes study.[6]

MASTERING *MISSION-DRIVEN* MARKETING

When you want to learn how to do something, you turn to the best for inspiration. In this case, Apple is undeniably the master – so let's close out this chapter with some "Apple Axioms" that illustrate the most important *Mission-Driven* marketing lessons we've learned from this icon for the ages.

Apple Axiom #1: STAND FOR SOMETHING OR STAND FOR NOTHING.

If you check out the online website, UrbanDictionary.com, you'll find one of the terms listed is "Apple Hater," whose definition reads in part, "Apple haters dislike the success of the company and attempt to undermine consumers." Yes, because Apple's success has created a furtive and ecspecaily huge band of followers, there had to be a backlash. Whenever a company like Apple, a company with a firm, fixed identity and, yes, mission, stands out from the herd, there will be those who hate it just so *they* can also stand out from the herd.

As long as your mission has the right combination of attributes (which we discussed in the first chapter), you shouldn't concern yourself if your marketing happens to alienate a small portion of your potential customer or client base. It's inevitable – and it also makes your mission seem that much more authentic in the eyes of the public. You're not afraid to lose a few customers that don't believe in your mission. As long as you're positive and pro-active, never defensive and angry, small pockets of protest won't make the smallest dent in your brand.

---

6. Koprowski, Evon. "Apple Is the Most Powerful Brand in the World, According to New Forbes Study", Storyism.net, October 12, 2012. http://storyism.net/apple-is-the-most-powerful-brand-in-the-world-according-to-new-forbes-study

Apple Axiom #2: **YOUR PEOPLE MUST REPRESENT YOUR MISSION.**

If you've ever been to an Apple Store, you know that the personnel is selling the Apple company culture just as much as its individual products. That's because Apple is careful to make sure their employees fully *understand and represent their mission.* In the words of one, "Sometimes the company can feel like a cult. Like, they give us all this little paper pamphlet, and it says things like—and I'm paraphrasing here—'Apple is our soul, our people are our soul.' Or 'We aim to provide technological greatness."[7]

Your marketing isn't just about selling your mission to your potential customers, it's also about selling your mission to your employees and representatives – even, in some cases, your vendors. Zappos is another company that takes this principle very seriously, being so careful to make sure their employees fully support their company culture that, in the past, they've offered them money to quit!

Apple Axiom #3: **KEEP THINGS SIMPLE.**

Is there anything simpler – or more iconic – than the Apple logo itself? And is there anything more brilliant than including a sticker of that logo in every iPhone box?

Apple's actual mission is a fairly complex one – and yet the company is brilliant at communicating its essential essence with incredibly basic messaging. How basic? How about introducing such seminal products as the original Macintosh computer, the iMac and the iPod with just one word – "Hello."

Okay, they got a little wordier with the iPhone – those ads used the tagline, "Say hello to iPhone."

You might ask, well, what does saying "Hello" actually have to do with Apple's Mission? Plenty. Each new Apple product has a certain distinct "cool" look that immediately reflects the company's mandate to continually create beautiful new gadgets that deliver as much cutting-edge style as technology. Simply showing one of their new products with a friendly greeting says to the average consumer, "We did it again!"

---

7. Anonymous, "Confessions of an Apple Store Employee", *Popular Mechanics*, December 21, 2012

Or, in other words, Mission Accomplished.

Apple Axiom #4: INFLUENCE THE INFLUENCERS.
In order to introduce the first Macintosh personal computer, Apple aired a special commercial nationally *only one time* – during the 1984 Super Bowl. And this was no quickie; it was directed by a major movie director, Ridley Scott (*"Alien," "Blade Runner," "Gladiator,"* etc.) at the then-unheard-of price of $900,000. "1984," which was the title of the ad, ended up in the Clio Hall of Fame and was named to *Advertising Age's* 50 greatest commercials of all time.

But before all that happened, just after the commercial was completed and before it aired, it was screened for the Apple Board of Directors. They *hated* it. As a matter of fact, they never wanted it to see the light of day. Jobs insisted, the spot ran for its single airing during the Super Bowl, and the rest is history.

The commercial was more than an advertisement for the Macintosh itself – it was designed to create a conversation about the transformation of society through PCs. As Brent Thomas, the art director of "1984" said at the time, Apple "had wanted something to stop America in its tracks, to make people think about computers, to make them think about Macintosh…This was strictly a marketing position."[8]

Apple's marketing has always been as much about reaching the intelligentsia as its customer base. By aiming at influencing the influencers, their marketing achieves a high degree of credibility and prestige that goes beyond the usual retail selling. "1984" made everybody talk about Apple, even though the ad itself disappeared forever (well, you can still watch it on YouTube). Its "once-and-done" nature just made it all the more compelling.

You also want your organization's mission to be understood and respected by those in a position to validate and amplify your marketing message. Third party validation is always an incredible positive for any marketing campaign. The more "buzz" you can create for your mission, the more you impact the general culture.

---

8. Burnham, David. "The Computer, the Consumer and Privacy." *The New York Times*, March 4, 1984

Apple Axiom #5: AVOID CONFLICT BETWEEN YOUR MARKETING AND YOUR MISSION.

Anyone who studies marketing remembers the "1984" commercial. But very few talk about its follow-up.

In 1985, Apple presented another "event" commercial for the Super Bowl, designed to capitalize on the massive impact they had made the year before. Apple actually placed full page ads in newspapers around the country, telling readers to make sure and watch during the third quarter for their new sensational commercial – and gave special cushy seats and signs to everybody in the stadium at the actual Super Bowl.

All of this ballyhoo resulted in one of the company's biggest marketing failures. This commercial was received so poorly, Apple didn't place another ad in the Super Bowl for another 14 years!

The ad was called "Lemmings", and its purpose was to introduce Apple's new Macintosh Office software. It did this by portraying hundreds of blindfolded businessmen and women walking off a cliff to their doom – insinuating that everybody using a PC instead of a Mac was, basically, a self-destructive sheep. Problem was, many more people fit into the former category rather than the latter. As one journalist put it, "Turns out that insulting the very people you are trying to sell merchandise to is not the best idea."[9]

"1984" dramatized someone changing the status quo in an exciting and vivid way; "Lemmings" dramatized hordes of people willingly walking into an abyss to die. One vision was stimulating – the other was just plain depressing.

Apple's mission, up until then, had been to inspire new ways of thinking and doing – "Lemmings", in contrast, was more of a scare tactic to motivate people into buying Apple products. It was a rare misstep by THE master marketer – and it demonstrated the necessity of keeping the spirit of whatever your Mission might be in whatever marketing you're currently planning.

---

9. Seibold, Chris. "January 20, 1985: Apple Goes to the Well One Too Many Times." AppleMatters.com, January 20, 2011. http://www.applematters.com/article/january-20-1985-apple-goes-to-the-well-one-too-many-times/

The melding of mission and marketing is an incredible plus for any entrepreneur, business or nonprofit organization. It reinforces all the benefits that your Mission brings to the table, while elevating your marketing above the crowd with a subtext that stands out. And that, in turn, makes you Uncommon among your competition.

About Nick

A 3-Time Emmy Award Winning Director, Producer and Filmmaker, Nick Nanton, Esq., is known as the Top Agent to Celebrity Experts® around the world for his role in developing and marketing business and professional experts, through personal branding, media, marketing and PR.

Nick serves as the CEO of The Dicks + Nanton Celebrity Branding Agency, an international branding and media agency with more than 2200 clients in 33 countries. Nick has produced large scale events and television shows with the likes of Steve Forbes, Brian Tracy, President George H.W. Bush, Jack Canfield Jack Canfield (Creator of the *Chicken Soup for the Soul* Series), Michael E. Gerber, Tom Hopkins and many more.

Nick is recognized as one of the top thought-leaders in the business world, speaking on major stages internationally and having co-authored 36 best-selling books, including *The Wall Street Journal* Best-Seller, *StorySelling*™.

Nick has been seen in *USA Today, The Wall Street Journal, Newsweek, BusinessWeek, Inc. Magazine, The New York Times, Entrepreneur® Magazine, Forbes,* FastCompany. com and has appeared on ABC, NBC, CBS, and FOX television affiliates around the country, as well as E!, CNN, FOX News, CNBC, MSNBC and hosts his own series on the Bio! channel, *Portraits of Success.*

Nick is a member of the Florida Bar, a voting member of The National Academy of Recording Arts & Sciences (Home to The GRAMMYs), a member of The National Academy of Television Arts & Sciences (Home to the EMMYs), The National Academy of Best-Selling Authors, and serves on the Innovation Board of the XPRIZE Foundation, a non-profit organization dedicated to bringing about "radical breakthroughs for the benefit of humanity" through incentivized competition, best known for it's Ansari XPRIZE which incentivized the first private space flight and was the catalyst for Richard Branson's Virgin Galactic. Nick spends his spare time serving as an Elder at Orangewood Church, working with Young Life, Downtown Credo Orlando, Entrepreneurs International and rooting for the Florida Gators with his wife Kristina and their three children, Brock, Bowen and Addison..

Learn more at: www.NickNanton.com and
www.CelebrityBrandingAgency.com

About JW

JW Dicks, Esq., is America's foremost authority on using personal branding for business development. He has created some of the most successful brand and marketing campaigns for business and professional clients to make them the credible celebrity experts in their field and build multi-million dollar businesses using their recognized status.

JW Dicks has started, bought, built, and sold a large number of businesses over his 39-year career and developed a loyal international following as a business attorney, author, speaker, consultant, and business experts' coach. He not only practices what he preaches by using his strategies to build his own businesses, he also applies those same concepts to help clients grow their business or professional practice the ways he does.

JW has been extensively quoted in such national media as *USA Today,* the *Wall Street Journal, Newsweek, Inc.*, Forbes.com, CNBC.com, and *Fortune Small Business*. His television appearances include ABC, NBC, CBS and FOX affiliate stations around the country. He is the resident branding expert for *Fast Company's* internationally syndicated blog and is the publisher of *Celebrity Expert Insider*, a monthly newsletter targeting business and brand building strategies.

JW has written over 22 books, including numerous best-sellers, and has been inducted into the National Academy of Best-Selling Authors. JW is married to Linda, his wife of 39 years, and they have two daughters, two granddaughters and two Yorkies. JW is a 6th generation Floridian and splits his time between his home in Orlando and beach house on the Florida west coast.

CHAPTER 17

FRAMING POSSIBILITY

BY MAY BAGNELL

"When you change the way you look at things,
the things you look at change."
~ Wayne Dyer

LIFE

I was born with a disability. I arrived in this world broken. Literally.

My mother, a woman of stature at just 5'2", went into labor on January 15, 1968. I was about to arrive on the scene at a sizeable 10 pounds! The birth process was not going to be easy on her. As was customary in hospitals, women in labor were given drugs to deal with the labor contractions. The combination of the medicine and my sheer size, proved to be too taxing for my mother. Her heart stopped.

Imagine the scene, she is pushing to deliver me and as my head was emerging she went into cardiac arrest. That labor room became an emergency room as teams of medical personnel arrived on the scene. Two lives hung in perilous conditions. Two women were fighting for their lives, together…one to start her human journey and one to continue hers.

Because her heart had stopped, everything else in her body came to a screeching halt including the womb that had been actively working to deliver me. As the one team rushed to revive my mother, another team raced to assess how to rescue me. My broad shoulders were trapped in her pelvis as her whole body went into lock down. The attending physician made the only choice that could save my life. He had to break my right clavicle. The procedure saved my life but it paralyzed my right arm. The function of my arm was absent as it hung limp.

Both teams were triumphant in the rescue of both of our lives. It was a day of receiving. We were both given the gift of this precious life -- however rough the start had begun. My mother now was faced with a choice. How would she look at this situation? How would she see my disability? She made the only choice *she* could. She chose to see me as whole, to see me living the life I was purposed to live. She prayed daily…not that I should heal but that my disability would not hinder me from my God-given purpose and meaning.

Those early days were not easy as a young mother, but she chose to see the situation differently. She saw the possibility not the disability. She dedicated herself to my 24-hour care of feeding, diaper changing, soothing and physical therapy exercises prescribed by the doctors. She remained focused on what was possible for my life.

One day, when I was about 3 months old, she was going about her regular routine of caring for me. She had left me on the bed momentarily as she turned to get something. When she looked back at me, she thought she saw my right arm move. But of course she thought, "no… that can't be…I must be imagining things." She had prepared to raise a daughter who knew no limitations despite her disability, but this? Could this really be happening?

That was a day of receiving the gift of a God-given miracle that the doctors had no explanation for. It was a day for receiving the gift of "seeing things differently" for both my mother and for me. While I regained the use of my arm, I was left with some restriction. But all these years, I have grown in gratefulness that I was the recipient of such a divine gift. My minor restrictions only serve as a reminder that *framing possibility shifts the focus from "what is" to "what could be"*.

What about you? What do you believe is possible in your life right now? Your work? Your family? Where do you lack vision? Where do you need to shed some new light? Are you in a place of fear or doubt? Be encouraged my friend. What I am about to share with you can help you shift your focus no matter your situation. The truth is…*You have the power to create a whole new way of "seeing" any situation. You see... the truth is...how you "see" is how it will "be".*

LIGHT

Much of what has been made visible to me about my work as a life coach, I gained through my work as a photographer. Join me as I take you through a photographers guide to framing possibilities for your life and business.

> **"When you change the way you look at things, the things you look at change."** ~ *Wayne Dyer*

Vision

All my sessions, whether photography or coaching, begin with casting the vision for what we will create. We plan and visualize the mood and theme we are after. This is foundational for all that will be created. From there we are inspired to add the items that will enable the vision.

Harnessing a vision for your life or business is key to establishing a framework from which to create. Your mind has the ability to experience feeling a future event. Think of a time when you were preparing for a long anticipated vacation. Perhaps it was a beach vacation. The more you planned and prepared, you could just about hear the seagulls, feel the warm sand under your feet and taste that Piña Colada! *You can use the power of your mind to cast a vision for your life and business.* Vision boards, whether hand made or on Pinterest, are key tools used by successful leaders to see their desires already manifested.

> *{Say: I am the co-creator of my life.}*

Lighting

So much can be said about lighting. While light is boundless, it can be harnessed to shed the appropriate amount of illumination for the subject, space and mood. The word photography literally means painting with light. Knowing how to be a light observer and how it falls on the subject will dictate the overall mood of the image. Where you focus your light relative to your subject will dictate the mood of the overall image.

In the canvas of your life, your creative tools are your thoughts and your words. They are the light sources you are casting to give form to any subject or circumstance you face. Do you look at your past with regret or longing? *Every time you think, you can be shaping and illuminating your future.*

{Say: The past is a place of reference, not a place of residence.}

Focus

For photographers, focus is the mother of sharpness and what you draw the viewer's attention to. Focus allows the photographer to highlight a particular aspect of the overall image and make it the star of the show. Without focus, the image is uninteresting, blurry and devoid of inspiration.

Situations in life and business can easily become blurry without the intended focus applied. However, there can be situations when you don't really want everything in focus. It can be distracting and overwhelming.

The lens of your life works much in the same way. *Focus on who you want to be in the circumstance, and watch your circumstance shift.*

{Say: I don't have to put everything in focus, only what matters.}

Composition

The composition of an image is all about how you want to have your subject appear in the overall frame. You have a host of possibilities... you can compose with your subject right in the middle, like all beginners will do, or you can master how to create a more interesting composition by training your creative eye. Either way, as the artist, you have the choice.

You have the choice on how you see any circumstance. *We all start at the beginner level but if you are willing, you can master how you see.*

{Say: The way I frame a circumstance has the power to change the circumstance itself.}

Depth of Field

DOF is used to emphasize part of the image or the entire scene to get the "big picture." In some situations, it may be desirable to have the entire scene sharp and in focus. However, if you desire to highlight only a part of the overall scene, "the details" for example, you utilize visual depth to make the subject stand out. One way photographers can utilize DOF is by selecting the appropriate aperture of the lens, the size of the opening through which light can travel responding to the lighting conditions.

In our human optics, the pupil is the aperture. When you experience very bright light, your pupil responds and constricts to limit how much light is allowed in. In dim lighting situations, your pupil opens wide to allow as much light in for your ability to see. The depth of your perception is necessary for your ability to integrate information. At times we need to see the big picture, the full frame, with a clear view. And at other times, we benefit from focusing on the details.

You may find yourself in a "dark" scenario. Sometimes the "light" is nowhere to be found. However, you can control the amount of light you let in by remaining wide open to what is possible. *You have the power to shift your visual depth to serve you and the circumstance at hand.*

{Say: In any given circumstance, I have the power to respond and remain open.}

LESSON

Recently, my husband and I took a short trip to visit our youngest son. We spent some time together exchanging ideas. Our son is a philosophy major in college, so these conversations are certainly a source of great intrigue. All three of my children have been used to be great mirrors and teachers in my life. As we conversed, I shared my thoughts on framing possibilities and the importance of what you choose to focus on, and he shared with me Plato's Allegory of a Cave. Fascinated by this allegory concerning human perception, I felt it was an instant tie in to my thoughts.

"When you change the way you look at things, the things you look at change." ~ Wayne Dyer

Imagine in your mind a dark cave. In the cave, 3 prisoners are held bound and cannot see anything except what is projected in front of them on a wall. They have been there since birth. This cave is devoid of light except for a fire that is burning behind them and the people carrying the objects which projects shadows on the wall—both of which the prisoners are unaware. To the prisoners in the cave, the projections cast on the wall appear real because, of course, if they have never seen the real thing, to *them*, that *is* that real thing.

One day, one of the prisoners escapes his dark existence of the cave. He is taken aback to discover by what he "sees" outside his cave. As he gets accustomed to this world, he comes to terms that his previous view was only part of the reality. He is fascinated to see a much larger source of light: the sun. Content with his discovery, and with his mind expanded, he cannot wait to return to the cave and share this great news with the other prisoners. Much to his dismay, they do not believe him and shun him for even bringing such ideas into the cave.

As I reflect on this allegory, I cannot help but see the connection. We can easily get lost in the cave of our own thoughts and negative beliefs. Operate this way for long enough, and over time, the shadows of those negative beliefs become reality to you. That reality becomes all that is possible. *But what you did not notice is that you successfully fabricated a reality based on a very small source of light.*

The key to framing possibility is the willingness to shift your focus and use the appropriate light source to help you "see" differently. You can focus on the problem or you can choose to focus on the possibility. We unconsciously live by a certain way of seeing. *You have the power to choose.*

Practice framing new possibilities to shift you from where you are now to where you desire to be. Be brave and courageous to walk out of the cave of limitations into all of God's best for your life.

Desire to be Uncommon, because now you know – how you "see" is how it will "be".

About May

Becoming personally involved with each of her clients, the versatile visual artist, life coach and personal brand leader, May Bagnell, has created a powerful niche as an in-demand lifestyle portrait and brand photographer. When May tells her subjects that they've entered the "no pose zone," this is their cue to smile, relax and simply enjoy the moment. Her unique artistry will do the rest—and make every memory live vibrantly in the process. Her storytelling ability to capture visual poetry is evident as she documents the lives of her client's *life celebrations*, *brands*, and *dreams* through Personal Branding and Coaching that leads to inspiring documentary films and imagery.

One of the most fascinating aspects of this ambitious entrepreneur's emergence as a world-class photographer and coach is the unexpected, serendipitous way her lifelong passion became a busy full-time career. Growing up in Miami, she developed a love for photography and people from an early age, inspired by her physician father, who took the family on numerous trips for vacations and medical conferences and shot hundreds of pictures to chronicle their adventures. May's favorite photos were those that captured life's happy moments, catching people in joy and fully expressed -- images that collectively told a story.

"The way it happened was like a dream come true for me," says May. "It's a career that is a joy to wake up to and do every day. Besides being personally fulfilling, the big payoff for me is bringing delight to the clients I am privileged to serve. My coaching work along with my photography work is very lifestyle-based. I'm always living moment-to-moment looking for that spark and personality that illuminates the day and allows me to best help my client really "see" themselves. Looking back, one of the most serendipitous things about my life is that the act of helping women with the birthing process, in my early career as a birth coach, in turn actually birthed my career in life coaching. I discovered that I could nurture this dream and love every moment of making it come alive and grow over the years. I am a true believer that *everything shapes us.*"

May, an International Coach and Photographer, has been mentored by some of the best in the industry. She has been taught by the Robbins-Madanes Center for Strategic Intervention, Divine Living's Gina DeVee, Landmark Education and others. May Bagnell works with her clients to move past limitations, embrace what is possible and tell their stories in a compelling way.

A big believer in *paying it forward*, May enjoys speaking and teaching about her experiences as a photographer, entrepreneur and her journey with God. "My heart's desire," she says, "is to encourage others that there is a divine plan. Being a part of creating what's possible we can help budding dreamers achieve their goals. It's all about finding where that passion lies, and it's wonderful to watch other women like me grow into their own God-given dreams."

You can connect with May Bagnell at:
may@maybagnellphotography.com

CHAPTER 18

"UNCOMMON FORMULA WORKS LIKE MAGIC!"

BY MARJORIE DICK STUART

Seven simple *"secrets"* to solve the mystery that has puzzled home sellers and confounded <u>most</u> real estate agents for decades... How to Get More Money for Your House?

What if everything you thought you knew about how to sell your house *(including what real estate agents have told you)* is wrong? For over 35 years I've listened to hundreds of sellers and learned many valuable lessons.

Let's begin with Janet...

Janet's mother promised to marry her father as long as he promised to move from Wall Street. And so they moved to Washington, D.C. Janet lived in the house on Idaho Avenue for over eighty years! She cherishes memories of reading comic books and playing checkers with her brother in the closet on the top floor, headquarters of their "secret club."

She grew up running through the Bishop's Garden watching the National Cathedral rise from a chapel to its towering presence on Mount Saint Alban. Janet remembers the McLean's summer estate "Friendship" and its private golf course before it was transformed into housing for workers during World War II and then converted to condominiums. The face of her Cleveland Park neighborhood changed before her very eyes!

And then, it was time to move. Janet's challenge: *How to keep eight decades of equity from slipping through her fingers, while stirred by a lifetime of emotions?*

SECRET #1: IT'S EMOTIONAL.

To poorly paraphrase Tina Turner, "What's *'emotion'* got to do with it?" …*Plenty!*

Consider that the sale of your home may be the largest financial transaction of your life. But it is much more than just business. First of all money is emotional for most of us, and the gain or loss of lots of money is even more so! Couple that with the fact that most home sales are triggered by a major life event...a birth, a death; a wedding, a divorce; a new job, a lost job; a retirement, a relocation; and you can appreciate that selling your home is very personal. And very personal usually means very emotional. And very emotional can be very dangerous in major financial matters.

Make sure that whoever helps you sell your house understands not just your situation but also your stress.

SECRET #2: PICK THE RIGHT AGENT.

Many sellers think that any agent will do. That's why some will pick a relative or friend, because they need a break – someone in the neighborhood or the agent that sold them the house – solely because of familiarity. And that's okay...if the agent you choose successfully represents dozens of sellers each year!

"...by the time you realize that your deal is challenging, you are stuck with whatever agent you have – and they may be over their head at that point."~ Bob (successful seller)

So who are you looking for? Someone who will make it *easy* for you to get more money, without the daily *aggravations* and ongoing *frustration* of uncomfortably surviving the continuing *disruption* in a house languishing on the market, *unsold*, week after week after week, sometimes even for months on end.

Yes, every single day, you <u>do</u> have to make your bed the moment you awake and wash your dishes immediately after each meal...nothing left *in the sink. And make sure to <u>always</u> lock the bathroom door!*

And how do you evaluate an agent? In real estate appraisals there is a guiding principle...*"highest and best use."* I stumbled across its value to my business and my clients' success by accident.

I was eight months pregnant with our son, Rhett. Now he's a freshman at Emory and a pitcher on the baseball team *(sorry, couldn't help myself... proud mama).* Anyway, I had high blood pressure and my doctor told me I had to stop working. Well, you know what happened next. That's right, a negotiation!

Four weeks of strict bed rest, in exchange for the telephone. I made seven sales in the next three weeks! How did I do it? ...With a lot of help! And I could still deliver my *highest and best*, trusted advice and expert negotiating. I discovered I didn't have to do it all. As a matter of fact, my clients were *better served* when I only did what only I could do. It changed my business and my life.

Find an agent successfully representing enough sellers, that he/she has the experience and expertise you deserve and has developed a skilled support team to assist with the thousands of details required of your sale.

A final tip: Don't hire a "yes" man. Find someone who will tell you what you need to know, not just what you want to hear!

SECRET #3: MENTALLY MOVE OUT.

Most sellers ask, "What do I need to do to get my house 'market' ready?" Make sure that the advice you get is based upon a proven track record of results. And if you can afford it, follow it!

Who wouldn't follow sound advice? You'd be surprised!

They loved the red walls in their dining room and so did all of their guests. That's the amazing property "dead in the water" with two different agents for over 191 days, over 6 months! Finally, the sellers hired me, after I advised them to repaint the dining room. They did. *We got two offers in just 27 days... sold!*

Is it really that simple? It can be. So what's the problem? Many sellers refuse to believe "staging a house to sell" makes a difference until they have already cost themselves tens of thousands of dollars. And it's more complicated. Once a house becomes "market-ready" it no longer *feels* like home to the seller. That should be a good thing, but it is uncomfortable nonetheless. Hence it is vital for the seller to *"mentally move out."* Let go and begin to move on. Start celebrating your move.

And remember...each time a buyer visits, *get out*! Allow the buyers an uninterrupted opportunity to enjoy your home without an anxious seller trailing behind like a puppy dog, or worse yet, leading them through with an aggravating sales pitch.

What did Janet do? She moved out and had her house staged by a professional. You are going to love what it did for her price...*keep reading*.

SECRET #4: THE POWER OF "PIN-POINT" PRICING.

"How much is my house worth?" You are not going to like the answer. No one really knows! Not you, not your neighbors, not your agent, and not even a licensed appraiser. Just about everyone has an opinion, but the only one that matters is your buyer's.

We operate in a real estate marketplace of buyers and sellers. Find an agent knowledgeable in your market who can provide up-to-date market activity, including recent sales, current competition and local conditions. Taking an objective look with an expert will usually lead you to the same price range.

And now for the most important part...remember these words: *"Better to under price by a dollar than overprice by a penny."*

How can I say that? Simple, it works. Time after time after time. What I discovered is that the market *self-corrects* and typically *competes* for properties just *below* top dollar, frequently paying *above* top dollar.

Earlier this year, David and Alison decided to leave D.C. for a new job. They wanted to sell their house for more than $1,400,000 and we did! Let me tell you how. We priced it at $1,385,000, generated multiple offers and sold it for $1,430,000!

What happens if you overprice? Nothing! *Buyers aren't stupid.* They are *value-seeking* missiles who won't waste time on an *unrealistic* seller. The market is *unforgiving*. Don't add to the *invisible inventory*, overpriced listings that nobody sees.

Okay, back to Janet. Sometimes, even I am surprised. The staging transformation was so complete, I recommended the *unthinkable* - raise the price. A little later, I'll tell you how that worked out.

SECRET #5: SHARE YOUR STORY.

Make sure your marketing resonates with your buyers. What do I mean by that? There's a very good chance that the "best" buyers for your house share a number of similarities with you, ranging from their "house-hunting" search to how they hope to enjoy and experience living in your home.

Tell them about *"Your frustrating search, scouring the newspapers, endlessly surfing the Internet and trawling the neighborhood until you discovered your home."* It's likely that your buyers are struggling through the same thing. Don't they deserve to be rewarded with your house?

One of my clients shared a *"home story"* in our marketing. Starbucks was so nearby she threw away her coffee maker. Guess what her buyer told me? *"The first thing I am going to do is throw away my coffee pot!"* Really?

Yes, really. Remember Janet? Can you see her reading comic books with her brother in their "secret" club? Probably huddled under the eaves with a flashlight!

*****Marketing is about connecting.*****

SECRET #6: SPEED MEANS MONEY.

Selling your home is not the time to wait for a *"needle in a hay stack"* buyer to miraculously appear, or "sleep" on the best offer you'll ever see.

I have developed a proven success strategy for home sellers who want to get more money. Let me describe it. Just please don't laugh. It is dependent upon *"market" acceleration*...speed.

It begins with a candid client conversation and continues with a detailed *"room by room"* review. This isn't the fast part. Recommendations are made and agreed upon, so that once the marketing is *launched* on a Friday and the home is *introduced* at a Sunday "open house," *multiple* buyers will compete to pay full price or more by Monday night, if not sooner. *By the way...don't sleep on it.* Sign it!

Unfortunately one of my recent sellers *did sleep on it*. On Saturday, a buyer offered her $10,000 *above* full price to sell before the Sunday open house. The seller refused. Lucky for her, the buyer came back with another offer on Monday, but *only* for full price. This time she signed it...*a ten thousand dollar loss in just two days!*

Perhaps some readers are skeptical. Just remember, this book is *non-fiction*. My clients have experienced the value of speed. Do your own research, I've done mine. Look beneath the surface of your friend's sale. You know, the one who waited month after month to sell her house and finally, proudly announced, "I got my price." *Whatever that means?*

Here's what the research shows. Houses either sell right away or very quickly *after* some change is made to the property or the price to reach market value. So what happened to Janet's after we raised the price? Two buyers wanted it right away and one was willing to pay the higher price.

Selling is about connecting fast!

SECRET #7: "UNDER THE RADAR" REAL ESTATE.

This is one of the *"hottest"* new marketing strategies for getting more money, fast!

Sometimes you can create more value with a house that is not on the market. I represented the seller when Kathy and John bought their home. They called me three years later when they were thinking of selling. They didn't need to move for about six months. Since we were just emerging from the "polar vortex" and nothing was on the market, I suggested we test the market early.

"You mean a *'pre-marketing' preview?*" Kathy asked.

"Exactly!" I agreed, noting the new phrase Kathy had just coined that I continue to use. It was her idea to order a *'Pre-marketing Preview'* sign.

We priced *aggressively*. I *quietly* told thousands about the house. A number were scheduled to see the house Sunday. But one buyer couldn't wait. He loved it. His wife was in North Carolina. It didn't matter. He offered $75,000 *more than full price*...Kathy and John didn't sleep on that one!

P.S. In case you're wondering, his wife loved it when she saw it. Lucky guy!

That's it, 7 simple "secrets"...to get more money when you sell your house.

1. It's emotional.

2. Pick the right agent.

3. Mentally move out.

4. The power of "Pin-Point" pricing.

5. Share your story.

6. Speed means money.

7. "Under the radar" real estate.

Remember each one!

And for those of you thinking of buying...that's another story for another day!

About Marjorie

Marjorie Dick Stuart is a residential real estate expert in Washington, D.C. with W.C. & A.N. Miller, exclusive affiliate of CHRISTIE'S INTERNATIONAL REAL ESTATE. She has represented hundreds of buyers and sellers in the Metropolitan area. Marjorie's sellers are rewarded with an average of 102% of *full* price in *only* 6 days!

Marjorie's husband, Bill, is her business partner. They are an **UNcommon** team. Think of Marjorie as *Michael Jordan* and Bill as *Phil Jackson*. Together, they grew their business through the 2008 economic collapse, guiding their clients to success during one of the most challenging real estate markets in history.

The Realty Alliance, a network of elite residential brokerages, recognized Marjorie's exceptional performance, ranking in the "Top 1%" of all residential real estate professionals in North America.

She was covered in a *Washington Post* series on creativity in the real estate market, highlighting three of Marjorie's most successful cases. She was also the guest expert on the *Post's* live, follow-up web-chat Q&A.

Marjorie has even been seen on the Success Today TV Show, hosted by media personality from the **Today Show**, Bob Guiney, which has been seen on ABC, NBC, CBS and FOX affiliates across the country.

She is a member of America's Premier Experts®, home to the nation's foremost "specialized" subject matter experts where her content is routinely featured and distributed to journalists across the country.

Marjorie is a featured speaker at Long & Foster's Annual Real Estate Symposium.

She serves on the Board of Friendship Place, dedicated to ending homelessness and rebuilding lives. (www.FriendshipPlace.org)

Marjorie is also a founding contributor, volunteer and a member of the Board of Cleveland & Woodley Park Village, "Neighbors helping Neighbors" age in place while remaining in their community within a supportive network. (www.ClevelandParkVillage.org)

For more information on Marjorie, visit: www.DCHomeblog.com

CHAPTER 19

PITTSBURGH – UNCOMMON CITY

BY ELMER DAVIS, JR.

OVERVIEW—TIED TO UNCOMMON PRINCIPLE

"Uncommon valor was a common virtue" is a quote from Admiral Chester William Nimitz in reference to the U.S. soldiers on Iwo Jima in 1945. In fact, all the way back to our Founding Fathers, Americans have taken approaches that were uncommon—in particular as it applied to achieving independence from England. They understood partnerships and leverage; they essentially borrowed from France to fund the war of independence. Our Founding Fathers married and balanced varied interests ranging from political to financial in order to achieve their objective of full independence from England.

They also required structure, so they created the Federalist paper, which led to the United States Constitution, and the concept of the Central Bank based on Alexander Hamilton's financial model. The goal was to take the best of the historical approaches and transform it to create a viable and sustainable model for the United States, the result of which is that the US Constitution is now the longest-surviving constitution and form of government in the world today.

APPROACH & METHODOLOGY

In much the same manner, you too can utilize a unique and/or uncommon approach to reach and exceed your goals—with tremendous long-term financial results. At our firm TBK Ventures, Inc., we have under our belt years of fieldwork with thousands of small businesses and found that 50% of them failed within the first five years. You actually learn more from challenging times than when things are sailing along smoothly.

In nearly every case, we found that the limitations of the owners translated into business problems associated with profitability—or lack thereof—in several key areas (refer to our publications "SuccessOnomics" and "Victory" for more detailed information on these and similar topics):

- Pricing—To cover true costs

- Expense Control/budgeting—To include break-even analysis

- Human Resource Productivity—50% of revenues go to pay people directly and indirectly; the excessive cost of miscommunication

- Asset Management—Poor return on capital and assets, 75% plow back of profits into the enterprise, financial intermediation, conspicuous consumption

At TBK we focus our attention on the asset management area to illustrate the optimal solution that we have identified in the current economic climate to address the above-referenced problem—and how that same system can easily provide a turn-key, independent and long-term opportunity to generate wealth for clients from both passive and portfolio income-producing assets. One approach is creating tools to utilize real estate to make a profit—enabling people to participate in ways that they wouldn't normally be able to do independently, particularly as outsiders to a market.

What do you need to know about the U.S. affordable housing market then?

1. The **market** is not providing an adequate number of **homes affordable** to middle income people. 2. The shortage is particularly acute in the rental **housing market**.

INVESTING IN REAL ESTATE: FORBES.COM RATES PITTSBURGH NO. 1 "MOST LIVABLE" CITY

One place that does offer an appealing market for affordable housing is the Pennsylvania city of Pittsburgh. Named the "most livable city" six times since 2000 by The Economist, Forbes and Places Rated Almanac, Pittsburgh has also landed on more than 200 "best" lists including "40 Prettiest Cities in the World" *(Huffington Post)*, "Most Entrepreneurial City in the America" *(Inc.)*, "Most Livable City in America" *(Forbes)* and "Best Places in the World to Visit" *(National Geographic)*.

Former Mayor Luke Ravenstahl announced that Pittsburgh has once again made its way onto the list of distinguished news sites that perform research and release ratings on cities' livability. Forbes.com rated Pittsburgh the number one 'most livable' city stating that "...jobs are plentiful, crime is low and there are myriad entertainment options."

Forbes.com gave strong mention to Pittsburgh's established university presence and low unemployment and crime rate. Also rated highly were factors including its affordability, a vibrant arts and cultural scene, and the ability to reinvent itself amidst a struggling national economy.

In compiling their list, Forbes.com measured five data points in the nation's 200 largest metropolitan statistical areas and averaged them to arrive at a final score. Those data points included: unemployment, crime, income growth, the cost of living, and artistic and cultural opportunities. Forbes.com utilized information from the Bureau of Labor Statistics, Moody's, the FBI, and Sperling's Best Places Arts and Leisure index.

"Our City has come a long way and I'm thrilled that Forbes.com has once again recognized Pittsburgh's unique position as a City that truly has it all – entertainment and affordability, but most importantly, safety and jobs," Ravenstahl enthused. "It's important that we look to these ratings as an opportunity to not only tell our good story and attract more people and businesses to Pittsburgh, but to roll up our sleeves and work on getting even safer, creating more jobs, and being more livable."

Pittsburgh Magazine: "Pittsburgh Ranked No. 5 Most Resilient City in the World" – New report by international development company Grosvenor Group has high praise for the city's adaptability.

Another day, another top ranking for Pittsburgh: First, data told us that Pittsburgh residents were living well. Then it told us Pittsburgh residents were intelligent. Lastly the report told us Pittsburgh residents were sinful. Now data is backing up our gritty reputation.

According to a <u>new report</u> by the international development company Grosvenor Group, Pittsburgh is the <u>No. 5 most resilient city in the world</u>. The report measured the ability of cities to accommodate change in areas such as governance, technical capacity and planning systems. It then balanced those numbers against city vulnerability to varying elements such as climate change, population growth and infrastructure decline. The Canadian cities of Toronto, Vancouver and Calgary landed the top three spots, followed by U.S. frontrunner Chicago and then Pittsburgh.

Pittsburgh's adaptive capacity score was 95 out of 100. The best part of this news is *why* the study was done in the first place: The London-based Grosvenor Group compiled the rankings to help guide its international clients on where to invest and develop real estate. Pittsburgh attaining placement so high on the list will certainly raise eyebrows.

Pittsburgh even beat Stockholm!

RENT COVERAGE IS A LITTLE EASIER IN PITTSBURGH

Rents nationwide have been climbing in recent years in response to the growing demand for rental housing; Pittsburgh is no exception. The city remains however a bargain compared with what renters pay in some other parts of the country.

The average cost of an apartment in the city of Pittsburgh runs about $838 a month, compared to average rents of $2,985 a month in New York, $1,970 in San Francisco and $1,045 in Chicago as per New York-based real estate research firm Reis, Inc. And those rental dollars go further in Pittsburgh.

"You can get a better home for less money in Pittsburgh than you can in Chicago or New York or San Francisco," reports Jon Pastor, CEO and co-founder of Rent Jungle, a North Shore-based company that collects data on rental rates nationwide.

"It's not just more square footage you get in Pittsburgh," he says. "But also you'll get a location in a neighborhood where young professionals want to live, with lots of access to bars, restaurants and activities like movies and shopping."

Since the Great Recession, Pittsburgh has been consistently rated as one of the nation's strongest housing markets. Still, rent in even the most desirable neighborhoods—Shadyside, Oakland, the South Side and Downtown—remains a far cry from what landlords are charging, on average, in other major cities.

Even looking just at cities near Pittsburgh, Reis data show the cost of renting outside the Alleghenies is much higher. For instance, average rents in Baltimore are $1,043, Washington, D.C. rents average $1,488, and Philadelphia's average is $1,058. An exception would be Cleveland, where the average rent is actually lower—$731. The figures include apartments of all sizes.

The large disparities among various major U.S. cities have a lot to do with income levels.

U.S. Census Bureau data show the median household income for Pittsburgh in 2011 was $37,161, while the median household income was $72,947 in San Francisco; $61,835 in Washington, D.C.; $67,204 in New York City; $54,525 in Las Vegas; and $47,371 in Chicago.

The U.S. Department of Housing and Urban Development recommends that renters spend no more than 30 percent of their gross income on housing and utilities. That means a person earning $37,000— Pittsburgh's median income—should not be spending more than $925 per month on rent and utilities.

A person earning the median income of $67,204 in New York would be able to afford $1,680 in rent and utilities based on federal government recommendations, and someone in Chicago earning the median income there of $47,371 would be able to afford monthly housing costs of $1,184.

People who live in high-rent cities, however, may need to allocate more of their income toward rent— sometimes up to 50 percent in large metropolitan areas. Individuals in rural areas—such as Knoxville, Tennessee where the average rent is $601 a month—may be able to allocate less than the recommended 30 percent of their income.

A ranking of nationwide apartment costs by Reis indicates that costs are lowest in Wichita, Kansas—where average rents are $517 a month— Oklahoma City ($564), and Tulsa, Oklahoma ($575).

"These are lower cost-of-living areas," states Brad Doremus, a senior analyst at Reis. "Incomes are lower, so you wouldn't see apartments in these areas get bid up like they would in higher income areas."

Not only are median incomes in New York City among the highest in the nation, the forces of supply and demand also play a role in pushing rental prices higher.

"There are more job opportunities in New York, but there's a lot more competition for those jobs and you have to pay more to live there," Mr. Pastor says. "A young professional may make 20 percent more in New York, but pay twice as much rent."

According to Rent Jungle, the more expensive rental communities in Pittsburgh include Oakland, Shadyside, South Side and Downtown. Mr. Pastor affirms that there are still bargains to be found in East Liberty, where rents have not caught up with the amenities in that neighborhood—such as restaurants and shops—which have improved in recent years.

Douglas E. Culkin, president and CEO of the National Apartment Association in Arlington, Virginia, says several considerations influence rents in any given location. "Beyond the basic economic principle of supply and demand, factors including market-specific cost of living, the local job market, quality of life and available housing options all exert upward or downward pressure on average rents," he observes. "Whether it's the flexibility to move for employment opportunities or the luxury of living a maintenance-free lifestyle, we are also seeing nationwide that now more than ever, Americans are making the decision to choose apartment living for their housing."

The rental market in Pittsburgh has been expanding with the conversion of office buildings and other underutilized industrial properties, reports Jim Eichenlaub, executive director of the Apartment Association of Metropolitan Pittsburgh. He points to several landmark buildings that have been converted to apartments, such as the Cork Factory in the Strip District, Heinz Lofts on the North Shore and the former State Office Building and the former Verizon Building, Downtown.

"Even with all the positive factors, it's still a competitive market [in Pittsburgh], especially with multi-family rentals," Mr. Eichenlaub comments. "Tenants can move. You always have that possibility. They still have to be competitive with each other."

Mark Popovich, senior managing director at Downtown-based HFF Inc., a commercial real estate broker with a national footprint, said the demographic that Pittsburgh is attracting to its rental market is young people who have graduated from college or who are fairly new in their careers—usually between the ages of 23 and 30.

"What we have now are jobs and a growing economy," he notes. "A lot of graduates coming out of Carnegie Mellon University and the University of Pittsburgh and other colleges now have the ability to stay in Pittsburgh and work, whereas previously—in the 1990s or early 2000s—there weren't a lot of employment opportunities in Pittsburgh. Our economy wasn't as robust then as it is now." Popovich adds, "Today there are opportunities for employment in high-tech jobs, corporate banking, accounting and energy-related fields, to name a few."

While Mr. Popovich acknowledged that Pittsburgh rents are on the rise, he said the fairly low cost of housing in the city limits how much landlords can charge. "When you look at the monthly rental rates for Class A apartments, you could afford a mortgage payment on a nice house," he asserts. "But the younger demographic would rather live in an urban rental in Shadyside, the South Side, the Strip District or Downtown. They don't want to be tied to the burdens of home ownership."

WHY PITTSBURGH HAS ALL THE RIGHT ATTRIBUTES

To reiterate, the following are some factors that make Pittsburgh a very desirable housing market in which to invest, especially when you can partner with an organization like ours, which knows the market inside and out:

• Most livable U.S. city for 11 consecutive years

• In Top 5 most resilient markets worldwide

• 50% of resident families rent

• Properties realize 3% growth per year

• Rents increase every year

• Inexpensive rehab labor costs/low average median family income

- The TBK team knows the market not by county or by zip code but rather has street by street knowledge acquired over several lifetimes of hands-on work in the local communities

- TBK can offer a turn-key solution with property management and tenant acquisition

CONCLUSION

TBK Ventures, Inc. offers exceptional funding tools; we can help you make money on real estate you don't even own, enhance your real estate investments and/or increase the profits of your business—all in alignment with our mission of *Engineering Profitability Globally Through Neighborhood Reinvestment.* We are committed to presenting our message in greater detail, offering educational seminars and training around the content featured here in *Uncommon* as well as in our other recent books *SuccessOnomics* and *Victory.*

About Elmer

Elmer Davis, Jr., MBA, ALM has over 25 years of experience in marketing and finance, including working with private and non-profit organizations, as well as Fortune 500 corporations. He began his business career in marketing with Bristol-Myers in Washington, DC in the early 80's, then moved on to work for industry giants like Mobil Oil.

He was a partner with Anderson, Philips, Davis, and Hoffmann in Washington, DC, NYC and Los Angeles, and served as Executive Vice-President and Chief Diversity Officer for Financial Dimensions, Inc. A graduate of the Florida A&M University School of Business and Industry, Mr. Davis holds a Bachelor of Science in Marketing, as well as a Master's of Business Administration from Howard University. He also recently earned a Master's of Liberal Arts from none other than Harvard University in Operational Management.

Elmer has conducted leadership-training forums for clients in numerous industry segments, including the public and private sectors and major Universities. Elmer has also written several articles, including Understanding the Communication Environment, The true costs of miscommunication, Effective strategies for business growth, Financial management for cash flow and profits, Embracing Workplace Diversity and Eliminating Employment Discrimination.

Elmer Davis, Jr., was chosen as a Mortgage Bankers Association National Diversity Champion in 2005 and a Heritage Who's Who in 2004. He is well-regarded as a facilitator of crucial information and trainer having worked with organizations in various industries providing specialized training to maximize profits through human resource productivity, asset management, pricing, and expense control. Elmer is a natural communicator and was a recent guest on MIT University radio WMBR.

His current company, TBK Ventures, Inc., has helped to control the costs and increase profits for businesses in the Pittsburgh, PA area and around the country. To obtain more information or arrange for individualized training, call: 855.293.0877 or email: edavisjr@post.harvard.edu. Or visit his website: www.elmerdavisjr.net as well.

CHAPTER 20

LOVE THE ONE YOU'RE WITH

BY TRACY COUSINEAU

From a young age, growing up in a humble, disciplined military family, I was taught many values and beliefs that I still carry with me to this day. As with many people, my biggest mentors growing up were my grandparents and parents. Later on in life, I had mentoring from other greats that I will speak of later. Through my father being stationed at a military base during the Iran hostage crisis, I had the opportunity to shake all of the hostages' hands after they were released and came back home to our great country. As a young girl, it was a day that I will never forget as long as I live: life-changing and transforming. For as far as the eyes could see, there were American Flags, ladies in yellow dresses and servicemen. My learning experience from that day was how short life is, how quickly it can be taken away and that we are never guaranteed another day – so you must make the most out of each and every day. This has remained with me through the years, and has been the foundation of my business to make the most of everyday and everyone that comes into it.

Later on in life, before starting my career in Real Estate, I worked for a large property management company. I was one of their agents that they sent out when a property was failing. My duties were to bring life back into the failing site. One of the problems that the company was having with this particular property was a lack of foot traffic – rarely was anyone coming to view the property. That was obviously one of the first things that I knew it needed to be fixed, but I knew would take a little time for advertising to gain traction and be absorbed. On my first day there, one of the company's executives came in and mentioned the title to an old song. He said that foot traffic was low, and it could be weeks before advertising was absorbed by the market, so you have to "love the one you're with." At first, and for years after that, I believed that in my heart, and always looked after my client's best interest. It wasn't until later in life that I took what the executive said, put a spin on it to a deeper, more profound meaning of life—one of my biggest core values in running my organization.

Loving the one you're with is much deeper than just simply spending time with the customer that you are with at the time. If your mindset is that your client is only a paycheck or that this is just a job to pass time, you are destined for failure. You have one of two options, change your mindset or get into a career that you love, one that you enjoy and one where you bring value into people's lives. One of the biggest gifts that GOD has given me was to be coachable and to always be learning. A majority of the things that I've learned in life has not came from me on my own; it has been a compilation of constant learning from seminars, conventions, books, speakers and mentors . . . Brian Tracy, Zig Ziglar, Tony Robbins, Jay Abraham, Darren Hardy, Jay Kinder, Michael Reese; the list goes on and on. All of these mentors have one thing especially in common, they strive to deliver the ultimate client experience.

It all starts out at the top and transfers throughout the company. When the head of the company strives to deliver an experience to their client that trumps any other experience that they've ever had, that is an experience that can't be matched by any other. When you truly "love the one you're with," you will treat them as if they were your immediate family members with whom you are doing business. Steve Harney, voted one of the nation's top 100 Most Influential Real Estate Leaders once said, "treat your clients as if they were your daughter, your son, your mother, your father, your brother or your sister." That resonated with me, when you are truly looking at your clients and helping them like you would your own family, there is no doubt that you will build lifelong relationships as you do with family.

My mentors have also taught me that running a business that's built on a strong foundation with solid core values and beliefs can't be done by one person. It's about your team, the people that work in the trenches next to you. As the late Zig Ziglar once said, "You don't build a business, you build people and then you build a business." The people that work within your organization have to believe in your vision, they have to feel the passion in their heart. When your team believes, it's a transference of energy to your clients. "Loving the one you're with" isn't only reserved for your clients.

The lifeblood of your company is the staff that delivers your message to the public daily … your employees. This happens when you hire employees that align with your core values, have high levels of integrity, work ethic and truly believe in your processes and procedures to build lifelong clients. Guess what you do when you find those wonderful people? Correct, you "love the one you're with." It is amazingly gratifying when you find these people or they find you and their experience is life-changing. The message that is delivered has to be one that is clear, precise and consistent.

When I opened my own real estate brokerage, it was exciting to immediately put in place mandatory training, meetings and conference calls to have our entire company on the same page. Our strategic plans that are backed by market research deliver unrivaled value to our clients that set us apart from the competition. The ultimate goal of our company is to maximize our client's experience and become the pre-eminent figure in our market place. We do that by having systems and procedures in place that are duplicable. In turn, through disciplined training, we can train our staff; then they can train other team members and then the message is delivered consistently by highly-trained professionals to the consumer.

In an industry that has lacked luster in recent years by the value that may be brought by traditional real estate agents, we have differentiated ourselves by bringing highly-skilled Expert Advisors that educate the consumer to a level that has never been seen before. As someone once told me, "you are either green and growing or brown and dying." My biggest suggestion to a new agent starting out would be to learn something new everyday. Discipline yourself to block your time out for a minimum of 10 hours per week to sharpen your skills within your trade. Leading into the last section of this chapter, here are ways that you can obviously break relationships and lose clients forever.

SEVEN SURE-FIRE WAYS TO LOSE A CLIENT FOREVER!

1. LACK OF INTEGRITY.

It takes a long time to build a high level of trust, although trust can start to develop within the first milliseconds of meeting your client. To really love the one you're with, trust is earned after they have experienced your services – after they have seen that you are the "go-to" source in your industry. As in personal relationships, the same holds true for business relationships, trust can be broken in seconds to an unrepairable point. Always hold the highest level of integrity, and honesty is truly the best policy. At times there are messages that have to be delivered that are tough, maybe even a mistake that you've made. Do the right thing, the truth sets you free.

2. INCOMPETENCE.

Imagine sitting in your doctor's office, you haven't been feeling well, and have flu-like symptoms. You're sneezing, coughing, have a headache and are drowsy. The doctor then in turn pulls out a cast, and starts to treat you for a broken leg. Of course, it makes no sense to treat you with a cast on the leg for flu-like symptoms. Are there times that your clients feel like you are misdiagnosing them? This usually happens because you are not asking the proper questions, not listening to your client's needs on a deep level and/or you simply may have not educated yourself to a high level within your industry. When you fail to learn, practice your trait, keep honing your skills and sharpening your proverbial sword, your confidence level will also appear low to your client. As a doctor would do, before you write your prescription, dig in deep and find out your client's true needs and wants.

3. TERRIBLE COMMUNICATION.

Have you ever went out to buy a product or service and in the middle of the process, it turns into a nightmare? You try calling the company's agents and they are avoiding your calls, or they keep sending you to different agents within the company or you're stuck in the dreaded automated recording system. This will drive the consumer nuts. They will, and deservingly so, move on to a company, that delivers better service. You can also make the consumer feel this way by forgetting to return calls and having weak follow-up systems. Make sure that your client understands the message that is being delivered and that both parties, you and them, have clarity. Miscommunication is as bad or worse than having no communication at all. Deliver a constant, clear and precise message to the consumer. It starts as early as the message that your marketing and advertising brings. Having all employees on the same page helps eliminate communication problems. It is confusing, and also becomes an integrity issue, when a company's employees are saying two completely different things.

4. YOU HAVEN'T EDUCATED THEM.

These days the consumer has immediate access to unlimited information through the Internet. We have the opportunity to educate ourselves today unlike ever before. This can also be a double-edged sword when information is conflicting from one site to the other. Even the most trusted sites in the eye of the consumer can inadvertently be misleading with information that is dated. When the consumer knows more information than you, they don't feel that you're the trusted advisor they want to work with. Always make sure that you keep up with all of the current data, market research, market trends and projections. Arm yourself and your client with visual information from credible sources so they have all the information needed to make intelligent buying decisions. As the old saying goes, "Be loaded for bear while hunting for rabbits." Be prepared and proactive, do your research.

5. THEY DON'T FEEL APPRECIATED.

The consumer has no obligation to work with you now or in the future. As business owners, they are our employers, we can't survive without them. I've seen many organizations fail because they didn't treat their customer, and usually their employees also, with respect. It may be from not listening, giving them the feeling of just being another number to the company or to just being flat-out dishonest, rude and/or condescending. After the transaction is completed, many companies have no follow up procedures to make the customer feel valued. So they ultimately allow the customer to feel as if they were just another transaction to their company. As my parents always told me, treat others the way you would want to be treated. Always follow up with your client after the sale to let them know that you are still there if they have any concerns. I've made many lifelong friends through an initial client relationship by giving them the attention and respect they deserve.

6. NO ACCOUNTABILITY.

There is no business owner that is perfect and makes no mistakes. At times, even third party influences that are outside of your control can reflect on your company. You must always research and monitor vendors that you refer your clients to, as it can place your company in a negative light if that vendor doesn't handle business and have as high ethics and core values as you do. When you make mistakes, admit them, make it right with your client, they will normally understand and respect you for it. The consumer doesn't enjoy doing business with companies that are full of excuses when problems arise. Instead, keep in mind that you can take a mistake made during the purchasing process and you can make that client your strongest reference by admitting and correcting the mistake.

7. YOU DON'T DO WHAT YOU SAY.

When you overpromise and underdeliver your services to the customer it becomes really frustrating for them. Even down to punctuality, the first promise that is usually made is to meet with them for an initial appointment. When you are late and in a hurry, you have already broken your first promise and are fighting an uphill battle. I learned this the hard way, being five minutes late to a retired military client's appointment. He said that I lost his business when I was one minute late, this was an eye-opening lesson learned that it was his perception that my time was more valuable than his. Make sure that your sales presentation is one that is educating, and lives up to their expectations after the customer's business has been earned. If it is nothing more than a sales pitch built on deception, this will give your company a horrible reputation. This does not build lifelong relationships and you will be ultimately out of business. **When you tell someone you are going to do something, do it and do it well!**

About Tracy

Tracy Cousineau is the leader of one of the nation's fastest growing real estate teams. She started her career in 1988 in property management – leasing apartments. Quickly she rose through the ranks of the company to become one of the company's top producers. In 1999, Tracy decided to take her career to the next level and jumped into the highly competitive world of residential real estate. Tracy being highly competitive and determined, quickly became a force to be reckoned with inside her marketplace. She built a successful real estate team that she developed, trained and taught. She did that for numerous real estate agents. During this time period, she won many awards and helped hundreds of families achieve their goals of buying and selling homes.

When the market started it's downhill spiral in 2007 within her marketplace, she was still selling many homes within the plummeting new construction market. In 2009, she gave birth to her third daughter, lost her mother to ovarian cancer, and her real estate market turned upside down. Tracy decided not to concentrate on real estate and took the next two years at an idle pace. This time period was unforgettable and was a time that a lot of strength was built from within.

In November of 2011, still in a dismal real estate market, Tracy decided to step back into the real estate market full-time. Tracy along with Jason Williford, her business partner, opened The Tracy Cousineau Home Selling Team and have not looked back since. Her sales volume has doubled three years in a row and is on track to be one of the top real estate teams in the state of Georgia.

In June of 2014, Tracy and Jason opened their own real estate brokerage, Real Estate Expert Advisors – a high-powered real estate brokerage of well trained, full-time real estate professionals. In the future, Tracy plans to open more branches of the brokerage. Her mission is to maximize the value that she brings to her clients. She has strategic plans backed by market research to give home sellers maximized return on their investment. In turn, her goal is to help home buyer clients of the firm find the perfect home, always negotiated at the best price.

CHAPTER 21

CLIENT RELATIONSHIPS... THE KEY TO REAL ESTATE SUCCESS

BY JOSH PAINTER, REAL ESTATE BROKER

One of the most important factors of being a successful real estate agent is the one that gets overlooked the most often. What is it? When we approach clients like they are a transaction. Sure, you may close a deal, but with that perception, it will probably be your last one. Not only should real estate clients demand more from their Realtors, but Realtors should also embrace being more for their clients. It's the best way to create a winning formula that starts to duplicate itself through referrals and clients remembering who you are because *you didn't just say you cared, you showed that you did.*

People enjoy doing business with individuals who demonstrate their positive qualities through their actions. Qualities such as reliability, accountability, genuineness, and follow-through lead to good business practices that allow consumers to put their trust into a Realtor for something that they are definitely considering more than a transaction. The buying or selling of real estate, or a combination of both at once, can be stressful and chaotic. With a Realtor that is looking out for the genuine best interests of their clients, it doesn't have to be that way. I'm grateful that this is something that I understood early on and it has made a huge difference in the way I conduct real estate business and the experience my clients have. Be a difference maker, not just a deal maker.

Whether you are an agent or someone who is looking for that Realtor that they can really establish a connection with, I'm excited to share with you some of the most important fundamental things that you can do to have the type of experience that you not only remember, but actually smile when you talk about it.

AN APPRECIATED CLIENT IS A GRATEFUL CLIENT

There are many ways in which a Realtor can show clients that they are appreciated. These are genuine and sincere gestures that show you value their relationship, as well as make it so they remember that you are the agent who makes things easier. Who wouldn't embrace that? I'd like to share some of my more favorite and most successful ways that I've discovered and implemented for creating positive experiences for real estate clients.

- Client appreciation program. With this concept, we create opportunities that are fun and meaningful to connect with our clients, who have also become our friends. Some of the most successful events include: quarterly picnics or dinners, and family movie nights.

- A borrow it, don't buy it program. Think of all the things that home owners may have to purchase just to use it once or twice? There are many items that fall into that category, including special tools, power washers, and even things such as bolt cutters. Our clients can come to our office and borrow these items and then return them. It's an amazing value that they appreciate and it gives us a chance to say hello to them and see how things are going. This type of opportunity doesn't happen with Realtors who are only worried about the transaction.

- A complementary van and trailer for clients who are moving to use. Having access to something like this is a real helper for the chaotic times that happen around a move. Many times, clients are selling one home and then going to the closing for the home they are purchasing right after. Even if they hire a moving company, what about all those last minute things that need to be moved? Putting them in a van or trailer makes things much easier. Supplying complementary access to these items is also an excellent way to give back to the community because you can let charities use them, too.

- Complementary notary services, faxing, and copy making. These are conveniences that clients definitely appreciate. They give real estate staff—which is very important to all Realtors' successes—and agents a chance to connect with clients and make their errands and "to-do" lists just a bit easier.

Ideas like the ones that I've found to be successful for building and maintaining relationships are so effective. They are simple and easy to implement, and clients appreciate them so much. If you were a client seeking out a new Realtor, would you consider the one who thinks of you as a transaction? Or, would you be inclined to go with the one that past clients have testified to having had great experiences with, consider them a friend, and refer them every chance they get? You'd be more likely to go with the one that made you feel comfortable and human nature dictates that Realtors who are referred are easier to feel confident in.

BE A SOLUTIONS PERSON

There's a pretty common saying that states, "A chain is only as strong as its weakest link." This is also true of real estate teams, and consumers understand that when they are looking around to establish a real estate relationship. Just like with any professional that someone may need to reach out to, they want to find "the one" and stick with them. The best way for Realtors to be this for their clients is to be a solutions person. Clients—do not settle for anything less from your Realtor, either.

It would be fantastic if all real estate transactions were smooth and seamless, but that is not the case, regardless of best efforts. Most of us can accept that. However, when things go wrong and a client is looking to their Realtor for solutions, a great Realtor will have those precious solutions. Someone who is focused on a commission check above all else will stutter and fumble, not really offering viable solutions that take everyone to the finish line—the closing, which is where the real friendship and lasting relationship between Realtor and client starts.

Honesty and quick thinking are two essential traits that a Realtor must have in order to navigate their clients through the unexpected surprises that can surface during a real estate transaction. You can be certain that if a Realtor cannot keep their composure during an unexpected event, a client is going to pick up on that and focused solutions become challenging problems.

- Evaluate the big picture. A true real estate professional, someone who is dedicated to client relationships and successful transactions will be able to assess a situation and find the best options for a solution. Realtors should have referrals and connections for:

  o Repair persons, including plumbers and electricians

  o Information on schools, utilities, and other pertinent contacts

  o Specialists in their region (exterminators, roof inspectors, pool maintenance, etc.)

I recall a situation that I came across with a client one time. They'd had their offer in on the home and it was getting time to close. Everyone was excited and everything was in place until...the pump on the pool went out. Of course, it wasn't a common part either, but through the connections that I had, I was able to coordinate a solution that worked so the property could still close on time and with a working pump for the pool. Without fast, reliable problem solving, this could have really put a damper on the transaction, but it didn't. Now, it's part of the client's story and shows how clients who surround themselves with the right Realtor can handle more situations.

- Think outside the box. This is a great skill to have and one that can start even before an offer is put in on a property. I was once in a situation where I had some clients who wanted a house so badly, but there were a lot of offers in on it. Waiting and hoping the other offers fell through was not really a proactive solution, and the other houses they looked at simply were not the one they wanted. We got creative. The clients wrote a letter to the homeowners, telling them exactly why they loved their house and wanted it. Guess what? It worked. Their offer got accepted, they closed and moved in, and today they have made a home there. Will this work all of the time? Maybe not, but creative ideas like this—the unexpected—can make all the difference.

Most stories about real estate transactions seem to involve making offers, or the details that come along with finalizing and closing the deal. However, many of the largest obstacles take place for people who are selling their homes right off the bat. For every seller that cannot get an offer on their home there is a buyer who doesn't realize that their perfect home is there. Why? It's all in the marketing.

SMART MARKETING IS THE SIGN OF A GREAT REALTOR

When a Realtor understands the full nature of their business they realize how important smart marketing is. It might be easier to start by defining what it is not. Smart marketing is not:

- Telling a client that you'll put their house on the market for an inflated price...just to see if you get any takers.

- Putting a house on the market without thorough evaluation and pre-listing work that will help ensure that Realtors are placing their sellers in a more optimal situation.

Pricing a home correctly right from the start is absolutely necessary. You cannot look at your neighbor's home that sold down the street and assume that your home is better here or less appealing there and determine a value. You need some information and facts, including:

- Condition of your home

- Decisions on if your home will be staged or not

- Your reasons for selling

- Current market conditions

- Nature and details of the neighborhood sales

All of those factors are major contributors to what a home should be marketed for right off the bat. When Realtors or clients make the assumption that comparing what a neighbor's house sold for is like comparing "apples to apples" they could be making a false assumption. You need to evaluate many factors and look at the small details, as well as the area the home is in. This is only done through research and evaluation. A Realtor who is willing to tell a client what they want to hear will eventually be telling them what they do not want to hear—"no offers are coming in."

How do we market a home smartly? Here are three points that you need to be aware of when it comes to smart marketing to move a home.

1. **Have a marketing budget**. It does take some money to sell a home and make sure it's being marketed to the buyers who it would appeal to. This includes taking professional photographs and knowing the best places to advertise. This conversation is important for a Realtor and client to have before a home is put on the market. A startling statistic about your average Realtor is that they will spend about $89 per month on marketing. This is a shocking number, and not in a good way. You cannot get professional photographs for that price and they are a <u>must have</u> for effective marketing. How many buyers do you think are willing to go take a look at a home with no photos or shoddy photos? Very few. It raises red flags and makes you wonder *what is wrong with this home that they won't even show it.*

2. **Understand where buyers look for homes.** Times have changed drastically when it comes to how potential buyers find the homes they want to look at. Once upon a time, a buyer would talk with a Realtor and come up with criteria for the homes they wanted to look at. Then the Realtor would actually go and pull out the <u>MLS book</u> and start looking through it, pulling out a few properties that fit the criteria, and then they would hit the pavement. Those days are over! Today, 90% of buyers already have an idea of what they want through looking on the Internet to start their search. That reiterates the fact that professional photographs and proper pricing are mandatory when the listing first goes out.

3. **Do not believe you get the same results if you use a listing service, compared to a full service Realtor.** We all want to save money. It's logical and it's smart. However, many people do not realize that if they try to sell their home by themselves first or use a listing service they are creating challenges when it comes to selling their home. Why? There are several reasons:

   • These services put whatever the seller wants on the listing, which is not always what the market reflects or based on expert advice.

   • Realtors are hesitant to show these properties because there is not a professional representing the buyer. Therefore, the property does not move.

A properly marketed home can sell quickly and at a price that is acceptable for everyone. It takes a dedicated, professional Realtor working for you when you sell and knowing where to find that perfect home that fits your criteria when you purchase. These agents also realize that satisfied clients are repeat clients and referral sources. Everyone wins with this approach.

EXPECT THE BEST

There is no reason that a client who needs help with either buying or selling real estate, perhaps both, should ever settle for mediocrity over a dedicated professional. With all the regulations and designations out there, it is easy to tell which Realtors are committed to their careers and which are focused on getting a commission check. Career Realtors know that every action they take and how they work with their clients is what will deliver client satisfaction and lasting relationships that benefit everyone. Client relationships are the key to real estate success.

About Josh

Josh Painter is an expert in all aspects of Temecula real estate and the area's leading real estate broker. He started his career in 2005 as a loan originator, where he quickly learned the "other side" of real estate. Josh has always had a passion for helping families realize their dreams of homeownership and knew right away that his strength is in working directly with clients to help turn their dreams into reality.

In 2008, he started selling homes in the Temecula Valley. From the beginning, Josh set himself apart because he genuinely cares about his clients. Josh's philosophy is that it's always better to work with friends and his goal with every sale is to create a solid relationship that lasts throughout his clients' changing real estate needs.

In 2010, Josh decided it was time to take the next step to better serve his clients. He earned his broker license and founded Pacific Lifestyles Realty. In one year, he sold an astounding 165 homes – more than any other agent in the Temecula Valley.

Today, Josh annually sells hundreds of homes. With 40 of the best local agents working for him, Josh and his team are able to sell homes for up to 21 percent more money than the traditional real estate agent and they are able to do it 26 days faster than the average for the area.

Josh makes sure that every client who walks through his door leaves knowing that their home is in the hands of a trusted friend. He understands why people move to the area. He has raised his family in Temecula and, when he is not working hard for his clients, he enjoys entertaining friends and family in his backyard pool, playing a round of golf on one of the area's renowned courses or enjoying the beauty of the local wineries.

Josh lives in the Redhawk community with his wife, one teenage son, one teenage daughter and one spoiled dog.

Contact information for Josh:
951-265-3524
www.amazingtemeculahomes.com

CHAPTER 22

RETIRE WITH A BANG, NOT BROKE!

BY JOE MACMUNN

A college education is the best route for most of us to achieve financial freedom in our lives. It gives us an avenue to opportunity – the chance to make that money we're going to need for that day when retirement is on the horizon and we've walked up each rung of our career ladder and we're staring out at the world, maybe wondering what's next.

I'll never forget how excited I felt when I graduated college in 1987 and landed my first real job. It was big time for me, a job making $30,000 per year as a mechanical engineer for an energy company. **Life was great**. *I had no student loans, a new car, and a sense of freedom that I'd been longing for.*

By 1992, I was going for my MBA, taking advantage of my employer's generous offer to pay for that valuable degree. I sure couldn't afford it on my own, it was $40,000. However, I did manage to save up $10,000 and felt that it was the time to start dabbling in the stock market so I could earn a better rate of return on those hard-earned dollars. Life was happening fast and I had to keep up.

By chance, a fellow student in my MBA program began to work and earn a better rate of return on that hard earned money than what I was currently receiving. This classmate worked for a small company that was known as EMC. I learned about it through his presentation for part of our curriculum. A light bulb went off and I knew it as the words flowed from his lips—that was meant to be *my first investment*. I bought $10,000 worth of the EMC stock. ***That is when my real education began.***

WELCOME TO THE WORLD OF INVESTING

Saving $10,000 is not that easy to do and let's face it, most of us are protective of how we go about investing this type of money, especially if we are just starting to learn the stock market. I was that person. I went down to my local Charles Schwab Office and opened a brokerage account, gave them a check for my $10,000, and then told them what I'd wanted to purchase. I'd done the research and was ready to go. This sounds like a pretty easy way to gain a client, doesn't it? Well, the reaction I got was such that THEY were doing me a favor. I left with a sour taste in my mouth about the experience and it worsened when I received confirmation of the trade and noticed a <u>$75 commission charge</u>! I didn't think there was any work on their part, and there really wasn't!

Well, what's done is done, right? Like many new investors, I was excited. I'd call in and dial in the stock ticker symbol to find out how my money was doing—daily. I'd get a 15 minute delayed quote. This was great because I didn't have to wait for the next day's paper to find out what was happening with it. Then I received another surprise; I was limited to 25 calls per day. This entire process was not working out for me and about a month later, I sold my EMC stock because I needed something that moved quicker, more at the pace I expected. ***If only someone would have cautioned me***…if I had held onto that stock for 6 or 7 more years, my $10,000 would have become nearly $1,000,000! . . . Evidence that hindsight can be very painful.

1993 comes and I haven't given up on investing, but I am looking for a smarter way to do it. I need to learn more and take control. An advertisement for a local seminar titled "Become Your Own Stock Broker" caught my attention. I went and immediately became interested in becoming a stock broker (part-time) and earned my series 7 and 63 licenses.

I loved the market, watching the "action," and talking to brokers in the office. How did I do that while being a full-time engineer? I maximized my lunch hours. Unlike today, I could only access information by picking up the land line telephone and calling. My lunchtimes centered around

15 minute conversations about the market and how certain stocks were doing.

Before I knew it, 10 years had passed. It was time to try something new in my primary career. No, I didn't become a full-time stock broker. Instead, I switched over to sales for one of the largest energy providers in the country. It was risky and it was no longer just about me. I also had a wife and two little girls to take care of. That was the very reason to change jobs! **In order to provide for them in the manner that I wanted to, something had to change.**

The job change meant that my old 401(k) was now portable. It was about $100,000 and I had to decide if I was going to transfer it into an IRA or invest on my own—a big gamble! It was time to be bold and I realized that there was *no better time than right now* to start planning for retirement, college educations, and all those incredible things we want to have in place as our lives progress.

My first trade was very lucky. I purchased $30,000 worth of a $3 per share stock. One week later, the stock shot up to $11 per share and I was so excited! I sold out at about $10 a share, made a great profit, and spent a portion of that on a new car. My confidence in my investment savvy was escalating.

It was time for trade number two. It was early 1998, and the stockbrokers at my office had been eyeing a stock for months; a $0.75 per share stock price with a company involved in computer security. I loaded up with 75,000 shares. After all, so many tech stocks were booming. This stock hit on all gears and in a few years it hit just over $60 per share. Yes! My account had 4 plus million in it. Not a bad return! I was creating a nest egg for my daughters, which felt great for me. I was a dad who wanted to create a legacy for them. Literally, within a day and a half, that number changed. Hello "tech crash" of 2000!

My beautiful nest egg fell apart and the stock quickly retreated to the low single digits. Although I had made a few years worth of salary, I clearly did not create enough profit for a substantial legacy, or even to last me my own lifetime. It did teach me so much and from those experiences I pulled away *seven valuable lessons* that everyone needs to know if they want to retire with income, and also leave that legacy for those they love.

AVOID MISTAKES – INVEST SMART

Knowing what to avoid is half the battle sometimes, isn't it? We know to stay off the highway because there are detour signs. Well, with investing for retirement, there are signs that give us an indicator of the best ways to approach saving. We just have to look for them and learn to read them. Here are seven smart solutions for better retirement: that's what it takes!

1. Focus on the right stuff!

Retirement is all about income because it will determine the kind of lifestyle you live in retirement. Did you know that more people fear running out of money before they die than death itself? Whoa! It doesn't have to be that way. It is critical to insure your income and this takes precedence over insuring your portfolio. Many people have heard of the 4% rule, but it no longer exists in this extended low interest rate environment. Why is that? Well, independent studies indicate that there is a 50/50 chance you will outlive your income over a 30 year timeframe if you withdraw 4% annually.

Income producing assets need to be a major resource you can rely on in your retirement. You can create an income stream that you cannot outlive!

2. Assess risk often.

Many people define risk this way: I could lose some money on this investment. No one tends to think they could lose their entire portfolio. I thought this for awhile, too, and it was my personal downfall. What risk does mean is that there is a range of possible outcomes you may see when you invest.

Plan for the worst and hope for the best! At whatever stage of life you are in, ask yourself: Can I afford to lose 75%, 50%, or 25% of my portfolio?

3. Know your fees and costs.

Many people do not know the true fees they are paying and end up paying more than they realize. Many mutual funds have numerous expenses, and unfortunately, a lot of these expenses are hidden. Even a detailed look at a mutual fund's prospectus cannot tell you everything you need to know about fees. There could be fees other than the expense ratios (the easy one to spot) including: transaction costs, trading costs, commissions paid on the transaction, the price per market impact of funds, and buying or selling big blocks.

Taxes also play a role in the expenses. Yes, you do pay tax on mutual funds that went down in value, too.

To find out what these fees truly are you need to work with a retirement specialist, someone who knows how to give you a complete breakdown of every fee and cost.

4. Leaving a pension or IRA to a surviving spouse.

People who take an income stream from this source, along with receiving social security, will find that their social security income will decrease if the spouse passes away. If SS decreases, the need to increase withdrawals from a qualified plan will likely be necessary. What happens next? There is an income tax liability increase, which means that the now single taxpayer will have to file for this with only a one-person exemption, one standard deduction, and their social security may become taxable!

In order to address this potential problem, draft a tax return with the parameters laid out. If problematic, plan accordingly with a qualified tax planner and financial professional to see what options are available.

5. Plan for taxes; don't just prepare them.

Tax planning is more than dropping off your paperwork in early April, saying hello, and cringing as you wait for the bad news—the number. With tax planning, a qualified tax preparer or financial professional helps you identify potential problems. Be proactive in trying to reduce taxes now and future tax liabilities by considering:

• If government spending will increase or decrease; and will that increase/decrease mean, higher or lower tax rates?

• The impact on your retirement when qualified funds have not been taxed yet.

• How your IRA distributions affect taxable social security income.

You need to know how to address these issues and what you can do to avoid surrendering the money you need for retirement to taxes.

There are three tax positions for your money: pay tax on your money now, pay later and pay never. Ask your financial or tax professional now! These important people need to work together to look out for your best interests.

6. Social Security planning needs to be done.

Numerous factors come into play when planning for social security. An example is the best way to show how impactful social security planning can be. What benefits do you want to take?

• Adam is 60 and Amy is 59

• Adam's full retirement amount if $2,335

• Amy's full retirement amount is $1,442

• Both are healthy

• Both assumed they should take benefits at age 62

Both take benefits at 62 and Adam has a life expectancy of 85, Amy of 92. Assuming 2% inflation you are looking at cumulative benefits of $1,333,749. Guess what they could have been with an optimal strategy? $1,822,823. That is a difference of $489,074 over their lifetimes!

What does this optimal strategy include? Adam would have filed and suspended his benefits at Amy's age of 66. At that time, Amy would file a restricted application for spousal benefits. Adam takes his benefits at age 70, then Amy switches to benefits based on her record when she turns 70. This is just one strategy and may not apply to you, but you must evaluate your personal circumstances before you can gain clarity. Personal circumstances include:

• Health

• Life expectancy

• Work history

• Ex-spouses

• If you are widowed

- Future employment
- Tax situation
- Savings
- Pension

7. Evaluate your advisor(s).

Is the advisor who helped you prepare for retirement the best person to get you through retirement? More times than not, the answer is "no." A majority of financial planners do the same thing—help baby boomers build their retirement savings. And, they've done a good job! Then things get more challenging. Once you retire, your portfolio can't afford to sit tight and be patient through any bear market. The luxury of waiting is over and you need to move on to preservation and income strategies.

Fundamental shifts in life mean you must have a fundamental shift in your financial strategies.

No one is all things to all people. That's why we take our children to a pediatrician, not a geriatric specialist; that's why we hire electricians for electrician work and not plumbers. When approaching retirement, stick with retirement income specialists. Not sure if your advisor is a retirement income specialist? Ask your financial professional:

- How will we create an income stream in retirement?
- If the market tanks 50%, what will my portfolio look like?
- What are the potential sources of income if there's an economic downturn?
- What guarantees do I have?
- How do I get distributions?

Every question is an important question. Get the information you need to know in order to be smart about your retirement and know what your income will do for you. Is it what you expected?

PASSION FROM EXPERIENCE

The passion and desire that I have to help ensure that all individuals retire with the income they need to enjoy life is all consuming. My interest started because I personally enjoy investing and it continues to grow, making me realize that this is my true calling. Being able to help people maximize their chances of retiring with money that will sustain them for their entire lives is exciting and rewarding. Plus, I couldn't have made a better decision for my happiness and my family's well being. It feels great when you can help someone else avoid costly mistakes that take away their valuable, hard earned income. We all have more control than we think—it starts with aligning yourself with a retirement income specialist. From there…everything becomes clearer and simpler.

About Joe

Joe MacMunn has always had a curious mind and driving desire to understand how things work. It suited him perfectly as he achieved his degree in Mechanical Engineering from the University of Massachusetts, Lowell, and through obtaining his MBA from Northeastern University. Joe's true calling was not in the engineering field. In 2001, he was compelled to go where he felt he could do the most good for people and that was the start of MacMunn Financial Management.

Today, Joe is a Retirement Expert and Registered Investment Advisor. Realizing the importance of helping people prepare and organize for retirement—from an early age—is a driving force for him. His specialties include: retirement income, wealth preservation, and estate planning. With the use of his G.P.S. (Guided Planning System) Joe has helped hundreds of individuals successfully plan for their retirement. His life experiences have taught him to be more conservative in nature and that helps give him the perfect perspective for his clients. His wife is also an intricate part of the business.

Education is something that Joe is extremely passionate about. He firmly believes in the studies that indicate how a college degree can lead to from one million to two million more in lifetime income. That's why another major focus in his business is on helping parents prepare for their children's future by setting up smart college funding options, as well as learning how to navigate through the complicated financial aid process more effectively.

Joe's expertise in helping people close the gap about retirement questions and options has made him a professional in the industry who is constantly sought out by local and national media. He has appeared on *The Today Show,* is heard on *Money Matters Radio,* and has written for *The Boston Globe, The Worcester Telegram*, and *The MetroWest News.* Now, Joe can also add "author" to that list.

One of Joe's greatest gifts in life are his two daughters, who are actually young ladies now. Not only are they a joy to have in his life, but they are also motivators for Joe's belief that a parent who wants to leave a legacy for their child can leave that legacy. Joe has also dedicated his time to volunteering for the Special Olympics and raising money for Leukemia awareness—two activities spurred on by his daughter with Down's Syndrome. A fitness enthusiast and adventure lover, Joe also enjoys opportunities to travel to some of the greatest cities in the United States, as well as to more tropical locations such as St. Lucia and Jamaica. Joe shows everyone that a little planning can go a long way!

CHAPTER 23

D.R.I.V.E. TO SUCCESS

BY PA JOOF

I came from humble beginnings. Born in the U.K. to "illegal immigrants," my family moved to the tiny country of The Gambia in West Africa. When I was six, my father found a way to bring us back to the U.K., thinking it would offer a better quality of life for his family. But without proper documentation, the challenges were many. My father couldn't get any of the blue collar jobs, and there was constant pressure to provide for his family.

After years of struggling to survive, we moved back to The Gambia, where we lived in the family home, cramped in a residence of 30 people. I shared a single bedroom with my parents and my younger brother. We slept on the floor, next to my parents' bed, and I'd lay there at night and dream of a better life and making a difference for other people ... of being an example for my people, instead of a warning. Success was not going to be a maybe. It was not a should. It was an absolute must!

Unfortunately, the people around me who tried to influence me at that time believed that opportunity existed... *but somewhere else*, somewhere *outside of The Gambia*. They weren't able to perceive a life beyond poverty, beyond their current condition. In my heart, I knew I would never settle for that belief. I knew that *poverty is a mindset*.

I tapped into an inner drive that compelled me to leave The Gambia and return to the U.K. at the age of 17. I worked full time as a cleaner to make ends meet and to cover my college expenses. The work was often grueling and exhausting, but my dreams, my vision, and my reason why kept me going.

THE ACCIDENTAL GIFT

Then an unexpected "gift" arrived: my 12-year old brother – who was sent by my parents to live with me. I could barely support myself and adding the responsibility of my brother was a role I wasn't equipped to take on. I loved the guy, but his presence often felt like a burden and a curse. I was a young man finding his own way, who wanted to have fun, not be a parent in what little free time that I had.

Consequently, I didn't care for him in the way that a teen living in the Hackney neighborhood of London needed to be cared for – he lacked supervision and guidance. I took out my frustration on my brother by being insensitive towards him and treating him harshly.

Then reality hit. I began noticing dramatic changes in his behavior patterns, such as smoking, piercing his ear, being distracted with girls, and hanging around the wrong crowd. My lack of presence and being a poor example drove him to find attention elsewhere, where he met his needs for acceptance, connection, significance and love. It was an awakening I didn't expect, and I knew I had to step up and take responsibility.

It was then that I realized: *My life isn't about me. It's about being an example.* And it was time I started with my brother. If I didn't show up, HE wouldn't show up. Our father always said, *"You are who you hang around with."* If I didn't show up as a positive force in his life, why should HE show up any other way than how he was then, with his *new peer group*? I knew the only way to reach and influence him was through his peer group. I had to be a role model who could help them make different choices that would lead to a better quality of life. What I initially perceived as a problem was really a gift that expanded my comfort zone. I had to step into the unknown and do what I had never done before. I connected with them and was able to create transformations in the group as a whole, individually, and in my brother.

My passion for uncovering human potential and the defining factors of success was ignited. I realized that magic happens when we take on problems to solve. Solving this problem forced me to grow and be a bigger person. I discovered that I became relentless when it came to creating miracles and that magic.

THE EVOLUTION OF D.R.I.V.E.

The adolescent youths who were my brother's peer group were a tough bunch to reach. Testosterone ran high and their "bullshit radars" were constantly going off. In their eyes, everyone had an agenda, and these agendas didn't include looking out for them or their well being. Life on the streets of Hackney was about *survival*, not about *trust*.

I knew why I had to earn trust with these guys, and I had a genuine desire to connect with and be accepted by them as a positive influence whose only intent was to be there for *them*. They were conditioned to question the motives of other people, but I found a way to be accepted and trusted, and became that positive influence they needed in their lives.

Experiencing and participating in this intervention helped me embrace the impact I could have on this group of individuals. Not only did it transform their lives, there was also a snowball effect in the community in which I lived. It was then that I realized I had a unique gift, but also acknowledged along with that came responsibility. Each experience from that time helped to affirm this and I began to recognize patterns. As long as you know your why and purpose, then you will discover that the gap between you and your mission is filled by taking action. This is how the metaphor of D.R.I.V.E. came about.

WHAT IS D.R.I.V.E.?

Think back to when you first learned how to drive a car. You probably felt some fear, but you learned to get over it, and push through until you could drive on your own. Basically, you expanded your comfort zone and the distance of where you could go.

I like to think of going through **Driving School** as a metaphor for *Life*. It's your choice to be a commuter, or a competitive race car driver and enter the *Grand Prix of your Life*. It is Surviving vs. Thriving. Put yourself in the driver's seat and customize a life that you can **rev up**, starting with answering some questions:

- Are you stuck in first gear, wanting to shift to fifth?

- Are you driving an economy car instead of a Formula 1 racing car?

- Will you design a customized vehicle that is built for you and equipped for your route?

- What do you need in your tool box to guarantee peak performance?

- Will you engage a Pit Crew to Coach you?

- Will you use regular or high octane fuel?

- How will you best utilize your Pit Stops to refuel and recharge?

- How will you go from Point A to the Winner's Circle?

- What is that one decision you need to make that will transform your life forever—one that will balance and complete your Wheel of Life?

WHAT ARE THE ELEMENTS OF D.R.I.V.E.?

D — Desire

What is the ultimate Goal you wish to achieve in your life? When your Purpose is about your Mission, then it becomes easy to evolve from Survival, Massive Action and Success.

This is when your reason WHY is so crucial. It will become your Driving Force that will push you to accelerate to reach your final destination.

R — Roadmap

How will you get there? First, you have to know your **starting point**, and what your **ultimate destination** will be. Think of a GPS that plots you to where you want to go. To successfully plot YOUR roadmap, you'll need to understand **The 3-R's:**

- *Reward:* Knowledge and experience helped me break away from the cultural belief that I was a victim of my own circumstance, stuck in a life with no possibility of change. I created a vision of what my life was going to be like, and made it compelling. I knew the **Reward** would be there, because I had the hunger and desire to achieve greatness.

• *Risk:* I had no money and spoke little English when I went to the U.K. I knew there would be many risks. Participating in my own transformation overpowered any consequences that **Risk** could bring. My belief in myself and my destiny of a greater life helped me step into my fears and take on any risk that came my way. AND, I learned how to enjoy the ride and embrace the wisdom I learned along the way.

• *Route:* We can get trapped in the mental detours that make us veer off course. There will be roadblocks along the way and you will be tested. But you also know the obstacles will build the inner strength you need to keep going onwards to achieve victory. Staying focused on your Desire will steer you back to the road to your destiny.

I — Identity

Your Roadmap will also shape your **Identity**. It will no longer be about being the person you think you should be or what others have told you that you need to be. It is the **essence** of who you are at your **core**. Who do you need to become in order to get your ultimate desire?

Understanding that it is a process, an evolution that comes through time and experience, will give you the patience to know that you are unique and a work in progress. A few things that I did to shape my identity were:

• **Surround myself** with people who were already doing what I wanted to do. Successful people leave clues!

• **Educate myself** through work experience and personal empowerment to become an expert in wealth building and wealth creation. I could not help others create wealth if I could not do the same for myself.

• **Master my public speaking** so I could effectively share my story and experiences with others and guide them through creating their D.R.I.V.E.

• **Find the heart of my message.**

V — Values

What is most important to you? Are you aligning yourself with what you truly value in order to reach your ultimate goals? It is the essence of who you are, and is reflected in how you show up in your daily life, for example:

- Being in peak physical health and condition.
- Having the financial freedom to help others.
- Being present each day with love, patience, and empathy.

You should also acknowledge when *life changes* warrant a fresh look at your values. What may have been important may have shifted because of a change in life conditions or stage of life.

E — End Game

This is about building and defining our *legacy* - something much bigger than ourselves and our personal needs.

The key is to be clear and precise about your **End Game**. Everything you've learned about yourself and what impacts you will determine how you can impact others. This has repeatedly helped me teach individuals how to turn their concepts into profitable enterprises in a relatively short time. So, envision and embrace the mark you want to leave on this Earth.

READY, SET, D.R.I.V.E. ... MY INVITATION TO YOU

Isn't it time for you to discover your D.R.I.V.E. and take the road trip of your life? To be able to Ignite *Your Purpose* and reach the *destination of your dreams*? Today is your opportunity to identify your goals and desires and how you can put your unique stamp on them.

I invite you to do something **BIG**. Something that *freaks you out*. To anticipate that something great is on the verge of happening. It would be an honor to be your Instructor and Guide in a Driving School that will give you the tools and teach you the skills and strategies to be able to adjust to those turns, hug the road, and lead you to YOUR Winner's Circle.

About Pa

Pa Joof's message of *Making It Happen Now* is a reflection of how he lives his life. He takes and embraces information and turns it into action NOW. Born to illegal immigrants in the UK, Pa's family was sent back to their country of his ancestry when he was just a child. In the tiny republic of The Gambia, he lived with little, but had a burning passion to help those around him. His humility comes from sharing the family home with 30 others, and understanding that the human condition is not permanent. As a international speaker, trainer and coach, he inspires, motivates and guides over 200,000 people worldwide to transform to a more wealthy and purposeful life. His life has been far from ordinary. He left The Gambia at the age of 17 and returned to the U.K., where he supported himself through University, earning a BA Hons. degree in Business Analysis.

He rose through the ranks in the corporate world, creating shared value for many people and leading to a position as Head of Banking for a Fortune 500 company. Pa was responsible for over $1 billion in assets. He achieved financial independence at the young age of 30 - a mere 13 years after leaving The Gambia on his own. His success speaks for itself.

Pa has created multiple businesses worldwide, creating shared value for many people and generating millions of dollars in revenue. He has guided many clients to the same ranks of success, creating multi-million dollar businesses in less than six months and taking big, established companies to the next level.

Pa Joof currently runs various companies that operate in different countries around the world. This is impressive for a man who swept floors in order to pay his way through University while supporting not only himself, but also his 12-year old brother. His background in the financial industry qualifies him to train others on the psychology of wealth and sustainable strategies to develop the right mindset. He is President of the **Wealth Institute**, which is an international platform of industry experts providing knowledge, know-how, mindset and empowerment towards high performance on a grand scale.

Pa is also a powerful leader in Personal Development, coaching individuals from CEO's, athletes, and politicians to peak performance on a personal and professional level. The wisdom he shares comes from the heart and stems from his real life experiences, and he sets the example by walking his talk. He possesses the unique ability to connect with individuals, revealing their best qualities and attributes. He discovered his calling of inspiring people and is a key visionary of the **Making it Happen Now Foundation**, working with young people and communities to give them the greatest possible opportunities.

His message of *Living Your Legacy* by *Igniting Your Power* is the foundation of seminars that he presents internationally, training and coaching tens of thousands of people. He has a unique style, engaging energy, infectious laugh, natural charisma and a larger-than-life presence that has a compelling impact. And his delivery produces results – *Making it Happen Now!* Pa was voted one of the Top 100 Business Leaders To Follow on Twitter and he has been ranked in the top 100 motivational speakers in the world.

Pa is humble, yet powerful. And he can turn on the fuel that ignites the brilliance to influence lives with high energy, passion, and D.R.I.V.E.

CHAPTER 24

HEALTHCARE SPENDING – TAKE CONTROL NOW!

BY PHYLLIS MERRILL

Mother always wanted to start out early, leaving home while it was still dark. The sprinkling system just finished watering the fields when we arrived. It was a cold, wet morning, barely light, the sun just peeking over the horizon and there I was, a six-year old girl, sitting on an upside down bucket, picking green beans. The cold, wet vines in the early dawn always made my hands freeze.

We made crop work a competitive game. It was me against my mother and sisters to see who could fill their bag first. Mother carried the heavy, full bags to the weighing station. My bag was weighed and a card with my name on it was punched with the appropriate number of pounds. We were paid three and a half cents per pound. Mother did her best to support us, working in the fields, Spring through Fall, but it was up to me to earn enough money to buy school clothes, shoes and the other school supplies that were needed. This was how I spent my summers until I was seventeen years old.

The only stores we knew were JC Penny's and the Sears Roebuck catalog. There were no discount stores in our small Oregon town. There were no sales and every item was purchased at full price. The money didn't go very far. It always seemed so tragic that it took so much effort to buy so little.

These early experiences, working in the fields, taught me to appreciate hard work and the value of money. I could not help but notice the difference in the quality of life of those who paid me compared to how we lived – barely scraping together a living. It informed me as to what lay beyond my circumstances. I grew up looking for ways to stretch my dollars and to get as much as I could for the money I spent. I have lived by the slogan, "Never pay retail or anything like it." I usually don't.

Later, in the process of building businesses, these lessons guided me. It has become a passion to find ways to purchase *anything and everything* at less than retail. To avoid being overcharged, like most business owners, I always negotiate the price for goods and services and before the check is signed, I make sure the invoices are correct in both price and quantity.

In the past 30 years, I have been involved in the administration of partially self-funded medical benefit plans. It never ceases to gall me how the medical delivery system is set up to thwart common and accepted business practices when it comes to paying fair prices. In the case of medical services the purchaser is simply not in control. Every business owner in America senses they are being gamed, but they have absolutely zero control when picking up the tab for healthcare. They may think they're doing everything within their power to obtain the best "discounts" for medical services, but why then are most businesses losing the battle?

We often hear how the system is broken. We recognize the need for transparency. A lot of energy is expended by organizations in pursuit of something better. However, the solution always proves to be elusive.

On March 4, 2013, *TIME Magazine* published the entire issue on just one topic: the egregious overcharging and the lack of transparency in medical facility billing. As I read the articles, I thought to myself, finally someone is spilling the beans on this ridiculous over-billing practice. I reflected on what it was that brought us to this point; the disconnect between value and price.

If we go back in time, the first medical insurance was an Indemnity Plan that paid a set amount for a specific type of medical event. Then came Major Medical, which at the time seemed revolutionary, and gave people a way to cover the cost of catastrophic care for the price of a monthly premium. It was up to the insurance company to pay for medical care and being an informed and responsible consumer was now not possible.

This created a disconnect between the billing and the payment of the bills. The disconnect is even greater now that it has become a right to have all major medical expenses paid no matter the cost.

Insurance companies then began negotiating with certain facility groups to gain discounts in exchange for driving the patients of an insurance plan to that particular facility. Don Merrill, Founder of MBA Benefit Administrators, Inc. tells of his experience when asked to consult with a large hospital system in Texas. In the early 80's, when the preferred provider networks were in their infancy, Don and a protégé were contracted to assist in setting up a provider network. It was a complicated process and in the end the hospital decided that they would give a 20% discount to those who used their network. In order to do that, they increased the billed rate for services by 20%, and only those who were part of the network could enjoy the discount. *The idea of discounting as a percent off of retail is genius because if the hospital needs more money they simply increase the billed charges and leave the discount percentage the same.* This approach is widespread today.

Furthermore, in exchange for discounts, most PPO contracts do not allow payers to audit a hospital bill. Hello unlimited mark-up! In hopes of gaining some control over runaway spending, some insurance companies have negotiated the price on DRG's (Diagnostic Related Group). Facilities, however, are still very much in control. Glenn Melnick, Professor of Health Economics, University of Southern California asks, "How do hospitals set prices? They set prices to maximize revenue, and they raise prices as much as they can - all the research supports that."

Another part of the problem is who acts as the watchdog? In general, administrative costs charged by insurance companies are based on the overall cost of claims or as a percent of premiums. *Insurance companies are not rewarded for keeping claim costs down.* Where is the incentive? Are they really working in your best interest?

Insurance brokers are usually paid the same way, as a percentage of the premium. Your broker may feel bad when delivering an increase to you, however, when your premiums go up, so does the broker's compensation.

So one has to ask, in the current climate of health care, in the ACA (ObamaCare) world of today, *who is on the side of the employer?* Not the government! Not the hospitals! Not the insurance companies! You're on your own!

Do you want to pay less for your organization's health care? Would you like to control your costs and put your savings to other uses? Do your employees want more freedom in choosing their providers?

If so, you'll need to make sure you observe some important points. After 30 years in the health plan management business, I've come to believe there are eight critical areas you need to focus on for strategic and long-term success.

EIGHT CRITICAL STEPS TO TAKE CONTROL OF YOUR HEALTHCARE SPENDING

1. **Insist on transparency from the insurer.** Insurance companies hold all the cards. There is an absence of adequate medical plan reporting by insurance companies. You may never really know the justification for rate increases because they are in control. You will pay for one bad claim year for the rest of your business' existence. Insist on total transparency from your broker, the insurance company and health provider facility. Tools are now available to help with this process.

2. **Demand transparency in the actual costs of the medical services you pay for.** There is a lack of transparency in medical billing practices by facilities. However this information *is available*. What is a reasonable profit to pay to medical facilities? This is crucial to keeping the costs down for your medical plan. When you know the facility's cost basis for each and every medical procedure, you can decide to pay less. Contract with a medical claims auditing and re-pricing service that has the information and resources to structure claim reimbursements with a reasonable profit margin for the facility.

3. **Use an independent administrator.** Find an experienced and qualified claims administrator who is not a stake-holder in the insurance premiums. If your plan (whether fully insured or partially self-funded) is administered by a large insurance company, you are not in control. The right administrator will work on a "flat fee" basis and provide you with complete cost transparency.

4. **Control the plan parameters.** Who decides what the plan will and won't pay? Do you have a say in this? If you are working with a traditional insurance company, you may have a choice between the plans they offer but you do not have control over the boilerplate conditions in the policy. Frequently, an individual's medical situation falls into a "crack" in the policy and payments are either limited or disallowed. Obscure plan limitations are found throughout many insurance policies. Look for a good medical plan administrator who will help you craft the plan of benefits to suit your corporate culture.

5. **Keep insurance plan reserves for yourself.** Unused reserves turn into profits. The question is, who will benefit, the insurance company or you? Remember, this is *your* money. You worked hard for it and you should keep more of it and you *can*- if you take control. Use a "partially self-funded" plan structure, strong medical management and a fair and transparent reimbursement approach to take charge of your medical plan budget.

6. **Eliminate network restrictions.** Are the medical providers on your Preferred Provider Network or Panel the best in their field? What if participants need medical care that is not found in your network? What if an accident occurs away from home? This is one of the major deficiencies in the current network-driven medical insurance system. If a plan participant has one of these unfortunate circumstances, both the employee and the plan pay for the lack of network discounts. Today, more and more insurance plans are further restricting and limiting networks in exchange for greater discounts. Remove the network requirements in your plan and gain control over medical costs by changing the way you reimburse the claims. This is the only way you can be assured the medical care needed by your participants is fully available to them at reasonable prices.

7. **Prevent claims with effective medical management.** There is a lot of controversy about the effectiveness of wellness plans. The major premise of "wellness" is prevention and believe me, if you can prevent a medical issue, everyone wins. Wellness plans may help by providing incentives to people who maintain a healthy lifestyle. The more difficult thing is to help individuals

with chronic medical challenges. This is best done with the help of a robust medical management company set up to assist, support and educate individuals with medical issues and to be their health accountability partner.

8. **Keep your broker on your side.** If your premiums go down does he get a pay cut? Keep the broker in your corner by paying him right. Negotiate a flat fee and tell the broker, "If you can get me a cost reduction, I will pay you for it," because in the end it will cost you much less!

If you have a business with at least 50 full-time employees, the integrated actions above provide the solution. As Amory Lovins, Chief Scientist of the Rocky Mountain Institute says, *"Integrated design of the whole system produces expanding returns."*

End your frustration and *take control*. These are your keys to success: No network requirements in the plan, State-of-the art auditing and re-pricing of claims based on the actual cost of the procedure, customized plans to fit your corporate character and experienced medical management to reduce and eliminate hospital claims.

Whatever you do make sure that financial incentives to all parties are aligned with your goals. Make everyone a stakeholder in helping you reduce costs!

Organizations that leverage this information will experience significantly lower costs, increased freedom of choice and healthier, happier participants.

Note: For a good tutorial on egregious hospital billing practices, I refer you to the March 4, 2013 *TIME Magazine* issue entitled, "The Bitter Pill. Why Medical Claims Are Killing Us" by Stephen Brill. It can be found at: www.theopensolution.com along with other information on how your organization can save 25% or more in year one on healthcare costs. Read stories about how other organizations have taken control of their healthcare spending. You can, too.

About Phyllis

Phyllis Merrill has been active in the health insurance administration arena for 30 years. She is the co-owner and CEO of MBA Benefit Administrators founded in 1987. MBA, as a Third Party Administrator (TPA) has experience in the administration of all types of benefit plans with an emphasis on partially self-funded group health insurance plans and serves a wide variety of businesses and organizations. MBA's unique expertise is the implementation of multiple, high-powered cost containment strategies with proven track records of success. These strategies go far beyond the usual self-funding plan and wellness program. Effective plan design, real long-term savings and superior customer service means clients of MBA stay around. The loyalty/persistency rate for MBA clients is more than a decade. (www.mbaadministrators.com)

In 1992 Phyllis founded Critique, a medical management, cost containment and patient advocacy service. Critique brings a level of transparency to patient care that has shown to substantially reduce costs of healthcare for participating organizations and their employees. Critique's nurse coaches' interactions with employees who are faced with chronic health challenges is a highly-effective health promotion approach. Engaging health issues early reduces and prevents costly hospital care down the road. (www.critiqueur.com)

The Open Solution™ was developed by Phyllis in 2012. The Open Solution™ is the synthesis of multiple cost-containment strategies and was developed specifically to serve organizations with 100 to 5000 employees. She leads an experienced team, which provides medical plan administration, medical case management and cost-containment specialists. (www.theopensolution.com)

Phyllis is driven and energetic and brings a different type of intelligence to the challenges of health care insurance. She is passionate about bringing cost transparency to the payment of medical claims, empowering organizations and consumers to take control of their medical care, paying only fair and reasonable prices.

Her long history in the health plan administration world has allowed her to clearly identify the flaws, abuses and the egregious pricing tactics of hospitals and other providers. She is a strong and passionate advocate for bringing transparency to business owners and reducing employee benefit costs.

Phyllis has spoken to thousands of healthcare and insurance professionals in an educational capacity and has been interviewed on major media outlets. She has introduced and guided hundreds of company founders, CEOs, CFOs and HR directors to the benefits and rewards of a properly structured health benefit plan. She is a leading advocate of the various cost-containment strategies now available to organizations to gain control of their healthcare dollars and reduce the cost of providing benefits to their employees.

CHAPTER 25

DREAMS WITH DEADLINES

BY PERMINDER CHOHAN

The clearer our brains are, the clearer the picture becomes for what we want out of our lives. This is true of business goals and personal pursuits. The big question is, "How do we go about creating clarity?" The answer—we must have direction and goals for what we want to accomplish in life. I learned this as a young man, moving from India to Canada with a Masters Degree but not knowing a single word of English. I'll admit, I was embarrassed at first. It was hard! Everyone spoke fast and it was impossible to keep up. I realized that it was up to me—no one else—to make the changes I wanted.

Realizing that I was the navigator of my brain's GPS, I got to work on making the change happen that I wanted to see. There were three specific, precise personal commitments I made to ensure this was more than a fleeting thought in my mind.

1. I told myself what I wanted to do.

2. I would be ready to do what was necessary.

3. I would start doing it!

Think about it, how can we go from Point A to Point B if we are unclear on where we want to go? It's like driving on an unfamiliar road in a haze of fog. That's why these three commitments carry over into everything I've pursued in my life, and are a driving force behind me being an effective team leader, mentor, and hopefully an inspiration to many.

I'm excited to share the principles and strategies that I've learned and used for many years to make changes and achieve goals. There are many small pieces to the puzzle that can be connected, creating an amazing picture of what we are capable of doing if we desire it and are willing to work to achieve it.

TWO STEPS TO START THE JOURNEY TO SUCCESS

I work in insurance and manage a very large team—over 150 individuals that work together. One of the first things that I do with new team members is sit down with them and talk about goals, or business plans, as we call it. My approach to this process is different to that of many people because I want people to really think about what they wish to achieve. I don't want them to write down a goal because it looks good to me. It needs to be a good fit for them and they need to understand why they want to accomplish it.

Through our discussions, we come up with ideas that are based on that person's strengths. We all have something we are good at. Our greatest successes will always come when we are utilizing our gifts and personal assets to make it happen.

After a goal is recognized, it is time to attach a deadline to it. You see, an open-ended goal is an idea that hasn't been put into action—yet! Without action, there is no accomplishment. That's the essence of dreams with deadlines. We need to:

Define a goal and give our goal a deadline.

Through my involvement in various team-leading roles, I've uncovered one of my greatest strengths, which is building quality teams that produce and deliver stand-out results. My strength is not sales and I'm not a salesman, although I started out as one. Knowing this has saved me a lot of wasted time and energy pursuing things not meant for me. I'm meant to be a teacher, someone who helps people realize their maximum potential through greater self awareness and specific goals with deadlines. It's a winning formula and I'm going to share the concepts that create the foundation. Everyone can build off this and start accomplishing goals, removing themselves from the long list of people who do not do this!

FIVE ESSENTIAL BUSINESS TRAITS

Our substance has a great deal to do with our success in the business world. All our qualities are a part of what makes us distinct; however, there are five main qualities that people who strive for extraordinary have. This group is more elite than it should be. We all have the potential to do this!

1. <u>Be strong.</u> Business is not a smooth, steady road that keeps on sloping upward until it reaches the pinnacle of success. There will be times when bad things happen. How will you respond? Some people grow fearful and stop. They aren't the ones who achieve great things. Those who learn, adapt, and keep pursuing are the ones who will make it through the rough times.

2. <u>Be effective.</u> We need to attract quality people in order to be effective in business. This can only be done if you are a quality person, too. In business, like-minded people attract. If you have a goal to be the number one sales agent in your field you do not hang around the person who is last. If you want advice on how to improve, you don't seek out someone who is declining. I never ask anybody to do something and assume that's enough. I show them how, so I can be effective.

3. <u>Be honest.</u> You're probably familiar with that saying, "Try it, you'll like it." When you work in sales, in particular, you cannot be honest with your clients if you're recommending something that you haven't tried. How could I offer a product to my clients without being in their shoes? If what I'm recommending is not good enough for me, it isn't good enough for them. This is honesty through action. Imagine how you'd respond if a client was face-to-face with you and they asked you why you didn't have that product. Would you be honest? Would you tell them that you personally don't use that product and why? It would be hard! Your entire business reputation is based on honesty—always remember that.

4. <u>Be dedicated to leadership.</u> I have yet to meet a person that doesn't want anyone to be like them, unless they aren't successful. Leadership is defined as: the action of leading a group of people. Action is the important word here! Leaders are

created through action, not claiming, "I'm a leader."

5. <u>Be confident to delegate.</u> If you want to take your business to the next level, you need to delegate some responsibilities to others. This means you need to trust them, which ties into being effective. Trusting team members to take on certain tasks is also a sign of strength. How do you trust others? By understanding individuals' strengths you can delegate tasks to the appropriate person. For example, the person that doesn't like to talk to large groups isn't the one to send out for a presentation.

Experience has taught me a great deal about delegating, in particular. When I was first in business, I wanted to do everything myself. The thought of asking for help was unacceptable. This was ineffective and my volume decreased—the worst nightmare a person in sales or a sales manager can have. I only had myself to blame!

After I began trusting people and recognizing their strengths, I began delegating and it made a significant, positive impact on my business. Everyone was winning and I wasn't spread thin. If you find that you're prone to "micro-managing," it's important to recognize that your business will suffer.

THE "BIG 4" MOTIVATORS

Staying in action mode to achieve your goals is as easy as 1,2,3,4. I assure you that if you're aware and active in these four things, you'll be able to reach any well-thought-out goal you give yourself.

1. <u>Surround yourself with success.</u> Be around people who inspire and motivate you. I challenge you to remember that you are who you associate with.

2. <u>Commit to regular communication.</u> As a team leader, I make sure our team meets once a week. This is an opportunity to communicate goals and dreams, keeping them vivid and alive. Anyone in a leadership role—or who aspires for one—should realize this. Your goals and dreams are attached to what your team does. When you communicate effectively, people see a clear picture and vision of what can be achieved! It's also important to focus on strength, not weakness. Our strengths build business.

3. <u>Always keep learning.</u> We cannot grow without knowledge. I want to be able to inspire people constantly, which is why I'm committed to learning something new each day. I also have a library of motivational and inspirational business books that I give to my team members to read as part of their goals. It's effective!

4. <u>Step out of the comfort zone.</u> If we don't step outside of our comfort zones we will always achieve the same results. So many people don't leave their comfort zone. They're afraid. It isn't easy to do things we aren't comfortable with, but our business rewards lie outside of our comfort zone. Only 8% of our fears ever come true. Why focus on that 8% when we could focus on the 92% of successful opportunities that we can create for ourselves?

LESSONS IN LEADERSHIP

There are many amazing, inspiring things that I've learned through the years. It's important for me to share these things with others. They are lessons that help us to keep our sanity, goodwill gestures, and have created a stronger team that I'm proud of as a team leader and a person.

Humor is important to have in life. Not everything in the business world has to be serious. Laugh and enjoy yourself, too. It's good for you mentally and is a natural generator of positivity. Humor also builds camaraderie, which is the foundation of a solid team.

One of the most exciting aspects of how I use my business team to bring about a stronger sense of community is through volunteering. Giving back to the communities that lend to our success is rewarding. It gives a presence to our business, all while being great for the heart and soul. It's one of the most effective ways to have the joys of our personal lives and business endeavors come together. I want people to know my team and I in person—not just from a billboard.

I've also realized that it's mandatory to have an open door policy when you're a team leader. There should never be a time when someone on your team doesn't feel welcome. I've seen plenty of stressed-out bosses and team leaders close their doors, using the workplace as their retreat from negative noise and commotion from the outside world. An open door policy does come with noise and commotion, but it's positive. People helping people and finding answers is what I focus on. I'm open-minded, realizing that no one person can be a master of everything. It's human nature to desire feeling important in some way, whether large or small, and I get this. In fact, I rely on my team to reveal their strengths to me and when they do, I incorporate them into our game plan.

The ultimate lesson in leadership is the one I've saved for last. We must be genuine with our purpose. We don't want our team to succeed simply because it means a better paycheck. Genuinely wanting others lives to be better through helping them realize dreams and goals is authentic success. Our best rewards come at unexpected times; doing something because it is "the right thing to do."

ASPIRE! PURSUE! ACHIEVE!

My life has given me many great opportunities. I have pursued some of them and passed on others. This is because I understand who I am, what I have to offer, and what dreams I want to fulfill. It carries over to how I lead by example, not with words alone. Nothing brings me a greater sense of contentment than when someone shares their thoughts about my leadership style with me. I've heard wonderful things, compliments focused on my sincerity, honesty, openness, and my trustworthiness. When people are not afraid to come to you it pays off in many ways, both in quality of character and in business growth.

Don't hesitate to be that person that aspires to pursue and achieve excellence.

About Perminder

Perminder Chohan is a firm believer in being genuine, honest, and trustworthy. It's these three principles that have driven him his entire life. He's a veteran insurance industry leader, working as a Managing Director with Desjardins Financial Security Independent Network (DFSIN) Richmond South office since 2009. His efforts for authentic success have been proven, building a team of over 150 agents and focusing on helping them achieve excellence through organic, grass roots efforts in sales.

Perminder Chohan was recently a featured guest on The Brian Tracy Show. The Brian Tracy Show, filmed in San Diego, California, features an interview format, hosted by best-selling author Brian Tracy, one of the country's leading business minds. The episode featuring Perminder Chohan recently aired on NBC, CBS, ABC and FOX affiliates across the country.

Back in 1998, Perminder started his career in the financial services industry, joining Registered Education Savings Plan Company. Within six months, he became their number one agent nationally. From there, things began to grow at a rapid pace, one which he kept learning from in order to become a leader to others in their pursuit of financial and personal success. Then he expanded into the life insurance industry, becoming a mentor and being instructional to over 200 agents.

Perminder's success is notable, but it did not come without a lot of hard work. Having been raised in India, when Perminder moved to Canada he did not speak the English language. He didn't shy away from embracing opportunity, though. He began creating challenges for himself that he was determined to conquer. Learning the English language was one of those challenges and he set goals for himself to make that happen! He fed off the energy that setting goals with deadlines gave him and realized that any goals he may have could be achieved through a solid plan, a commitment to success, and, of course—much hard work!

Community involvement is another thing that Perminder is passionate about. He is a tireless supporter of many activities and events that are important to the South Asian community in the Greater Vancouver Area. His generosity and sponsorship include: fundraising for twenty different charities in the area, sponsoring sports activities and teams year after year, and even bringing fan favorite Bollywood acts to Canada to perform. He is also invited to present at awards ceremonies that honor achievement.

To his community and work environment, Perminder is definitely a valuable contributor; however, to his family he is considered a loving, caring father and husband. When asked about the factors of his success, he always expresses that none of it would be possible without the support of his loving wife, Deep, and his children, Henna and Armaan. Together, the entire Chohan family finds joy in being involved in their community and giving back.

Career Awards:

GAMA International Awards

Agency Builder Award 2013

Agency Builder Award 2014

Agency Achievement Award 2014

National Management Award 2014

Desjardins Excellence Awards:

Recruiting Award 2013 and 2014 – was declared number 1 in Canada

Business Growth 2013 – Was declared number 1 in Canada

Excellence below 50 Associates 2013 – number 2 in Canada

In-force Growth 2014 – Was declared number 1 in Canada

Excellence below 50 Associates 2014 – number 1 in Canada

CHAPTER 26

ATTRACTING THE LIFE YOU WANT FROM THE BOARDROOM TO THE BEDROOM

BY PIA WASHINGTON

Law of Attraction – *What you radiate outward in your thoughts, feelings, mental pictures and words, you attract into your life.*
~ Catherine Ponder

When I was a teenager I used to think I was psychic. I remember countless times when I would have a vision of something in my head, I would verbalize it and then it would happen. Starting at the age of thirteen when I first met Levett, and I told my best friend and my sister, "I am going to marry him." Of course, they laughed and said you are too young you don't even know him, etc. but I knew in my heart that we would be married. I saw us growing old together. Levett and I were married in 1993 and continue to have a strong, successful relationship. I would have the same results in my academic pursuits as I excelled in high school and then went on to become the first person in my family to attend and graduate from college. Similarly, I always knew that I would have a successful career as a financial professional and that is exactly what I did.

Then in 1995 we started our own business. Our mentors in that encouraged us to read books that introduced us to the principles of leadership and success. I finally realized that I wasn't psychic at all; I had been manifesting through the Law of Attraction. Once I understood the creative control I had over my own life experience, I would continue to master the Law of Attraction and use it in every area of my life. Financially, I had climbed the corporate ladder rapidly and was on a leadership fast track. By the age of 26, my husband and I were able to build our first home. The convertible Mercedes that was on our refrigerator was soon in our driveway.

After our youngest daughter was born, I decided to make enough money from our business so I could take a break from corporate America and have more time at home with our four kids and I achieved that goal as well. As I continued to have success in my business as well as in my personal life, people began to ask for my advice. In 2010, I began my coaching practice, co-authored my first book with my husband on relationships, and became focused on helping others to have success in their careers and personal life. Everyone is capable of achieving their goals in the areas of finances, health and relationships regardless of background, intelligence level or innate ability. **And I am excited to share with you how to achieve the life of your dreams from the boardroom to the bedroom!**

THREE COMMON PRINCIPLES FROM AN UNCOMMON PERSPECTIVE

1). *Purpose*

You have to have a dream to make a dream come true.
~ Dexter Yaeger

The first step is to determine precisely what you want. Finding your true life purpose involves uncovering your dreams and aspirations; reflecting on your values, motivations and reflecting on what you are passionate about. Each of us has a unique life purpose that drives our energy, thoughts, needs, wants and choices, and which is waiting to be discovered. Once you discover your purpose, you must align it with your vision and goals. Purpose is the reason why you are here, vision is the daily expression of the purpose and goals are action items that help you realize your vision and purpose. For example, my purpose in life is to inspire others; my vision is to inspire others by helping them maximize their potential to experience true love and happiness, and one of my goals associated with this is to publish the book, *Attracting the Life You Want from the Boardroom to the Bedroom.*

Your purpose should be aligned with your needs and desires. Your purpose tells you what you should do. Your needs (money, shelter, clothing) dictate what you must do. Your desires (enjoyable work, passion) dictate what you want to do. Taken individually, each of these areas will only point you in a general direction, but when you put them all together, you will find it easier to set the specific, practical goals that form your life vision. This way you will be setting goals that help you fulfill your purpose, meet your needs and do what you love to do. Don't be afraid to dream, build and reflect upon what you want to do, be or have.

Having an all-obsessing sense of purpose is an essential element of success, so once you discover your purpose, stay focused. Your thoughts, goals and energy must be concentrated without let up. Refuse to downsize dreams -- you have the power to do, be or have anything you choose. Whether it is wealth, success, great relationships or better health, you can have anything your heart desires. Go to bed with a dream and wake up with a purpose!

2). *Image*

If you think you can or if you think you can't, either way you are right.
~ Henry Ford

I have always had a strong self-image and I never doubted my ability to achieve my goals. Once we moved from Ohio to California, I continued to achieve success in my career, business, relationships and personal life. In 2005, we had just built a million dollar home in a gated community, our marriage was stronger than ever, the kids were well adjusted and doing well in school and we had just successfully opened a wine retail store and purchased a territory to grow the franchise. Our wine store was by all accounts successful; our weekly tastings were crowded, people loved the wine and the atmosphere of our tasting room. When the recession came, our shopping plaza was hit hard and major retailers were closing their doors. For the first time in my life, I had a fear of failure. I began to say things like, "We can't afford the monthly overhead" and "Our business isn't going to make it." As a result of my fears and limiting beliefs, by the end of 2008 we were closing our store and relinquishing our franchise territory.

We all have hidden obstacles that hold us back; fears, negative self-images or limiting beliefs that come from our own subconscious based on our past experiences, failures, humiliations, circumstances or the way others have reacted to us. The term limiting belief refers to beliefs that place limitations on your ability to take action and achieve your goals. Call them your inner critic, negative thoughts, excuses, or mental blocks, it's all about the programming you have in your subconscious mind.

Some examples of limiting beliefs are:

- "I don't deserve to be successful."
- "All the good men/women are taken."
  ...and, the worst of all,
- "I can't afford it."

Our image of self determines what we can or can't accomplish; what is difficult or easy and how other people respond to you. Just as certain and scientifically, as a thermostat controls temperature in our home, our actions, feelings, behaviors and abilities are always consistent with our self-image. Like limiting beliefs, and negative self-image, our fears also keep us from achieving what we want in life. Fear of success, fear of rejection and fear of failure are just a few examples of fears that hold us back. In fact, most fears are only figments of the imagination or False, Evidence, Appearing, Real. In reality, we have no limitations on what we can achieve, but we must first eliminate our fears and limiting beliefs. You can keep trying to succeed in life while ignoring these obstacles, but until you change your core beliefs and self-image your efforts will be futile. The snap-back effect states that you cannot outperform or escape your self-image. And even if you do escape briefly, you will be snapped back like a rubber band. The control of self-image is absolute and pervasive and the snap-back effect is universal. Your self-image is the foundation upon which your entire personality, your behavior and your circumstances are built.

In order to achieve your goals and create the life that you want, you must identify and clear all subconscious blocks and improve your self-image. The process of eliminating subconscious blocks is simple, but it will take time. First, you must be aware of and catch any beliefs that are not in line with your goals and desires like, "I don't deserve to be loved",

"I can't afford it" and "I am a failure." Second, stop and cancel the limiting belief or negative thought immediately. If necessary, literally say "cancel" or "stop" out loud. Finally, after you catch and cancel, you must create a new belief statement. Always state the new belief statement in the present tense as a positive affirmation. "I deserve to be loved"/"I have more than enough money for everything that I want"/"I am successful." Repeat this process of catching, cancelling and creating until the subconscious is retrained. It will take a minimum of 30 days but don't stop. Consistency is crucial. Eventually the subconscious will accept the new belief statements as fact, you will improve your self-image and start manifesting your goals.

3). *Law of Attraction*

"We cannot solve our problems with the same thinking we used when we created them."
~ Albert Einstein

The law of attraction states that "like attracts like" and that by focusing on positive or negative thoughts, one can bring about positive or negative results. This is true for relationships, career, personal goals and all aspects of life. It is the attractive, magnetic power of the Universe that draws similar energies together. This law manifests through your thoughts by drawing to you thoughts and ideas of a similar kind, people who think like you and also corresponding situations and circumstances. The law of attraction can work for you or against you. You get what you think about, whether you like it or not. You can take advantage of the law of attraction to achieve the life you want and make conscious choices toward achieving your goals and realizing your life purpose. Through creative visualization, positive affirmations and gratitude you can manifest anything in your life. By visualizing a mental image of what you want to achieve or by repeating positive statements, which are called affirmations, you create and bring into your life what you visualize or repeat in your mind. In other words, you can use the power of your thoughts, feelings, mental pictures and words to attract the life and the love that you want.

Ralph Waldo Emerson declared that "the ancestor of every action is thought." Thought is the original source of all wealth, all success, all material gain, all great discoveries, inventions and of all achievement.

Your predominant thoughts determine your character, your career, your everyday life. Your beliefs create your attitudes, your attitudes create your thoughts, your thoughts create your feelings, your feelings create your decisions and your decisions create your life. Change your beliefs and you can change your life! One of the most effective methods of bringing the subconscious into practical action is through the process of making mental pictures – using the imagination – perfecting the image of the thing or situation in the physical form. This is commonly referred to as visualization, and it is key to bringing the things that you desire into your experience. Once you change your thoughts and visualize your goal you must pay attention to how you feel. It is important that your feelings are aligned with your desires, and when they are, you feel good. If you are giving your attention to the lack or absence of your desires you will not feel good. Feelings of gratitude, love and appreciation are the most powerful emotions you can emit to manifest the life you want. There are no exceptions to the Law of Attraction. Your relationships, finances and health without exception are the result of what you have attracted into your life.

Everything you want in life – joy, love, health and wealth – is already within you. There is nothing that you cannot be, do or have. Simply determine your **Purpose**, improve your **Image** of self by eliminate limiting beliefs and practice the law of **Attraction** to manifest your desires. Remember, today's actions and attitudes determine tomorrow's options and opportunities. Now is the time to take control and create the life that you want from the boardroom to the bedroom!

About Pia

Author of the book, *Attracting the Life You Want: From the Boardroom to the Bedroom,* Pia Washington is a dynamic speaker, coach and attraction specialist dedicated to helping people produce extraordinary results in their lives, careers and organizations. Pia is a results-oriented professional with over 20 years of experience across a wide range of industries including Media & Entertainment, Technology, Biotech, Retail, Financial Services, Healthcare and Manufacturing. As a finance executive, she has achieved extraordinary results for many Fortune 500 companies including NBC Universal, DineEquity, Amgen, Guitar Center, Wellpoint, JP Morgan Chase, Exxon Mobil and Eaton Corporation.

Pia is the loving mother of four children and she has been happily married to her junior high school sweetheart, Levett, for over 20 years. Levett and Pia are principals of The ECI Group which provides consulting and coaching services to Executives, Couples and Individuals. Together the two co-authored the books, *Shades of Love: Portraits of Successful Marriages* and *Love is Never Enough: The Five Essential Elements of Effective Relationships.* The vision for their coaching practice is to inspire others to maximize their potential by living an authentic life. The couple has appeared on THRIVE with Sandra Bishop, KKZZ AM 1400, KISS FM 102.7 and numerous Internet radio talk shows. They also publish a relationship blog at: Lovesneverenough.blogspot.com.

Pia is an active volunteer with several community-based organizations. She is also founder of *Novus In Tutum: New Path, Safe Haven* which is a foundation that provides support services and transitional housing for women and children in crisis. Pia earned a BS in Finance from The University of Akron, attended Case Western Reserve University's prestigious Weatherhead School of Management and she received her relationship coaching credentials from The Relationship Coaching Institute. Pia is committed to helping others use Passion, Inspiration and Attraction to achieve the life of their dreams from the boardroom to the bedroom!

You can connect with Pia at:
Pia@PiaWashington.com
www.twitter.com/Piavet
ECIGroup.coachesconsole.com

CHAPTER 27

THE NEED TO PURCHASE LONG TERM CARE INSURANCE

BY RODNEY JONES

If you are undecided about whether long term care insurance should be a part of your financial portfolio, then meet Bob and Ann. Bob was the CEO of a nation-wide grocery chain. He retired with a comfortable pension and a healthy portfolio of secure assets. Upon retirement Bob and his wife of 50+ years, Ann, were looking forward to traveling the world and enjoying the rest of their lives together.

Shortly after retirement, Ann became ill with cancer and went downhill quickly. Bob immediately called me to ask about the long term care policy I had persuaded them to purchase to protect the income and assets that they had worked a lifetime to accumulate. I informed Bob that Ann's benefits from Medicare and her supplemental insurance were limited and his decision to purchase the long term care insurance was a good one.

Approximately two weeks later I received another call from Bob saying Anne had just been admitted to the hospital. He again asked me to re-affirm that if Ann needed extended care, that her long term care policy would pay for this care. Again I shared with Bob not to worry, that Ann had full coverage, and everything would work just the way we had planned. Bob was relieved and shared with me that he would not be able to take care of her at home. Soon Bob called me to inform me that Ann could no longer feed herself, bathe or dress without assistance. Ann was moved to a nursing home facility. I contacted the facility and coordinated for Ann's benefits to begin. The facility required Bob to pay over $30,000 up front before her long term care policy claim was even filed. After several months in the facility, Ann's long term care policy paid out several thousand dollars for Ann to receive excellent care. The long term care policy prevented Bob from having a stressful financial crisis, while allowing him to concentrate on his bride during the last days of her life. Bob would call me almost daily to inform him of the payments being sent to the facility.

"Rodney, I don't know what I would have done without the long term care policy that you sold to us, thank you." said Bob S.

Even to this day, Bob calls me to thank me for convincing him to purchase a long term care policy.

The need is real. The protection of financial ruin is real. This is why I sell long term care.

Now let's meet Jim and Sharon. When I met with Jim and Sharon, Jim was 63 and looking forward to retirement. Sharon was just a bit younger and also looking forward to Jim's retirement so they could spend more time together and travel. Jim was an Account Executive at a Fortune 500 company. They lived in a beautiful home in an upscale neighborhood. Jim was very active and liked to cycle. He and Sharon would often spend the weekends at special cycling events around the country. With no children at home, Sharon would often go with him. When I met with Jim and Sharon, they felt with Jim's excellent pension and their accumulated assets they did not feel that long term care insurance was necessary right now.

I specifically remember Jim saying "I am not going to a nursing home." We agreed to meet in a couple of years to put Jim on Medicare and a Medicare Supplemental plan. Well, shortly after Jim's retirement, I received a phone call from Sharon requesting a meeting. Which we did. Again, I stressed the issue of long term care insurance, but was shot down again. Approximately three months later after Jim's retirement, I received a call from Sharon that Jim was in the hospital, he had a stroke and was paralyzed on one side of his body. His cycling days and their retirement dreams had both been shattered. Sharon kept in touch with me with hopes that Jim would recover and everything would be fine.

I didn't think much more about Jim's situation until about three months later when I received another call from Sharon with a much deeper concern in her voice. She informed me that Jim had been moved to a home and they advised her that Medicare and her supplemental insurance were done paying for their part and that she would need to start paying over $8,000 per month if she wanted Jim to stay in the facility that he was already settled in. Sharon vividly said, "I can't care for him in our home and I don't want to move him into another facility." She then asked me, "How long do I have to pay this kind of money?"

I sadly replied "As long as he is there or you run out of money and he goes on welfare."

There was a silence on the phone, I told her I was sorry and we ended the call. Approximately five years later I received a call from Sharon. Jim had passed away and she had depleted most all of their assets, including their nice home and she was living with her daughter and son-in-law. The sadness in her voice from the loss of Jim and the financial ruin put an empty eerie feeling in my stomach. She shared with me that she missed Jim, her home, her privacy and her independence.

Any prospects or clients that I meet with, I share that the most financially devastating Event that can happen to them at this stage of their lives is "the cost of long term care".

Here are:
The Top Three Reasons Why Individuals Purchase Long Term Care Insurance:

1. <u>Family</u> - they want to insure they won't become a physical or financial burden to their families.

2. <u>Nest Egg</u> - they want to protect the assets they've worked a lifetime to accumulate.

3. <u>Home</u> - they intend to stay at home as long as possible and want to avoid going to a nursing home.

About Rodney

Rodney Jones helps his clients to see and achieve their financial goals. He was brought up in a blue collar manufacturing culture where the norm was to graduate from high school and work at the foundry like past generations, but Rodney had greater ambitions. Rodney attended Southern Illinois University and Butler University. In 1990, Rodney earned his designation of Life Underwriter's Training Council and began educating clients and professionals on insurance and finances.

Rodney owns two business entities, RL Jones Insurance Group and RL Jones Financial Group. Both of his successful businesses are centered on the philosophy: "If you have the desire to protect and grow your assets, then he has the desire to show you how."

Rodney has helped several hundred clients to protect their assets and reach their financial goals. Rodney's clientele spans from small business owners to laborers and their families.

Rodney is a highly sought-after speaker and trainer. He was selected as one of America's Premier Experts® and has been on several media outlets including highlighted appearances on ABC, NBC, CBS, and FOX affiliates. He has also been selected to participate on several Advisory Boards of Fortune 500 companies. Rodney balances his time between his clients and educating professionals in his field. You can connect with Rodney via email, rjones@gordonmarketing.com or via phone, 317-626-4902 or 1-800-388-8342: Ext.302.

CHAPTER 28

LET THE JOURNEY BEGIN

BY STACIE WIDHELM

For as long as I can remember I wanted to live in a big city surrounded by the hustle and bustle. I dreamed of being an actress that could make a HUGE global impact on peoples lives. Fast forward 25+ years and I am a single mother living in a small town, owning my own fitness business, and I am NOW on my way to being who I want to be and where I want to be. I tell you this because for the first few years after having my kids, I thought for sure I was going to be the person who would live paycheck-to-paycheck and never have the big chance to help people out, and that scared me.

Reading through my journey you will see that there were times when I would take a big step forward (example would be starting my own business) and then there are points in my journey where I am sitting still (these were times where I was struggling). One such time I can recall would be just this last year, after being on maternity leave, I came back to a business that began to struggle because while I was gone no one was marketing. Instead of thinking that I needed to quit and find a secure job, I started researching and looking for ways that I could impact more lives than just the population of my current city. Had I decided not to continue with my journey while sitting still or struggling, I would not be where I am today. Now don't get me wrong, there have been quite a few wrong steps that took me backwards, but nonetheless, I used those as lessons, turned myself around and the next step was in the correct direction.

I would like you to take a different look at the journey you have embarked on in life and see if you are still on the right path; have you given up because you didn't think you would ever become great? Do you continue to take the same step over and over but never move forward? Do you have ideas, but no one believes you are capable of turning those ideas into reality? Instead of believing that you will never reach greatness, read this chapter to learn different steps you can take to keep you moving in the right direction. Success is not something that happens overnight, and any successful person will tell you the same thing. I am not writing this today as a person who has gotten exactly where I want to be, because I am still taking my journey, but I AM writing this chapter based on the fact that I know the possibility is still there and no one can take the desire and drive away from me.

First, a little about me and my life. My name is Stacie Widhelm, I grew up in small town Hastings, Nebraska, and was always ready to move on to the big city. I always felt like there was more out in the world to experience. I am a single mother of three amazing and beautiful girls. I am a fitness coach, a business owner, a motivational speaker, a teacher and a student. I have always been the entrepreneurial type of person and knew that the smarter and harder that I worked, the more successful I would be. The one thing that I did not ever think about was what success really looked like and meant to me.

My idea of success started to form one day as I was working for my parents after moving back from living in Dallas for seven years. I was sitting in the back office and thought to myself that, "Wow, here I am, 29 years old and I am going to be punching a time clock for the rest of my life if I don't step up and do something about my current situation." My first step was to find something right here in my small town that no one else was offering. I wanted to mix my fitness background, my passion for helping people get better, with a twist that most people had not thought of in this small rural town, YET. From this thinking would come my in-home personal training business *Fit 4 U Fitness*. My first client came from my garage sale, when I handed her my business card so she could call me back and let me know if she wanted a certain item. Instead she called back and asked if she and a few of her friends could meet with me about my in-home training. At that point, I needed to write up a contract, get some prices together, and buy some equipment. My crazy schedule of working full-time for my parents and training in-home clients during my lunch hour, evenings and weekends began. It all started with taking that first step of thinking outside the box and not letting anyone deter me.

1. Take the first step.

It doesn't matter if you have all of the steps in place, you just need to take the first step. You have a good idea and the desire to pursue it, and then the details will take care of themselves. We can spend so much time preparing for the perfect trip that we never take that trip.

I ran the in-home training business for six months before I came across another business model that would allow me to help more people at the same time. The word "boot camp" had not made its debut in Hastings and I was ready for the challenge, and was excited to learn from two great fitness professionals, John Spencer Ellis and Kelli Calabrese. I was scared and doubtful if it would work for me, but I knew that if I wanted to keep growing and helping more people then I would need to take this step. I packed my bags and headed out to California to learn how to get my Adventure Boot Camp set up and ways to ensure my clients success. I started my first camp and it was a success! Being trained by Kelli and John, I learned that you need to look further than just your city limits to find people to learn from. I started finding top-notch coaches to learn more about my trade, but also learn about how to run a business and be successful.

2. Always have a team of mentors that you can continue to learn from.

Watch how they do business and how they communicate and relate to their audiences. I have had coaches that have come and gone from my professional career. They have all taught me so much about where I want to be and how to get there. If I had just stopped at my core education I would have fallen short and therefore not have been able to help as many people as I have thus far. When you put together your team of mentors, include people not just from your industry, but ones who can teach you about relating to other people, mentors who can teach you how to control your mindset, and also those mentors that will help you hone your trade – whatever it may be.

I was working A LOT! I would be up at 4:30am, coach a session, and my last client would come to my house at 8:30pm, and then I would finish up with any business that needed to be done. In between those times, I had clients, marketing, bookkeeping, not to mention housework, getting my kids to school, getting them home from school, feeding them and all of the other odds-and-ends type jobs that you do to keep a business and a family organized. There have been a few times in my career where I had the feeling that I should just go and get a normal job and do the 8-5 like most people do. At those times, it was like someone was kicking me in the gut, because I knew deep down that the lifestyle those hours would create would not work for me and the vision I had for my life and my family.

I always wanted to be a stay-at-home mom. Since that did not exactly happen, my second best option was to create a schedule that would allow me to be there for my kids at the events and times that really matter. My focus on business may change, but how I want my life to look will not change.

3. *Know what you want your life to look like and then build your business around that.*

This took me awhile to figure out. It was not until I started working with the ever genius Brian Grasso and Carrie Campbell that I came to realize I was only chasing the money, but didn't realize what reason I wanted that money to serve in my life. Once I figured that out, different opportunities started to arise and they all fell in line with how I envisioned my life to look.

Until I had my youngest child, who is now seven months old, I would have these huge disappointments where I felt like I was working so hard and doing everything right, but was just not getting a break. I would get so sad and feel completely lost. I thought that people did not believe I was credible because of all these insane reasons that were only true in my subconscious reality. I remember sitting on the phone with Carrie Campbell talking about the CTSM program, my daughter was nine days old, and in my conversation with Carrie I remember telling her that I knew I could do so much more, but something in my sub-conscious had to be holding me back and I needed to figure it out. I joined their program and now I have added the tools that enabled me to figure out how to be more in control of my mind. Wherever you are in your journey,

I recommend this should be your first step, and every other step will be so much easier to take and to figure out.

4. *If what you perceive as reality does not feel good, then it is probably not accurate, and you should really take time to work on yourself first.*

This step here is truly powerful. If you feel like you are struggling even though you are taking all of the right actions and you offer a great product or service, take the time to invest in yourself, and figure out why and what is causing you to have the beliefs that you do.

After I decided that I needed to work on myself, I felt my life changing and the path that I was once on was taking a different direction. It was not that my end destination was different, but the steps and actions that I once felt were important to get there were no longer that important.

I had been doing pretty well in my business, but felt like all I ever did was work and never had enough time for myself or my family. Once I sat down and figured out what was important, it took the fear out of me when I made changes to my business that would initially affect my income, but in the long run would get me closer to the life I would like to create.

Taking those steps were not easy at first, because I had been working with a team where you would not succeed unless you were putting in 60+ hours a week. This is not what I wanted to do for the rest of my life at all. The next step I took was to find someone who I could relate to in regards to mindset and what it takes to be successful. By finding this person that I respect for what they stand for, I have been able to re-define my definition of what success means to me, and therefore re-direct the steps that I take on this journey called life.

5. *Find people to work with and learn from and who you feel comfortable working with.*

If you do not get a good vibe or are not inspired, then chances are you will not be able to implement what they are trying to teach you anyway.

As I started to change the way I looked at my business, I could see that instead of stressing over the events and programs that I was offering, and worrying that I was not going to profit from it, I would now organize, and once it was organized I would let it go. What I found was that I was able to become more passionate about what it was that I was really offering, rather than worrying that if I didn't make money back then I couldn't pay the bills.

> ### 6. *Be passionate about what you are offering and the rest will fall into place.*
>
> Like I said in the beginning, I am always learning and therefore some steps seem out of place, but I wanted to give you the idea that you don't have to have it all right before you do actually get started on your journey to success.

While I was starting to feel more confident in myself and my business, I felt like I was all over the place with ideas, but I couldn't figure out why I was just not getting the BIG items done. Then I learned that I needed to once again look at what I wanted my life to look like, what I wanted to achieve and then pick three reasons out as to why I BELIEVED that I could not achieve them. After looking at those reasons, then I had to step away from my own mind and would act like I am someone else giving their perspective on my "excuses" for not achieving what I really want to achieve.

BAM!!! Things started to happen.

> ### 7. *Step outside yourself and plow through the reasons you are giving yourself for not achieving what you really want in life.*
>
> This process is not something that you can do once and think your life will be peachy and perfect. They are steps that you must take day in-and day–out, but YOU ARE WORTH IT . . . and so is the life that you want to create.

While my journey is not yet over, it has at least begun and it all began with just the first step . . . then taking the next . . . and the next . . . and the next. I have not let any of my life circumstances stand in the way of what I truly wanted and neither should you. Take these steps and apply them to your life wherever or whenever you feel them needed.

LET THE JOURNEY BEGIN!!!

About Stacie

Stacie Widhelm is a passionate health/wellness coach and speaker who has been empowering clients of all ages and fitness levels for more than a decade. She is the proprietor of **Fit 4 U Fitness** and **SRW Mind, Body Performance**, Hastings, offering training in large and small groups as well as individually. Stacie has most recently put her talents into the forthcoming book, *Change the Habit, Change the Body,* centering workshops and speaking engagements around its tenet that simple changes in daily activities and mindset will make large fitness and nutrition goals attainable. She is continually expanding her own training and education so she can better serve her clients and help them get results in the most efficient, least intimidating way.

Stacie says, "There is nothing more amazing than helping someone reach a goal. When clients talk about results -- having more energy, dropping a jeans size, making it through the day without drinking pop -- those achievements feel like my achievements and they are huge."

Stacie works with athletes in their prime, seniors, youth, and everyone in-between designing programs to meet individuals' unique needs and helping clients reach their personal goals. Stacie is certified through the ISSA (International Sports Science Association), IYCA (International Youth Conditioning Association), and also has BioForce HRV, RBT Band, and IYCA Speed and Ability certification. She has also trained under Mike Robertson (Bullet Proof Knee/Access and Correct). In addition, she is MPI (Mindset Performance Institute) level 1 certified.

Stacie is available for consultation classes, workshops and speaking engagements focused on fitness, nutrition, health and wellness and mindset.

Email: fit4u@widhelm.com

CHAPTER 29

BUILDING UNCOMMON PROTECTION INTO YOUR ROLE IN CORPORATE AMERICA

BY STEPHEN VAN VREEDE

THE RISE OF THE CORPORATE "ENTREPRENEUR"

Let's face it. The world of "work" is more uncertain than ever. It penalizes you for things you often can't control ... for being too "old," too experienced, too qualified, too "educated," too "expensive." It might not reward you for this certification or that title. On top of that, corporate hiring processes are a sophisticated mess (to put it mildly), internal cultural and multigenerational conflict is commonplace, and many companies are struggling with how to retain their top talent.

As a result, professionals now make an external career move every 3 to 4 years. That means the average 30-year-old with 35 years (or more!) left in the marketplace can expect *10 or more company changes* before he or she retires. Even if this professional were to beat the odds with an internal promotion or two, by say double, he or she could still be out in the market every 6 to 8 years.

If all that corporate "goo" isn't bad enough, then there's the job market "zoo" to contend with.

It's difficult to get solid stats, as they vary by market/industry, but the general trend is that you can expect to spend one month job searching for every $10–$20K you make in salary. So if you make $100K/year, you could see your job search take anywhere from 5 to 10 months. And that is when you're conducting a fairly aggressive search (20+ hours/week)! If you're more of a "passive" seeker (employed and putting less than 5 hours/week into your search), then the road could be much longer.

BUT THE GOOD NEWS IS THAT
IT'S NOT ALL BAD NEWS!

Each day I work with professionals across the globe dedicated to building in career protection, and they are achieving *tremendous* results. Just like the rest of us, they face many of the same limitations: age, gender, level of experience, geographic restrictions, lack of credentials, market instability, and so on. The difference is in how they approach these limitations and build in their protection from the storm.

IS THERE REALLY SUCH A THING
AS CAREER "PROTECTION"?

People tell me that "job security" is a myth today or that if you work for someone else, such as a corporation, you can't really control your fate. And I understand what they mean.

IT SEEMS LIKE SOMEONE ELSE
IS HOLDING ALL THE CARDS

What they don't realize is that this is what an entrepreneur faces everyday, all day, for his or her entire career. The entrepreneur may well be "the boss," but this boss is all alone facing an unwelcoming market that doesn't care whether this entrepreneur makes it or breaks it, sinks or swims.

Therefore, he or she must figure out how to get strategically positioned in the marketplace to protect against the economic downturns (or even upturns), perception/cultural shifts, internal power struggles, and any other winds of change that, without a doubt, will blow.

The entrepreneur is rarely able to stop these winds; in fact, quite the opposite is true. He or she must face them head on over and over again.

THE RISE OF THE CORPORATE ENTREPRENEUR

As I said, there is good news. If you plan to remain in the corporate world, you really can build in some protections. But first you have to do something that's hard: Change your thinking.

DON'T BE FOOLED.

Corporate culture sometimes lulls us into thinking we are "safe" when we aren't or that this advanced degree or that certification will keep us "marketable." I've worked with many executives, MBAs, and other educated professionals who've had the rug pulled out from under them only to face a market that isn't so welcoming.

They came to a point where they had little choice but to do something different. It was time to shift gears.

YOU'RE GOING TO NEED MORE OF AN "ENTREPRENEURIAL MINDSET" THAN PERHAPS YOU'RE USED TO

The first step in becoming a "corporate entrepreneur" begins by accepting the market for what *it is*, not for what it *ought to be*.

Accepting "what is" is an important shift in your thinking!

Once you do that, leaving behind how it was when you first started out or how it should be, then (and only then) can you begin to do what every good entrepreneur *must* do:

BUILD A CLEAR STRATEGY

Here is what differentiates most professionals (entrepreneurs and corporate workers alike). Without a clear strategy (free from the "how it should be" or "how it used to be" mindset), you're like a row boat tossed about out in the open sea or a leaf floating in a strong wind. You have an idea of where you'd like to go, maybe even some plans for how to get there, but you keep getting sidetracked by the waves and storms.

STRATEGY GIVES YOU BACK SOME CONTROL

Empowerment is a wonderful thing when focused productively, and that is what good strategy offers. It provides confidence (not overconfidence), because you're looking at the market for what it is and adjusting with it as it shifts. It reduces emotional drama (overreacting to trends or getting sucked into corporate "speak") and frees you to focus on providing better service to the companies you serve.

SO HOW DO YOU BEGIN TO BUILD THAT STRATEGY?

I believe the best strategies are built from action, not from "over-analysis." In other words, you have to get out there and start doing some research and you have to build some pipelines to keep you alert.

Too many people rush to build strategies based off of just what they think they know.

So to help you get into this action mode, I've put together a 5-step overview for getting started:

1. Create Pipelines of Opportunity.

Entrepreneurs understand the importance of pipelines, and therefore corporate entrepreneurs should too. Pipelines bring ongoing opportunities and valuable information even when we are not "in the market." They show us our position in the marketplace and the trends that really matter. Without them, our world becomes small, which means our understanding of the market around us is narrow. So we need pipelines to broaden our scope and give us a more accurate picture of our industry and our place in it.

There are many ways to create "pipelines." The best come in the form of strategic introductions (aka "networking"), which we will discuss shortly. Another can be joining or building a "career management" group that is dedicated to passing along opportunities/information to fellow members. Recruiters (yes, that frustrating bunch) can also be a strong pipeline, but you must (1) be properly matched with them and (2) begin to form relationships while you're still employed.

2. Learn How to Watch Market Indicators.

When it comes to career management, people often talk about "soul searching" and personality "assessments," which have a place (we all want to love what we do and be well suited for it), but the corporate entrepreneur also recognizes the law of supply and demand because despite the human element playing out each day in the corporate world, ultimately what drives the market is supply and demand. Like it or not, you are part of the bigger marketplace, and it is affecting you, maybe even more than you realize.

It might not be sexy, I know, but watching market indicators in our respective industries can show us what's coming so we can prepare for it. (I've witnessed many professionals, well-educated and well-paid, get hit by this issue because they didn't see it – or refused to see it – coming.)

3. Build a Personal Brand.

Thinking your work history will speak for itself trips up corporate professionals often more than any other issue. The reason is because the corporate structure pretends to be paying attention to what you do. From yearly reviews to promotions to awards to mentorships to special rewards like trips and stock options, companies act like they're watching AND remembering your achievements. And sometimes maybe they do.

More than likely, though, when you want to cash in on all that watching and remembering, you might be surprised to learn that people, by nature, are forgetful.

Entrepreneurs learn this every day. To make sure clients and prospects remember and value the services provided (and refer others!), they must develop a brand and know how to communicate it effectively.

It's really no different inside the corporate compound as management often doesn't perceive us the way we do. And although they gave us kudos for that stellar accomplishment, when it's time for a raise or promotion, we find out just how much they remember.

Yet, as a corporate entrepreneur, you'll be anticipating that. You'll recognize the way things are (not the way they should be), and you'll help guide your "customers" (co-workers, management, users, etc.) down memory lane because you'll have the documentation, portfolio, statistics (aka "personal brand") ready to prove (or re-prove) your relevancy.

4. Don't Get Trapped in the Networking Loop.

It's simpler to build connections today thanks to social media and its role as a networking tool. Of course, traditional networking groups still exist, and almost every profession on the planet has an association or two you can join. The reason is because professionals have been told, and rightly so, that networking is the most beneficial way to find a job.

The problem, though, is that these professionals either struggle to make connections (online or off) or make plenty of them but struggle with what to do with them once they have them, turning tools like LinkedIn (where we "stash" all these contacts) into nothing but a Rolodex.

And like a Rolodex that turns in a continuous loop, that's where most professionals are trapped when it comes to networking. It just keeps turning as new names are added in, but nothing more happens.

A corporate entrepreneur has the ability to build strategic connections that turn into opportunities. All thanks to the pipelines that build momentum, the market indicators that drive direction, and the personal brand that asserts value. As a result, the corporate entrepreneur can better identify and attract the connections that make the most strategic sense.

From there, he or she can move into what is the most underused tool by today's professionals but arguably the most effective way of creating opportunity and avoiding the job market zoo: the informational interview.

5. Ace the Informational Interview.

Many professionals think informational interviews are only for young people looking to research a field or for those changing industries. What they don't realize is that often top executives *only* land their next positions through informational interviews because they put you in control of creating opportunity.

In a traditional, formal interview, the interviewer asks the questions and seemingly holds the power. In an informational interview, you ask the questions and do the "vetting." Your goal is to have the contact lead you to someone else or some type of potential opportunity, and you achieve that by putting the other person in an important place: the role of helper.

Believe it or not, most professionals generally enjoy being a resource to others. As long as you don't take advantage of their good graces, respect their time, and leave desperation out of it, many will find ways to help you. As I work with my client members to guide them through the informational interview process, I see this play out beautifully because individuals generally enjoy helping each other, particularly in today's environment where so much is stacked against the professional.

A Look at How It Could Be
When corporate entrepreneurship works best ...

Meet Ahmed, a Project Manager in his 40s. He is a single dad with two young children. Ahmed has gone through some rough times in his career. He worked for two Silicon Valley startups that went bust. Then after landing what he thought was a "safe" gig with a Fortune 100, he was promptly laid off.

His stints of unemployment have been hard on his family. Therefore, after starting his latest role with another tech company, he's vowed he'll handle his career differently this time. Although he certainly wants his current role to work out, he doesn't want to be caught off-guard again.

Thankfully, his job hopping has left him with contacts spread across his field, so he's invited several to join together to touch base monthly via LinkedIn on latest trends, developments, and opportunities. Ahmed also has kept in touch with two recruiters who were well matched with him during his last search, and he's set up reminders to check in with them routinely.

With those pipelines active, he's scheduled biannual career strategy consults to keep his résumé, LinkedIn profile, and other documentation updated, and to help him massage his personal brand and assess the industry info he's received from his pipelines.

Ahmed also has taken it another step and has defined parameters for his ideal employer type near his current home. He's then reached out and introduced himself to contacts at those employers and set up informational interviews, creating yet another pipeline.

It's taken some work to get up and running, and it continues to require some nurturing, but Ahmed appreciates knowing that when the times comes, he'll be in a much better position for making a transition. Thanks to his strategy, it's more protection than he's ever had!

ARE YOU READY TO JOIN THE RANKS?

The days of "putting your head down, working hard, and not burning bridges = climbing the corporate ladder" might be fading. But it doesn't have to be negative. In fact, the corporate entrepreneur finds positivity where others see none! I witness these professionals leverage the power of the entrepreneurial mindset to rise above the chaos and protect the careers they've worked hard to build (and the livelihoods that their families depend on).

You can succeed in today's environment if you know where to begin.

You don't have to become overly ambitious or lose yourself in your career. But the best defense is a good offense.

Corporate Entrepreneurs understand what it takes to be "UNCOMMON" in Today's world of work.

WILL YOU BE ONE OF THEM?

About Stephen

Stephen Van Vreede helps his technical client members craft and communicate their unique story ("personal brand") and leverage the power of networking in today's complex job market. Before becoming an entrepreneur, he spent his days climbing the corporate ladder at a GE Capital Company, where he engineered the growth and rapid technological advancement of a large-scale international operation.

Stephen was struck by the volume of candidates that struggled to present themselves successfully in professional interviews. An even bigger surprise was the realization that corporate hiring and retention policies resulted in an often convoluted and chaotic process (what he calls corporate "goo") that left hiring managers and candidates frustrated and confused. So, with his wife, Sheree, in 2001, he decided to jump off the corporate ladder and embark on an entrepreneurial adventure in the résumé and career services field, where he could be an advocate for professionals.

Over the past 14 years, Stephen has shaped his member solutions to succeed in an ever-changing market but with unique differentiation and value delivery at the core of all client member messaging. Starting out under the No-Stone-Unturned umbrella, where they served professionals across a wide spectrum of industries, he and Sheree soon recognized a gap in the career services industry in serving the technology, manufacturing, and engineering markets and knew they could fill that gap.

Thus, ITtechExec was conceived, where Stephen now serves as President and Chief Solutions Architect. He and his specialized team work with technical professionals, managers, and executives with 15+ years of experience. Stephen and Sheree have recently also launched NoddlePlace to focus on emerging technical professionals with 5–15 years of experience. At both ITtechExec and NoddlePlace, they not only craft résumés but also portfolio solutions, which are proving to be much more effective in the technical arena. In addition, they offer one-of-a-kind, "concierge" NoNonsense® job search agent solutions that build immediate momentum in the marketplace for their members once their brand messaging is in place.

Stephen holds an MBA from Villanova University, a Bachelor's degree from the University of Maryland, and a Six Sigma Black Belt Certification from GE. He is an Academy Certified Résumé Writer (ACRW) and a Certified Professional Résumé Writer (CPRW). As a Certified Online Professional Networking Strategist (OPNS) and Micro-blogging Career Strategist (MCS), Stephen is an expert in career marketing through social media forums like LinkedIn and Twitter.

Stephen's work has been featured in multiple CIO.com and TechRepublic.com résumé makeover series. He has been a keynote speaker at industry conferences and has served as an expert contributor on technology career, résumé, and personal branding topics for articles featured by CIO Magazine, CIO.com, Dice.com, and other publications. Stephen is a Board Member for the Career Thought Leaders, a think tank for the now, the new, and the next in the career field. He is also passionate about service in his local community, where he serves as an elected official on the Town Council.

You can connect with Stephen at:
Stephen@ITtechExec.com
www.linkedin.com/in/stephenvanvreede
www.twitter.com/ITtechExec

CHAPTER 30

CREATING AMBASSADORS THE CONTRARIAN WAY

BY SUA TRUONG

How a moment of inspiration turned an unconventional idea into one of my biggest referral lead generation systems. Where can you get a fully qualified lead and instant trust from a referral source that you just met? Imagine getting a referral from your competitor! The client is already pre-qualified and you know their story as well as having the instant trust being passed on to you by your very own competitor! How can you get that? Well I have been doing just that.

My very first referral from one of my competitors generated $26,000 from a single transaction the same week.

MY 'A-HA' MOMENT: HOW DID I COME UP WITH THIS IDEA AND PROCESS?

It was during a heated discussion with one of my colleagues about how unfair some bank advisors have it when it comes to receiving exceptions at the bank branch level for loan approvals. The broker channel would not be able to get the loan approved because we would not be able to request the exception to be made. It was quite an unfair advantage in this circumstance. Somewhere along the discussion, the comment about them being a competitor instead of working with the brokers really irked me. I thought to myself, "Why should they be our competitors instead of working together with us (the brokers)? There are plenty of customers to go around for everyone. Yes, perhaps there are some things that the bank advisors can do that we cannot do as an independent broker. However, there are many things that we can do that they cannot do either."

More and more questions floated through my mind that morning. Can the banks approve every loan that goes their way? Of course not! What happens to those people that were declined by the lender? What reasons could they possibly be declined for? Could I help them and rectify the situation? There is always a possibility!

I knew there were hurdles that had to be overcome before asking for referral business from the bank representatives. It is well known in the industry that selling away (referring business out) is frowned upon and even explicitly disallowed. Banks do not refer business out for fear of liability issues that may be created outside of their control which may come back to haunt them. I knew this from my own personal experience, having previously worked at one of the large financial institutions. If bank representatives were caught referring out business, they may have faced termination of their employment. How do you overcome these challenges?

I will share with you five simple, yet highly effective processes to creating your own ambassadors the contrarian way.

I. Tactics & Targets to Consider:

- Why would a "competitor" give me five minutes to listen to my proposition?
- Who should I approach at the bank? Front line staff or senior managers?
- What benefits could they achieve by "investing" their time with me?
- What do I have to do in order for the bank advisors to be able to refer business to me?
- What critical questions do I need to ask?

I knew that if I found out the "why," the "how" would take care of itself.

WHY: What win-win message do I want to convey?

The biggest hurdles to overcome are:

a. Trust - How can a bank advisor trust that you will not do anything that will damage the relationship that they have with the client and the client's feelings towards the bank (my employer)?

b. Confidence - Are you full of hot air or are you capable of getting the job done? How confident do I feel that you know your craft and are not just talking a good game?

II. <u>Strategies to Overcome the Unspoken Objections:</u>

For me, it is more a mindset than a sales process. I approach the "competing advisor" as if he or she was my colleague. I am there to let them know that I am on their side and can prove it to them. I talk from the heart and not from a speech I have memorized. In sales, people only buy from people that they know, like and trust. Winning over an ambassador is no different.

When I first meet my new partner, I get to know about them and why they're where they are today. Yes, I view them as a partner before I even meet them! I would share my own story about why I am doing what I do today. If they are in a service-related business, they must care about people or in some way feel good about what they can do. Doesn't everyone want to be a winner or feel like a winner? Of course!

Find out what motivates them to do what they do each day. Most people don't go to work just for the hourly pay that they receive. There is a driving force behind them. Is it their family? Is it their recreation or leisure activities that they enjoy and have to work to fund those passions? Do they have future goals or plans? What are they?

The intention for probing them with these questions is always to "do good." When I am there, I am all-present (not just physically there). I am mentally focused on getting to know this person and dig deeper when they respond to my questions. How do you know you are doing it right? You are there to serve others. Find out how you can be of service to them. What is his or her purpose in life? What value can I bring to this person and their network? How can I increase the value that I can bring to my network by connecting with this person? What is the message that I learned today? I have this mentality whenever I network with people.

III. <u>Be Open and Be Vulnerable:</u>

I am not shy about why I am there to meet them. Don't pretend that you're there for anything else. Be open about why you are there. My approach is to find out what they can do fast and spend more time on helping their clients. I need to dig as deep as I can during our discussion. Find out how they feel when they cannot help the client. Does it affect them? How does it affect their company or image? How would they feel about going above and beyond their role?

If you use the F.O.R.M. method during any conversation, both people will feel as if you are going to be great friends. The FORM acronym stands for Family, Occupation, Recreation and Message. I like to get to the message part the most. I find out what really drives them. We all can connect better at that level. It's genuine and from the heart. It takes practice at first, but the more you do it, the better you get at it. At first I was horrible at this whole process. I practiced in front of the hallway mirror, in my car by myself (out loud), with my family and every opportunity I get. Eventually it becomes a part of who you are. Then it becomes FUN!

IV. <u>Become Top of Mind:</u>

Now that you have made a good impression, you must have a strategy to be on top of their minds for future opportunities that may arise. How can you overcome "out of sight, out of mind"? What are you doing to be remembered when they face a situation that they cannot resolve within their company?

Here are some tactics that I have used to achieve my goal:

- Drop in with coffee and donuts for colleague and staff.
- Invite to events to help them network (Clubs, Toastmasters, etc.).
- Make notes of your top 10 or top 20 clients' needs and help fill them from your network.
- Reconnect on intervals 3-6 months for coffee or lunch.
- Send out birthday card with gift card for coffee, do the same for their children if that applies.
- Call them on their birthday and wish them a wonderful day (… who does that anymore?).

- Send Christmas cards, or recognize special occasions important to them.

This list is only a few of the things that I have done over the years. Many activities that I have done did not cost me anything. However, the receiver's perception of that gesture is priceless. Most adult children don't even call their parents and wish them a happy birthday. How important would your colleague or client feel if you called them on their birthday and wished them a wonderful day? The "good" feeling that they receive from this action will carry them through the day. The experience may even last the entire week. You cannot put a value on that.

The most powerful thing that anyone can do actually costs nothing except time. One realtor I know does especially well and he does not advertise. He doesn't need to, because 100% of his business comes from referrals in his network. How did he achieve this? He created lists of needs of clients or potential candidates he comes into contact with. He knows what drives them and what their goals in life are. He then finds way to help them achieve those goals by connecting people in his network that can help make those dreams possible or at least get closer to it. When one of his clients got laid off from work and he knows another colleague that is looking for someone with that work experience, he would connect the two people. He filled the needs of both people and it would cost him nothing except time. How can you place a value on his act of kindness and thoughtfulness?

Even the best real estate marketer in the world would have a tough time winning the loyalty of this client away from that realtor. When the time comes to buying a property, they will always remember what he has done for them and will feel more than obligated to have him as their realtor. The client will have no doubt or even consider anyone else. Why do you think that happens? My friend understands that building a great foundation will develop into a lifelong relationship. People will do business with those that they know, like and trust. It is simple as that. Whatever you do, do it with the right intention to help others and the universe will return the kindness in multiple ways.

V. <u>Instill a Contrarian Mindset:</u>

What really amazes me is that we all want the same thing. We all want people to love us, care about us and be helpful. Nobody likes to be treated like another victim or as the next sale, so why do it that way? The sale is the start of a relationship. It should not be considered "closing the deal," but as the "opening of the relationship." This is how I approach my competitor and clients. I have contacted nearly every one of my competitors over the years and even take them out to lunch to get to know about them and understand their strengths. I have even referred clients to them freely under certain situations. My client will know that I will not be compensated for doing so and they will understand what kind of person I am. These same clients will come back to me in the future. I assure you that they will. Why? Because they know I truly care about them and place their interests first before the almighty dollar. They know my competitor won't feel the same way.

I believe we're meant to be on this earth for one purpose only, and that is to give something of ourselves and to leave this world a little better than when we arrived. We cannot take money with us and it will disappear once we're gone. Creating an impact on others for the better, improving their life or the world that we live in...now that's inspiring and will live on forever. I truly hope to see more people open up and do business with heart and soul. Yes, that's different—perhaps contrary to what we're taught in business schools.

If the son of a poor immigrant can use these simple ideas to become #1 in his community, imagine what you can do!

About Sua

Sua Truong helps alleviate stress for his clients throughout the challenging process of financing their property so that they can enjoy their life and focus on their family or their business. They have full confidence in him and trust that he will always do what is in their best interest. His integrity is the cornerstone of what he does and why he has been so successful in such a short period of time as a mortgage broker. In just under four years, he has become the #1 Mortgage Broker in his community.

Sua has built his career on doing what is right for his client rather than what is best for his wallet. Helping people has been the biggest motivating factor in his life and he feels on purpose whenever he makes a big difference in their life. This mindset is what led him to his moment of inspiration where he came up with an idea to generate leads from his competitors. He calls it "Creating Ambassadors the Contrarian Way." He found a way to enlist his competitors to refer unlimited clients to him and yet both parties can still come out as winners. He has helped senior managers and advisors from nearly every major bank as well as other brokers from competing brokerages. These competitors have referred to him fully qualified business prospects on a daily basis.

Sua is a graduate of Kwantlen Polytechnic University. Although his love was in computer systems technology, his passion has always been about helping people. As a senior mortgage broker, he mentors and trains mortgage brokers. As the President of MoneyMasters Toastmasters (2014), he helps inspire and mentor potential leaders. Outside of work, he helps fellow real estate investors by organizing and teaching at the fastest-growing Real Estate Investment Club in his area.

Sua is a regular contributor to the local community newspaper and trains other professionals at his local real estate office. He has spoken on Fairchild Radio Vancouver as an expert on mortgage financing. As far as he knows, Sua is the only mortgage broker trainer that will allow outside brokers from other offices to freely attend his training. You can tell he truly believes and does what Zig Ziglar teaches: "You can have everything in life that you want, if only you help enough other people get what they want."

You can connect with Sua at:
www.SuaTruong.com
www.Meetup.com/SurreyREIC
www.SharingBankSecrets.com
www.linkedin.com/in/suatruong
www.facebook.com/sua.truong

CHAPTER 31

INDOMITABLE

BY TANJA N. REID

Once upon a time there was a skinny, bow-legged, brown-skinned girl with long arms and a big butt. Some people teased her about these features and she spent her life struggling with insecurities. Well, eventually I grew into those long arms, the legs are still bowed, just not so obvious, I'm not exactly skinny now, and the butt doesn't seem so big anymore.

As a young child growing up, I only had one dream and that was to make it to the Olympics and become a professional athlete.

I was an energetic child with an endless supply of energy and an insatiable appetite for competition! So when I was about 9, my stepfather decided to start preparing my siblings and myself for sports by playing soccer with us in the backyard. He eventually put us in organized sports and soccer soon became my first love!

As I grew into my awkward body, I became more athletic, playing every sport in school, but to me, nothing was more fun than soccer.

By the first year of high school, I was spotted by a track club coach and he immediately told my older sister, who was already training with him at the time, that I should be running track. I think the soccer world and my step father would agree that although soccer was a good sport for me to start with, I was often outrunning the ball more and missing goals because I couldn't slow down fast enough to get control of it. It became evident that it was time for a transition. Besides that, there were no scholarships for girl's soccer at the time and it seemed like it would be a dead end for me anyway. So I reluctantly gave up my first love and adjusted to the training regime with Mississauga Track and Field Club.

During my sophomore year, I was approached by my high school coach and was told that I should probably focus on one sport now if I wanted a future as a *Track & Field* athlete. I gave up all the other sports without complaining. This was the best decision I ever made! Although I did get a knee injury competing in long jump the following year at the Regional championships and was told by a doctor that I would never run again, I did run again, even won the Ontario high school championships known as *OFSAA*! But I NEVER jumped again!

My performances led to US recruiting opportunities, which turned out to be a blessing in disguise, when I was rejected from the Kinesiology program by all three of the Canadian Universities that I applied to. Apparently this was a very competitive program and only the very best students were being accepted. So at that point, a full scholarship to the University of Iowa was my *only* option.

I was so grateful for the opportunity and my Jamaican sprint coach there was the perfect match for this native Jamaican girl. He and the strength coach trained me so well, that in my first year I packed on the "freshman 15." I literally gained 15 lbs, but it was lean muscle and I barely recognized myself. My nutritional plan was an unhealthy "all you can eat diet," combined with 2-3 hours of intense daily training, plus competing every weekend in four events! My first year running at Iowa qualified me for the 1994 Commonwealth Games Trials in Victoria, British Columbia. I made the finals and was chosen to run first leg of the 400m relay at the Games for Team Canada! That was probably the most epic experience of my life! The opening ceremonies, spectators, special guests, athletes from around the world in customized uniforms with country flags waving, music, lights, cameras, just like the Olympic opening ceremonies I used to watch as a young girl!

A year later, I transferred to the University of Georgia and my sprint times qualified me for the 1996 Olympic Trials, and my 100m time even gave me a first place ranking in Canada! I was finally getting closer to my dream, but I didn't feel ready to compete. My Iowa and Georgia coaches encouraged me to do it anyway - they believed I was ready and convinced me to go for it! I reluctantly went to the trials for them, not so much for me because I knew I was burnt out from a long collegiate track season and there were also psychological obstacles I was facing at the time. Well as my luck would have it, I missed the 100m (a long story, I'll share another time) which was the race that I was expected to do well in. I was devastated, but managed to pull myself together and convince the officials to still let me compete in the 200m. I ended placing 5th in the final and did *not* make the Olympic Team.

The pressure to perform and disappointment I felt afterward were just too much to handle. I really wanted to hide from the world! Sadly, that was the last race of my career. I discovered I was pregnant a couple months later and figured that was probably a sign to give up on my dreams. So I left University my senior year, gave up my scholarship and forfeited my last year of NCAA eligibility. I realized that motherhood was way more important.

Physically I gave up, but mentally I held onto my dreams. After my first child was born, I dove straight into the domestic life! Then had 2 more children, each born 22 months apart. Since being a stay-at-home mom was something my husband and I agreed upon, he worked full time to make sure I could continue to stay home with the kids and begin homeschooling.

One day in the winter of 2004 I looked in the mirror and realized I'd been carrying around an extra 20 lbs of post pregnancy weight for the past 7 years! I didn't like the changes that pregnancy brought to my body, but I really wasn't taking care of myself either. I didn't work out anymore and my diet was only somewhat healthy. I became more insecure and suffered from postpartum depression. Child bearing was a beautiful gift, I know I should've loved myself more, but the truth is that I didn't. I decided to make a goal to get my body back in shape, so I entered my first fitness competition. Little did I know, it was the biggest fitness competition of the year at the time – called FAME – which was held in Toronto.

My daily training started off really slow for the first couple weeks, literally doing:

1 pushup

5-second planks

5 lunges

30-second jog and simple stretches

When that got too easy, I did:

2 pushups

5 squats, 5 lunges

10-second planks

60-second run

This was a very humbling experience to start from nothing after all my body had experienced before, and the results weren't coming fast enough - I almost gave up! But I made steady progress, so after the 4th week, I created an *overly* intense fitness-nutrition plan, which included healthy meals, daily cardio, weight training, pilates and tae-bo.

After 3 months, I lost 15 lbs and dropped my body fat to a competitive level. Competing on stage in a bikini with heels for the first time was scary and exciting! I'm not sure how I placed out of the 250 girls, but it didn't matter. I did it for me and that was the greatest victory!

Training and dieting for the fitness model competition wasn't something I could easily maintain and I didn't like the body judging element, so I set out on a mission to find a better way to eat, train and be healthy with no extremes! A year later, I signed up for a Fitness and Nutrition course with an online college. After 2 years of study and equipped with new knowledge, I got my diploma!

In 2007, I had my 4th child and decided to train in the martial arts school that my other three kids were involved in. After 300 intense hours of training and studying, I received my Black Belt Chief Instructor and School Owner Certification. I honestly felt that I had now found my niche! I felt passionate about training and teaching others what I had learned. It challenged me and changed my outlook on life as each belt level gave me something to look forward to. My new goal was to open a martial arts school, which wasn't easy, and I've faced many obstacles trying to get something established.

I actually worked at a gym for a year, then started my own personal training business privately and charged what I thought was a fair price and made enough in my part time to maintain the bills in our household. I created my own hours around homeschooling the kids and often trained outside, in my home or at my client's homes. It was a freedom that I enjoyed and it gave me the flexibility to be a full-time mom again and have a career. I loved sharing my passion for health and fitness, but having my own martial arts studio was still my ultimate goal and it had somehow replaced my Olympic Dream. I've accepted the fact that I may never be on that podium, but I'd found a new podium to stand on with pride and that was my journey to finding my calling!

Now fast forward 4 years and 5 kids later, I still train, consult and teach privately, eat well-balanced meals and discovered efficient ways to fit exercise into my busier life. Here are 6 valuable tips I learned, that can make your health and fitness goals easier:

1. **Love Yourself!** Don't compare yourself to anyone and don't look to others for approval! Love and accept who you are now and where you are now, first. At 42, I've finally accepted my body and now embraced the things I once thought were flaws! Self-love is the first key to success.

2. **Create short-term goals.** Start off with one change at a time until it becomes a habit, then create another change. Before you know it, your entire lifestyle will have changed for the better!

3. **Sleep well – Eat well**. Get balanced macronutrient meals with natural foods containing 1 cup of good carbohydrates, 4-6 oz of organic protein and good fats. Drink purified water. Avoid processed foods, sodas and refined sugars.

4. **Keep Moving!** I don't always have time for gym workouts, so I do stairs, squats, lunges, leg & calf raises, arm curls, push-ups, planks, martial arts techniques across the kitchen while I'm cooking, cleaning or on the phone. If you watch TV, try them during commercial breaks of your favorite show! Little things really do add up! I also dance with my little ones! Just picking three to five songs could give you a 15 to 30-minute intense dance workout depending on how much energy you put into it. It'll relieve stress and release some endorphins and serotonin (the happy hormones) as well!

5. **Don't be afraid to "fail."** Feeling the pressure of success from people or society expecting success from me resulted in my "failure," which ultimately helped transition me so I could discover a better place to learn, grow and nurture myself without seeking or needing the approval of others.

6. **Be Patient and Relentless!** An important lesson I've learned is that consistency, dedication and perseverance are important keys to success! There is no magic potion. No short cuts to good health. Don't be afraid to start with baby steps. These are stages of development. So start wherever you're at and gradually increase the difficulty. There's no rush, no pressure! Good health isn't about competition, so take the time you need to improve. It's your life!

Remember there's more than one way to get in great shape - more than one path you can take to achieve optimum health. When you get to know yourself and your body really well, you'll figure out what works and what doesn't. The secret is finding the path that works best for you and sticking to it!

About Tanja

Tanja N. Reid is a 42-year-old Jamaican-Canadian, busy, homeschooling mother of five children, ages 17, 15, 13, 7 and 2. She's been in the fitness industry for about 20 years as an athlete, coach, trainer and nutrition consultant.

Tanja was a full-scholarship Track athlete at the University of Iowa and the University of Georgia. She ran for Team Canada at the 1994 Commonwealth Games in Victoria, B.C. and ended her track career after she competed at the 1996 Olympic Trials. She has a diploma in Fitness and Nutrition – which she received after having her third child. Then she became a certified Black Belt Martial Arts student, certified Chief Instructor with school owner training from Choi Kwang Do Martial Arts International (CKDMAI) after having her fourth child.

The former NCAA All-American collegiate athlete and former Canadian sprinter, combines her background in track & field, fitness, nutrition and martial arts techniques to create a balanced, back-to-basics, keep-it-simple holistic approach to obtaining optimum health.

Tanja believes that anything is possible and lives by the idea that success is a result of setting your mind on something, never giving up and taking the necessary steps to accomplish your goals. She is very passionate about health and fitness and helping others achieve their goals. She's currently studying to become a Relaxation Therapist, while training for her 2nd Degree Black Belt.

Tanja loves cooking, baking and experimenting with new recipes or finding creative ways to make traditional meals and desserts healthier! Tanja also enjoys reading, writing, relaxing on the beach, watching movies, and playing games and sports with her kids. Her hobbies include drawing and painting with watercolor, acrylic and oils, on canvas. She currently resides in Ontario, Canada with her five children.

You can connect with Tanja at:
https://twitter.com/blackbeltnubian
https://www.facebook.com/tanja.natasha.reid

CHAPTER 32

FIVE MYTHS ABOUT RETIREMENT INVESTING

BY THOMAS F. HELBIG

Independent financial advisors and retirement planning specialists know one thing for sure. Most people they meet who are already retired or nearing retirement have no idea how many options there are for investing their hard-earned nest egg. In fact, what I've discovered is that there are five myths that most retirees and pre-retirees believe to be true.

1. All advisors are the same.

2. You don't need a second opinion about your retirement portfolio.

3. You need a million dollars to warrant an advisor.

4. The right time to call an advisor is when you're retiring.

5. The bigger your nest egg, the more income you'll have in retirement no matter where the money is invested.

Examining these myths will help retirees and pre-retirees begin to get a sense of what they should consider as they prepare for their retirement. First, let's try to understand why preparing for retirement is important. The answer seems obvious. You want to have money in the years following your full-time employment. But why is there pressure to plan now? Retirement is 5-10 years away. What's changed in recent decades that makes retirement planning so important?

The main reason planning is a necessity is that the old pension plans went away years ago. At one time, companies all offered a guaranteed pension plan for their employees. They provided retired employees with an income even after they stopped working. Guaranteed pension plans went away as 401(k)s became more popular. Now companies are turning all of the responsibility over to employees to fund their own retirement. The pension safety net is gone.

Wall Street has a lot of money and power. They were the ones that funded and spent billions of dollars convincing politicians to push the 401(k) so that Wall Street would become the 401(k) gatekeeper. No allocations beyond Wall Street securities are available to someone with a 401(k) which means Wall Street controls the money. Most of them don't offer savings accounts through banks and they don't offer a safe annuity through an insurance company. Wall Street controls 100% of the money in 401(k)s and they get all the fees.

When the stock market started to crash in 2008, people with 401(k)s had nowhere to go. They weren't ever given an alternative where they could have kept some of their money safe. The truth is that when Wall Street crashes, everyone loses money in their 401(k), and Wall Street still gets paid. It's as if the fox is guarding the hen house.

So, when investors have the option, perhaps when leaving a job or retiring, it's important to roll a 401(k) into a safer IRA. Once your nest egg is rolled into an IRA, a whole world of investment options opens up including savings accounts and insurance company vehicles that protect the principle while allowing for growth.

Right now, there are 10,000 baby boomers retiring every day and it's going to be that way for the next twenty years. In fact, over the next twenty years we'll actually have more retirees than people in the workforce. Mathematically, social security can't survive without changes because there will be fewer people contributing money than people drawing from it. That's a fact.

Even if you're already retired or retiring tomorrow and you believe social security will last for the remainder of your life, you still need to plan. People who didn't make a comprehensive, well-thought-out plan for their retirement in 2008 when the stock market crashed often lost over half of their life savings. They were planning to retire that year and they found that they'd have to keep on working for another 5-10 years because they couldn't live off of social security. Seems like a good reason to make a plan, right?

Knowing the five myths of retirement is important because it can mean the difference between a comfortable, worry-free retirement and a retirement where you're living day-to-day, paycheck-to-paycheck.

TRUE OR FALSE:
ALL FINANCIAL ADVISORS ARE THE SAME.

Wall Street brokers are educated and trained to sell stocks, mutual funds, ETFs, REITs, and variable annuities. These are all securities which means two things for investors. Your money is at risk and you'll be charged fees on a regular basis. In fact, brokers get paid regardless of whether you make money or lose it because the main goal for a Wall Street broker is to make money.

On the other hand, an independent financial advisor puts your best interests first because they don't make money via fees added to your account. What's more, independent advisors aren't controlled by Wall Street, so we can educate investors on all the financial products available to them. Not to mention that independent advisors are educated in non-Wall Street products like hybrid annuities, fixed index annuities, and other insurance company products. They can manage and provide the only financial investments available today offering safety and growth at the same time on the same dollar.

Investors need to understand that there are three features in every investment: safety, growth, and liquidity. A perfect investment would be if investors could have all three, but that doesn't exist. You get to pick two out of three.

In a bank account you have safety and your money's liquid. You can pull your money out anytime you want. But you give up growth. In Wall Street you have growth potential because your money's in the market and your money's liquid, you can pull it out anytime you want, but you give up safety. You could lose your money. With fixed index annuities, also called hybrid annuities, you've got safety because your principal is guaranteed, and you've got growth potential because they link to a stock index but your money's not actually in the market. You have to give up a little liquidity because the insurance company that's holding your money takes your money and buys 10-year Treasury notes. So your money's tied up for 10 years. But it's possible to withdraw 10% per year if you need it without any penalty. And, after 10 years is up, your money is 100% liquid. It's the only financial vehicle that gives all three features of safety, growth and liquidity after 10 years.

As an independent advisor, we know that hybrid annuities are a powerful option for pre-retirees and retirees. There are different types of annuities though and investors must be mindful. Wall Street sells a variable annuity which gives investors all the risk of the market and high fees. What most people want after they are educated on the difference of both is a fixed index annuity which came into existence twenty-one years ago back in 1994. Once again, independent financial advisors provide investors an advantage because we can match a wide array of products to the needs and concerns of the investor.

Independent financial advisors might seem too good to be true. If they don't collect fees, how do they get paid? That's a great question. There aren't any fees on these accounts. The insurance company pays a one-time finder's fee when a new account is open. The insurance company pays the advisor, not the investor. And independent investors have the added luxury of a good night's sleep knowing that their clients are well-taken care of and invested in ways that make sense for their particular needs.

TRUE OR FALSE:
YOU DON'T NEED A SECOND OPINION
ABOUT YOUR RETIREMENT PORTFOLIO.

We get second opinions on our health. We deserve a second opinion on our wealth. Just be sure that when you go to get that second opinion, you're visiting someone who can offer and educate you on all available financial products.

Most people are working with a Wall Street broker and/or have their money in a Wall Street product. Because of this, investors need to take a look at how much money they can afford to lose in the next market crash. Most people can't afford to lose any money but they still have 100% of their money in the market, at risk. Some brokers will reassure their clients that their money is diversified. But unless their money is diversified outside of a Wall Street product, the money isn't safe.

When an investor comes to an independent financial advisor, they are shown what they can do differently and provided with a personalized, structured income plan. This plan shows them that based on the total sum of their nest egg, if they were to roll their money into a safer alternative, they could see a guaranteed annual income for life at whatever age of retirement they choose. Guaranteed. The promise of safety and a guaranteed retirement income are reason enough to get the right second opinion before retirement.

TRUE OR FALSE:
YOU NEED AT LEAST A MILLION DOLLARS
TO WARRANT AN ADVISOR.

You don't have to have a million dollars to warrant an advisor. The money you have means everything to you whether it's $100,000 or a million dollars. It's your life savings and you want it to be protected because it's your safety net. This means you need to work with an advisor who will not turn you away just because you don't have a lot of assets. You want to work with an advisor that will protect your assets and show you what can generate the most guaranteed income for the rest of your life.

Many people assume that because they don't have a million dollars in the bank a financial advisor won't be interested in working with them. While this may be the truth for brokers who depend on fees for their livelihood, this couldn't be further from the truth for most independent financial advisors. No one is turned away because if advisors can help them we are happy to do it and we know that we will be paid.

The truth is that the biggest reward for me is not how much money as a financial advisor I will get paid. It's the testimonials and letters on our conference room walls that thank us for helping protect our clients' nest eggs during times of Wall Street turmoil. It's knowing that our clients can be comfortable in retirement. They have the financial stability they need and the peace of mind they deserve as they enjoy retirement.

TRUE OR FALSE:
THE RIGHT TIME TO CALL AN ADVISOR
IS WHEN YOU'RE RETIRING.

Retirement is a life-changing event which means that investors must make a plan and change their investment philosophy. Part of the philosophical change that must take place is the type of investment advisor you choose and when you begin a relationship with that person. If you choose a Wall Street broker, they will sell you Wall Street securities and all securities carry risk, some might say significant risk. If you choose an independent financial advisor you'll be choosing someone who can educate you about all the different types of investments and the risks they carry. In turn, they can help you determine what is appropriate for you in terms of risk level.

There's a financial Red Zone where retirees and pre-retirees are concerned. The financial red zone happens in the 5 year window before you retire and up to the 5 years after you retire. This period is crucial and it shouldn't be any less than 5 years before you retire.

Start planning and working with an independent advisor and have them put together a plan that shows you, based on your current assets, what kind of guaranteed income they can drive for you to live off of based on the retirement date you give them. Wall Street can't do that. Wall Street just sells optimism based on hypothetical returns – but nothing is guaranteed that way.. The financial Red Zone is the time to get in and get a second opinion from an independent advisor.

When you're nearing retirement, it's important to become more conservative. Lowering your risk is important because if there is a downturn in the stock market when you're about to retire or when you're retired, your hard-earned nest egg can be wiped out. That's the money that has to last you the rest of your life – sometimes 30-40 years. That nest egg has to provide you with an income for the rest of your life.

TRUE OR FALSE:
THE BIGGER YOUR NEST EGG, THE MORE INCOME YOU'LL HAVE IN RETIREMENT NO MATTER WHERE THE MONEY IS INVESTED.

Lifetime income becomes a very important part of your world-view in retirement. Retirement income is the driving force behind your retirement lifestyle. Your retirement lifestyle depends on the amount of guaranteed income you have coming in for the rest of your life.

This is the point in life where hybrid annuities, these fixed index annuities, are so useful because they protect your principal while offering growth on your account. They allow you to generate income for the rest of your life. No matter what.

The alternative is a Wall Street account. Remember, they'll sell you optimism. But guess what happens when Wall Street crashes again? Your income goes down because your portfolio went down. Simply put, you can't have a guaranteed income from a non-guaranteed account.

You can only get a guaranteed income from an account that's guaranteed not to lose principal. A hybrid annuity can offer a higher guaranteed income payout with less money than a larger portfolio invested with Wall Street.

Wall Street used to have a 4% rule on withdrawal in retirement. On a balanced portfolio of stocks and bonds, a retiree should be able to withdraw 4% a year for income and you've got a 75% chance you won't run out of money. However, there's a 25% chance you still might run out of money.

In July of 2011, Putnam Investments, a mutual fund company on Wall Street, changed that rule and now the withdrawal rate is no more than 2.7% if you don't want to run out of money. How could you afford to live off 2.7% unless you have a million dollars or more? You couldn't.

With a hybrid annuity based on your age, you can withdraw between 5-7% per year guaranteed income for life. So you're going to have more income coming in guaranteed on a smaller portfolio. Why? Because it's contractually guaranteed. There's no risk of losing your principal. It's not the size of your portfolio, it's the guaranteed income you can depend on to provide a good, comfortable lifestyle. One you can count on.

By using a fixed index or hybrid annuity you're creating your own private pension. With the old pensions, the check you received each month was coming from an insurance company. The old pension plan was an immediate annuity. It guaranteed you an income for life but ran out at your death. Investing your money with an insurance company has been considered safe and reliable for many, many years. Independent financial advisors believe it remains a safe and reliable investment today. However these new hybrid annuities give you the best of both worlds. It will provide you a guaranteed income the rest of your life and when you die the remaining principal still goes to your loved ones. And you can start and stop your income at any time with these accounts.

The next step to planning for your own retirement is to talk to an independent financial advisor. You deserve a second opinion from someone with a wide variety of options who is ready to educate you and help you retire comfortably and with peace of mind.

About Thomas

Thomas F. Helbig, a Retirement Planning Specialist, is a native of St. Louis, Missouri, and founder and CEO of Retirement Advisory Group. For 28 years he has focused on helping retirees and pre-retirees preserve and protect their wealth, and generate more guaranteed lifetime income regardless of Wall Street's performance. Today, Thomas is a nationally-recognized trainer and keynote speaker on the subject.

Thomas is no stranger to recognition and accolades. He was recently featured as an expert guest on the TV show "America's PremierExperts." The Show, filmed in Orlando, Florida, was seen on NBC, CBS, ABC and Fox network affiliates around the country. Helbig discussed how he is helping his clients achieve a worry-free retirement.

Helbig is the best-selling author of *The Boomer's Guide to a Worry-Free Retirement*. He has been featured in *USA Today, Newsweek, The Wall Street Journal, St. Louis Magazine* and *The St. Louis Post-Dispatch* as one of the leading retirement planning specialists in the country.

Additionally, because of his expertise and significant contributions to his industry, he was recently featured in *The Wall Street Journal* as one of the country's leading "Trendsetters" in the financial services and retirement planning world. Thomas was also featured in *Forbes Magazine* in the January 21, 2013 national edition as one of America's Top 20 Premier Experts in the country.

Thomas F. Helbig is also an approved financial advisor through the National Ethics Association and has been named a Five Star Best in Client Satisfaction Wealth Manager three years in a row in the *St. Louis Magazine*. This is an honor less than seven percent of all the wealth managers in his area have achieved.

CHAPTER 33

DO THE MATH...WHEN IS $1,000,000 WORTH MORE THAN $4,000,000?

BY BRADFORD D. CREGER

Let's start by asking a simple question. What do you know about investing for retirement? Most people know only what they have heard reported by the financial media and religiously repeated by their CPA and/or stockbroker. We have been brainwashed to think that our ONLY investment option for retirement is "putting our money at risk" in traditional Wall Street investments inside a tax-deferred retirement plan.

The next question I'd like to ask is, "Does the perfect retirement investment exist, and if it does, what would it look like?" Most people I have asked this have said it would include the following characteristics:

1. Market-like returns with no risk of loss of your money. Said differently, you want the upside of the markets with none of the downside.

2. Liquidity, control and access. You want to have the money set aside. But you also want to be able to get to it when and if you need it without penalties.

3. Tax advantages. You don't want to pay any tax on the growth of your investment and you don't want to pay tax on the income generated by it. And of course, if possible, you'd like a tax benefit when funding it.

Does this investment actually exist?

You would be hard pressed to find it on Wall Street. Your broker can help you make the standard retirement investment in stocks, bonds and/or mutual funds. But in doing so, you're being asked to risk 100% of your money to achieve a target return of 7-8%. Later, when you begin to withdraw your money during retirement, you'll be limited to the 4% safe withdrawal rate and you'll be paying income taxes on every dollar you receive.

What could you do differently? One option to consider, which offers all of the advantages described above, is Equity Index Universal Life insurance or EIUL. That's right. I am actually saying that life insurance may be the perfect retirement investment. But don't take my word for it. Let's examine the reasons why many Americans are increasingly turning to EIUL to fund for their retirement as well as education for their kids and grandkids.

Let me show you the math and how $1,000,000 in an EIUL can be worth more than $4,000,000 in a traditional Wall Street invested retirement account!

Let's first examine having your money invested in stocks, bonds or mutual funds. You get the ups and downs of the Wall Street rollercoaster with no performance guarantees. Their argument is that, over time, your account will grow more because the average growth rate on these investments is greater than your other options. This might be true. The average return might be higher, but is that what really matters? Wall Street will tell you that it does…

Let's first understand how using average returns when comparing an investment might be misleading. If I could guarantee an investment that would deliver an average return of 25% for 2 years… would you invest your money? Everyone I've ever asked tells me they'd absolutely make this investment. But is this a good investment?

To answer this you have to look at the returns that actually matter. If you put $100,000 into an investment and in the first year you gain 100%, you doubled your money. But what if during the second year the investment lost 50% of its value? By Wall Street standards this is a 2-year average rate of return of 25%. You still have your original $100,000, but you haven't gained a penny and therefore your real rate of return (or RRR^{TM}) is zero. As you can see what really matters is NOT average returns but rather the RRR^{TM}. Your "real rate of return" or RRR^{TM} is what translates into how much money is in your pocket.

How does volatility affect rates of return? With increased volatility your *RRR*™ will be increasingly lower than your average rate of return. In other words... eliminating volatility will yield better investment results over time.

What are you really looking for in an investment? You want high average annual rates of return with little or no volatility. What does "little or no volatility" mean in English? You want to avoid negative returns. Avoiding negative returns will not only improve your average return but it will dramatically increase your *RRR*™ thereby putting a lot more money into your pocket – and correct me if I'm wrong . . . isn't that every investor's ultimate goal? With EIUL, your investment can only go up in value or remain flat – you are guaranteed not to lose money. Yes, you read that correctly – you get the upside of the markets with no risk of losing money.

Wall Street will not tell you this story. Rather, they'll turn your attention away from volatility and focus on their higher average rates of return. With EIUL, you <u>might</u> have a lower average rate of return but by eliminating volatility you can actually outperform traditional Wall Street investments where it actually counts – your account values.

Now that we know a little about *RRR*™ and market volatility, let's discuss safe withdrawal rates. Many have heard that the safe withdrawal rate for "naked money" (i.e., an investment with no performance guarantees), is only 4%, but most do not know why it is only 4%.

In a nutshell, the safe withdrawal rate is limited to 4% primarily due to market volatility. When you lower expected volatility – you can increase your safe withdrawal rate. The problem... you can't lower the expected volatility to near zero and still get the upside of the markets without using EIUL. To lower volatility one must both keep the expected annual earnings as consistent as possible and above all, avoid negative returns. If you invest in the financial markets you will always be subject to the risk of loss. When using EIUL – you cannot have a negative return based on market performance. You get either the gains of the market (up to a "cap rate") or a zero. How is this done, you ask? You are not actually invested directly in the financial markets but rather in options on an index (like the S&P 500). When the index return for the year is positive, your index option is "in the money" and you get the gains – when the index return for the year is negative you receive nothing on that option. By using index options you can capture the upside of the markets with no downside risk. What is a cap rate you ask? A "cap rate" is an upper limit on the return that is available on the index option. You may be wondering why there is a cap rate on an EIUL index option. The simple answer is that it decreases volatility. The detailed answer is that it relates to pricing and the transfer of risk.

What kind of returns can you expect on these index options? Most EIUL policies offer a year-to-year index option with a 0% floor and an annual cap rate of around 12%. Simply put, the 0% floor ensures you will not lose any of your investment to market volatility. If the markets go up, you win. If the markets go down, you don't lose. Because EIUL can eliminate market losses, you can increase the safe withdrawal rate up to near 10% (or more in some circumstances.)

With $4,000,000 in your retirement account and a safe withdrawal rate of 4%... you can withdraw $160,000 each year. Let's not forget that this $160,000 is subject to income taxes. If we use a tax rate of 40%, this leaves you with only $96,000 to spend.

Let's compare that to $1,000,000 in your EIUL with a 10% safe withdrawal rate which delivers $100,000 in spendable income. But wait... isn't there income taxes on this withdrawal? The answer is NO! You can access your money in EIUL without paying income taxes. Additionally, the money coming from your life insurance will not subject your social security income to taxation. This cannot be said of distributions from your pre-tax retirement account which can cause up to 85% of your social security income to be taxed.

EIUL allows one to get the upside of the markets with no possibility of losing money to market declines. Your safe withdrawal rate is significantly higher than your typical "at risk" retirement investments and there are no income taxes paid on the money coming out. With these significant tax and investment advantages why on earth is anyone still investing the majority of their retirement assets with Wall Street in a pre-tax retirement account? My guess... a misunderstanding of how the numbers actually work? Wall Street has been great at changing our perceptions about the long term consequences of market losses. Wall

Street calls a loss of 10% or more a "correction." They tell us the values were too high – and a "correction" is good. Really? I think that's just a loss of 1/10th of your money.

Remember, when you lose money your *RRR*™ goes down. You first have to make up lost ground before you can start growing your retirement account again. Wall Street would have you think that their outsized annual returns will make up for these losses... but do they? Let's look at some numbers...

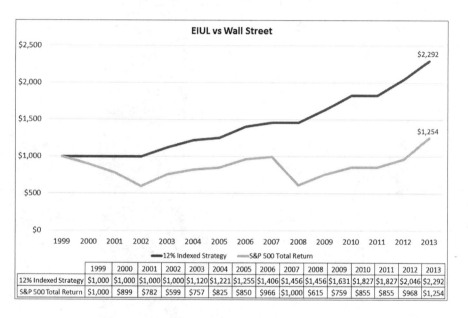

	1999	2000	2001	2002	2003	2004	2005	2006	2007	2008	2009	2010	2011	2012	2013
12% Indexed Strategy	$1,000	$1,000	$1,000	$1,000	$1,120	$1,221	$1,255	$1,406	$1,456	$1,456	$1,631	$1,827	$1,827	$2,046	$2,292
S&P 500 Total Return	$1,000	$899	$782	$599	$757	$825	$850	$966	$1,000	$615	$759	$855	$855	$968	$1,254

Figure 1: December 31, 1999 to December 31, 2013, 1-year point-to-point measurement, 12% growth cap rate and 0% floor (minimum crediting rate) for the indexed strategy vs S&P 500 index. Source: Wikipedia, December 2014.

Figure 1 shows the difference between an indexed strategy and the S&P 500 index. In this example, $1,000 was invested on December 31, 1999. Over this 15 year period you would have made $254 in the S&P 500 index where you would have made $1,292 in EIUL – all with no risk to your money. How is this possible? When the markets are negative the index strategy holds its value – and when the markets begin moving upward again, the EIUL does not need to play "catch up." This is incredibly powerful.

Did I cherry pick a time frame to make this look good? Let's look at the last 20 years instead.

Year	S&P 500	$100,000	EIUL Index	$100,000
1993	7.06%	$107,060	7.06%	$107,060
1994	-1.54%	$105,411		$107,060
1995	34.11%	$141,367		$119,907
1996	20.26%	$170,008		$134,296
1997	31.01%	$222,728		$150,412
1998	26.67%	$282,129		$168,461
1999	19.53%	$337,229		$188,676
2000	-10.14%	$303,034		$188,676
2001	-13.04%	$263,518		$188,676
2002	-23.37%	$201,934		$188,676
2003	26.38%	$255,204		$211,317
2004	8.99%	$278,147		$230,315
2005	3.00%	$286,491		$237,224
2006	13.62%	$325,512		$265,691
2007	3.55%	$337,067		$275,123
2008	-38.47%	$207,397		$275,123
2009	23.49%	$256,115		$308,138
2010	12.64%	$288,488		$345,115
2011	0.00%	$288,488		$345,115
2012	13.29%	$326,828		$386,528
2013	29.60%	$423,569	12.00%	$432,912
Average:	9.33%		7.73%	

Flat Growth:	9.33%	$595,370	7.73%	$443,336

Figure 2: Annual returns for the S&P 500 index. Source: Wikipedia, December 2014.

Figure 2 compares $100,000 invested in the S&P 500 index versus a 1-year point-to-point 0% floor, 12% capped S&P 500 index crediting method over a 20-year period. The first two columns show $100,000 invested in the S&P 500 index. The next two columns show the EIUL index crediting method.

At first glance you might believe that these numbers show that Wall Street is where you should be investing. Just look at the <u>average</u> rate of return and compare 9.33% in the markets versus 7.73% in EIUL. Wall Street wins, right? But remember it's the *RRR*™ that counts and compare $423,569 versus $432,912 in EIUL. These ending values are almost the same. If you can get to nearly the same place with no risk using EIUL, why take the risk with Wall Street?

What's even more important is the predictability of the ending values. Because your investment isn't subject to market losses, EIUL gives you the ability to better predict the approximate size of your retirement nest egg.

If you project the S&P 500 annual averages out as a flat rate – you might expect your ending account value to be $595,370. In reality you ended up with only $423,569 – which is nearly 30% less than expected. If we compare this with the expected and actual results of EIUL… there is only a 2.4% difference. I ask, which investment makes retirement planning more predictable? Are you comfortable gambling with your future investing in the Wall Street rollercoaster or does it make more sense to eliminate risk yet still get market-like returns using EIUL?

How about liquidity, access and control? Did you know that you can get money out of your EIUL at any age for any reason without paying taxes or early-withdrawal penalties? Can you borrow money out of your retirement accounts? Some you can, some you can't – but when you can, there are strict rules and limitations on the amounts. Did you know that Disneyland, McDonald's, J.C. Penny, Foster Farms and The Pampered Chef were originally built by borrowing the cash values from their founder's life insurance contracts?

How about the tax advantages of life insurance? Another reason to consider EIUL is that from a tax perspective, it has the same tax advantages as the Roth IRA. You pay tax on your investment up front and then you will not pay any more taxes on the money coming out during retirement. The biggest difference? You can put as much money as you want into EIUL and there are no income limitations – anyone can fund EIUL and get the same tax benefits (provided they can qualify for the insurance.)

It's even better for some business owners who can fund EIUL with dollars that are only 60% taxed up front. In other words, about 40% of the money going into an EIUL is never taxed. This retirement planning opportunity is a Section 79 plan and it is the most tax-advantaged way to save for retirement.

I ask you… when is $1,000,000 worth more than $4,000,000?

With EIUL you pay nothing in tax when you make a withdrawal and, because you cannot lose money in the markets, the safe withdrawal rate is about 10%. If you had $1,000,000 in your EIUL, you can withdraw about $100,000 a year throughout most of your retirement. Because there are zero income taxes due, you get to spend the entire $100,000. Remember, on the $4,000,000 in a traditional retirement account we netted only $96,000 after taxes…

It seems clear to me that $1,000,000 in an EIUL is worth more to you during retirement than $4,000,000 in a traditional retirement account.

When you consider that $1,000,000 is much easier to save than $4,000,000… you will not have to set aside nearly as much to have a comfortable retirement. While a regular retirement account may offer the immediate gratification of a tax deduction, the only math that matters (i.e., your after-tax spendable income during retirement), shows us that it just isn't as wise of a retirement investment as EIUL.

About Brad

Bradford D. Creger is passionate about his work - he does this because he never wants anyone to go through what his parents did. Brad's father was diagnosed with Parkinson's in his late forties and he was forced to retire at 51. Although his father was an investment advisor, they didn't have their financial or estate planning done correctly and his mom lost everything caring for his dad. Because his father focused solely on investments, he did not have the right disability insurance or any life insurance. Their estate attorney didn't insist on anything other than a simple will and the result was disastrous when his dad was disabled. Their accountant didn't pay attention to his mom's business, and instead of selling and living off the proceeds, her business bled dry. This was a very tough life lesson for Brad, and he was committed when he became a financial advisor that he would not only focus on the things he could be paid on, but his client's entire financial picture.

Brad first acts as a financial architect, and does a comprehensive wealth management assessment and then a complete written plan. He then acts as a general contractor and coordinates the services of other experts and professionals such as the client's CPA, attorney, TPA, banker, etc. He also will assist when it comes to the insurance and investment needs of his clients.

Early in his career Brad took a comprehensive look at his brother's finances, so that there would not be another financial tragedy in his family. Among other things, he made sure that his brother had proper disability insurance, and eight months later his brother was disabled. Because he had the right policy, his brother has been receiving payments for the past 19 years, and will continue to draw on it for 15 more.

Brad is currently the President/CEO of Total Financial Resource Group, Inc. (TFRG), an independent diversified financial services firm with their main offices located in Pasadena, CA. Brad began his financial services career with Cigna Financial Advisors in 1993. During his first three years, through Cigna, he clocked over 2000 classroom training hours which was 20 times more than the industry standard.

Brad has delivered estate and business succession planning services through numerous investment brokers at PaineWebber, AG Edwards, Morgan Stanley, Dean Witter, Prudential and Crowell Weedon for their Southern California VIP clients, and has created a body of estate planning law known as Contingent Ascertainable Standard Language (aka – Springing Special Needs Provisions).

Brad has been featured in *Forbes, Financial Planning Magazine* and *Pasadena Magazine* and has been seen on ABC, CBS, NBC and Fox affiliates as well as *The Wall Street Journal's* Marketwatch.com, CNBC.com, Morningstar.com, Moneywatch.com, Yahoofinance.com, TheBostonGlobe.com and TheMiamiHerald.com.

Brad obtained a BA in Economics from UCLA and has the designations of:

AAMS®, Accredited Asset Management Specialist

AIFA®, Accredited Investment Fiduciary Analyst™

CFS®, Certified Fund Specialist®

CLTC, Certified in Long-Term Care

Brad is a Registered Principal with First Allied Securities, Inc., a registered broker/dealer (Member FINRA/SIPC) and an Investment Advisory Rep for First Allied Advisory Services, Inc., a Registered Investment Advisor. CA Insurance License # 0B22199.

bdcreger@tfrgroup.com
626-795-9600
800-984-TFRG
www.tfrgroup.com
www.taxednever.com

CHAPTER 34

THE POWER OF GIVING BACK

BY DR. VINCENT J. MONTICCIOLO, DDS, MBA, JD

Using our talents and opportunities to help others is essential to a fulfilling life. In dental school I was only focused on mastering the art of treating patients, but when I started practicing, it lead to a huge question. How can I make a positive difference in my community? Combined with my career and my desire, I came up with the answer. I decided I could use my dentistry skills and my practice to help those in need of dental care in Port Huron, Michigan, the location of my first dental practice. The first step to accomplish this task was to choose the date. The best date I noticed on my calendar was the day after our ultimate day of thanks— Thanksgiving. Giving someone the gift of a more confident smile was the best way to start the season of appreciation. Although I might be biased, as a dentist, I believe that our smiles are a reflection of our souls, every bit as much as our eyes.

THE CALL TO SOMETHING GREATER

In 1998, our family relocated to Florida, for an opportunity my wife, Dr. Natalie Monticciolo, had in her field of dermatology. Michigan then became a place to visit. Every year we would travel back to Michigan to visit family and friends. On those trips, we would talk about what we were doing to help those in need and this lead to a desire to do more. Both of us agreed that BIGGER would be BETTER. Once we became established in Florida, we started contemplating how best to make it happen. We picked a new holiday to hold our event on. It was Valentine's Day and I coined the name, *Dentistry from the Heart*, for my event. We held our first event with the help of my staff and one other dentist who volunteered. On that wonderful day we saw almost 200 patients. And this event hasn't stopped growing since!

A TRIPLE WIN

Going bigger and better has helped us realize the triple win we receive from good deeds. It is an amazing feeling that stems from the awareness that ideas which are powered by a genuine desire to help others can evolve all on their own. Initially, we didn't advertise in the media; it was word of mouth through churches and centers that helped people who could not afford their own dental care. During those days, I became the face behind *Dentistry from the Heart*, but without amazing volunteers, none of it could have come together. The result has been a triple win!

- **Communities win:** Helping people who live in our communities receive the basic dental care that they need (extractions, fillings, and cleanings) creates an instant awareness of how much it means to others. The needy we help are grateful. We are equally thankful for the opportunity to help them, too. At these events, the energy is so positive and appealing. Reaching out to those in need feels amazing and inspires others to pay it forward.

- **Patients win:** Nothing makes us feel better than when we get feedback from our patients, telling us how proud they feel that we are their dental care provider. Our patients are a part of the community in which we do business. That makes them a wonderful outlet for helping us remain connected to the public in a positive manner.

- **Our dental office wins:** This was the most surprising win of the concept. I hadn't really thought of it directly, but realizing that my practice wins when we reach out to the community has given me a great platform to spread the message about what we've been doing. The ultimate compliment I receive is from new patients. They mention that they saw our event on T.V. and were so moved by the charity. They knew that we needed to be their new dental office. The adage of "no good deed goes unrewarded" is definitely applicable.

This event is now an annual one. It has never been promoted through paid advertising. To do this, I had to get creative. Over the years, I was invited to lecture on practice management at dental conventions across the country. I always took some time to mention *Dentistry from the Heart* at these events. Dentists were interested, eager for more information, and willing to host these events in their own neighborhoods. Our first milestone was when we grew to the point where we were holding nearly 50 events per year.

TAKING IT FURTHER

We needed to keep the spirit of our mission aligned with our passion. The numbers dictated the need to hire more staff and streamline the systems. In order to do that, we became a 501(c) charity in 2006. It was the only way to effectively keep up with the demand and desire to have more *Dentistry from the Heart* events. There were a few things we wanted to ensure when communities were hosting an event.

1. **Events had the same feel.** We wanted the experience and process to be consistent. This was done through developing a strategic plan on how to prepare for the event, and making the day of the event as smooth and seamless as possible.

2. **The charity wouldn't be vulnerable to legal risk.** Since this is dental care, we needed to make sure things were being done consistently and within local and national dental regulatory laws. Our events are for providing dental needs that help deliver smiles! We do this through a lot of prep work for quality dental care, in a healthcare environment. This is easy for a regular day at the office and considerably more complex for a day that will be busier than anything most of us have experienced.

3. **Bookkeeping and record keeping of events.** In order to keep our 501(c) status, it is necessary to keep accurate records for all the *Dentistry from the Heart* events. Anyone who has worked with a charity understands the importance. This is achieved by having a follow-up with the participating dental offices afterward, so we can get all of the necessary data to keep our records in order.

4. **Their event wouldn't overlap with others in their market or area.** Months of planning goes into a *Dentistry from the Heart* event and we are grateful for everyone who commits to holding one. Therefore, we guarantee their event date for a 3-month exclusive period in their area. This way, the media attention is focused on the event and gets the press it deserves. Communities are also able to organize, plan, and prepare for the big day.

With our four criteria in mind, we created a marketing package for dental offices that wish to host an event. These are helpful because they contain the following: press releases, commercials, billboards, banners, t-shirts, donated dental products, and detailed instructions on how to take the event from idea to completion. This is organized through *Dentistry from the Heart*. We work to train the volunteers on what needs to be done. It has proven itself to be highly effective and the results show there are now over 250 annual *Dentistry from the Heart* events in 50 states and 5 different countries. Our marketing packages are available in English or Spanish to accommodate all our different markets. More languages will come as we continue to grow.

BIG EVENTS — BIG ORGANIZATION NEEDED

To give perspective, our local event in New Port Richey draws at least 500 people who are standing in line from the night before, ready to receive their free dental care. A plan has to be in place and the planning starts months before the day of the event. It may sound chaotic, but it is also FUN!

To host an event you need:

- **Staff:** Staff and volunteers are essential. Various dentists, hygienists, assistants, and other dental personnel from neighboring practices also volunteer, along with my office team. Dental assisting school students get credit hours for the work they do, another winning element. The volunteer staff also prepares the paperwork for the registration of patients, manages patient flow, and prepares sample bags for the needy.

  Smile Faith Foundation is a great charity that helps us with providing assistance and organization. They are focused on people who are down on their luck, and help to provide personal and career counseling, as well as access to dental care. What better way to find a job than with a confident smile on your face? During the event, they hand out coffee and hot chocolate to those in line awaiting their free dental care. They have been an integral part toward keeping our event festive.

News crews televise throughout the night as additional patients continue to arrive. The staff arrives at the site at 4:00 a.m. We open our doors at 7:00 a.m. and continue until everyone has been seen. There is a one hour lunch break in which the volunteers get a great meal from food donated by local restaurants.. Plus, this is the perfect time to take a photograph of everyone who has played a part in bringing the *Dentistry from the Heart* event to fruition. Many additional photos, videos, Facebook updates, and tweets are uploaded to remind us of the amazing experience that everyone has encountered. All can be viewed via: www.dentistryfromtheheart. org and associated links.

- **Dental Offices:** Over the years, we have come across different weather conditions. We have now incorporated tents, porta-potties, and heater systems, when necessary. Systems are also in place to ensure that dental operatories are constantly turned over for maximum efficiency. One staff person assists the dentist and another cleans and sterilizes the room for the next patient.

- **Process:** The events are first come, first served to any patient in need. Our registration staff distributes patient intake and medical history forms. Upon completion, a number is given to each patient to keep the order and to ensure their spot in line.

This past year, our individual event helped more than 500 people and over 600 teeth were extracted. This was achieved with the help of 16 dentists and 100 volunteers. Without them, these events would not be possible. The desire to give back to their communities keeps the charity growing. It's the reason *Dentistry from the Heart* has become an annual affair that the entire community gets excited for and thus, wants to help!

BEYOND THE DENTAL WORK

How do we keep the patients happy and energized when they are waiting their turn? That's a question that many of you may be wondering. We've come up with some great ways to keep this as enjoyable as it is necessary for those who can't afford dental care. Some of the favorite ideas that are incorporated into our events are:

- Massage therapy from students at local massage schools
- Music and DJs to keep people dancing and laughing
- A tooth fairy is present, bringing laughter and lots of lively conversation
- Free skin cancer screening, which my wife provides, along with a sample bag that contains soaps, toothbrush, toothpaste, a t-shirt, and sunscreen
- Blood donation is always something that is important. At our event, those that donate blood get priority in line. This gives patients an opportunity to give back to their communities on the day they are receiving needed dental care.

THE VISION KEEPS GROWING

Today, *Dentistry from the Heart* has a full-time staff that works diligently on the coordination and organization of all our events, which are global! A few of the things they do in a given day are:

- Answer calls from people who are in need of dental care. They direct them to the event nearest to them.
- Organize and coordinate all the marketing packets. Each event has unique marketing and has to be customized to the event, including logos of sponsors and contacting the various media outlets about the event for press releases and publicity.
- Follow-up after the event with the dental offices for bookkeeping, as well as ideas on how to further finesse and grow the event. Each event allows us the chance to continue to improve.

As the charity continues to grow, I have increased my time and support. I love being actively involved in this concept that started so small and grew so big. For the most part, all funds that I contribute and donations that are given by the community and office go toward running the charity. This is the driving force behind our tag line, which is: **Smile. It's free.**

A CALL TO ACTION

When I decided to hold the first Florida event back in 2001, I never imagined that it would grow to reach every state, as well as Puerto Rico, Canada (which holds an average of 15 events per year), New Zealand, United Kingdom, and Ireland. To date, *Dentistry from the Heart* has provided more than 15 million dollars in free dental care. Nothing is more humbling to me, my family, and my staff, then seeing dentists willing to volunteer their time which allows *Dentistry from the Heart* to flourish.

The true **Power of Giving Back** is something to make you smile!

About Dr. Vince

With a passion for learning that is equal to his passion for helping others, Dr. Vincent Monticciolo has created a life where his skills and purpose are combined. Graduating from the University of Detroit School of Dentistry, Dr. Monticciolo received many awards and was selected to the Honors Clinical Program. In 2001, he earned his Masters Degree in Business Administration. Also, in 2013, he earned his Law Degree, all while practicing dentistry full-time and taking various continuing education courses.

In addition to his family and sedation dentistry practice, Dr. Monticciolo has been driven by opportunities to lead through example, which were first shown in his days as a part-time faculty member at the dental school he'd once attended. Over time, his drive grew into leadership and a commitment to serve his community, and it was there that everything really fell into place for him.

As inspiration to help struggling individuals who could not afford dental care took shape, Dr. Monticciolo found a way to improve the community he lived in by offering free dental care to a few needy individuals. It was an incredible experience and Dr. Monticciolo, along with his wife, Dr. Natalie Monticciolo, began to think of how they could take this simple concept and make it grow into something larger. After relocating to the Tampa, Florida area, *Dentistry from the Heart* was formed in 2001. It has become synonymous with Dr. Monticciolo's energy and efforts to embrace giving back. Since then, Dentistry from the Heart has become a charity that helps coordinate over 250 events in all 50 states, as well as internationally.

Furthermore, in 2012, Dr. Monticciolo started Dental Care Delivered, a mobile dental service that provides care to residents in assisted living facilities and nursing homes around the west coast of Florida. It is another step to ensuring that more people can have the smile they deserve, regardless of their circumstances.

Today, Dr. Monticciolo lives with his wife and two daughters in Palm Harbor, Florida. Aside from his charity work, he enjoys spending quality time with his family and practicing dentistry. Seeing how his daughters beam with pride when his *Dentistry from the Heart* event makes the news every year, featuring him, the founder and spokesperson of this charity, is a great reminder of the impact he has on those less fortunate.

Honors and Awards

- Honors graduate at dental school

- Academy of General Dentistry Outstanding Student Award
- Comprehensive Dentistry Award
- Frances B. Vedder Society Crown and Bridge Prosthodontics Award
- Omicron Kappa Upsilon (National Dental Honor Society)
- Alpha Sigma Nu (National Jesuit Honor Society)
- Class President in Dental School

Memberships and Societies

- American Dental Society
- Florida Dental Society
- West Pasco Dental Society
- American Society of Dental Anesthesiology
- Society for Special Care Dentistry
- Academy of Dentistry for Persons with Disabilities
- American Society for Geriatric Dentistry
- Florida HealthCare Association

Contact information
You can reach Dr. Monticciolo at:
www.dentistryfromtheheart.org
www.happydentistry.com
www.dentalcaredelivered.com
vmonti@happydentistry.com

CHAPTER 35

HOW TO BE
SUPER AMAZING!

BY DIEGO NICHOLAS

What is success?

The notion of success is different for everyone.

- For some it may mean landing a dream job or having enough disposable income to travel the world.
- For others it might mean just being able to buy a house…any house.
- It might mean having a job that pays your bills after years of struggling to make ends meet.

No matter how we define it, everyone has dreams about finding success.

The problem is that most of us don't know where to look for the how-to instructions to be successful. I used to feel that people got lucky or were gifted with better skills than me, until I realized that I could be just as successful as the most successful people out there! I just needed to learn how, believe it was possible and to work toward being successful (or as I like to think of it, work toward becoming *Super Amazing*).

I didn't have the best start in life. I grew up in Casper, Wyoming with my mom. My parents divorced when I was small and my dad was out of the picture for most of my life. I have two half-brothers who lived primarily with their biological father. This meant that much of the time, my household consisted of my mom and me. I will admit that if it was not for her, I would not be where I am today. Also my Grandparents were like my parents when my parents were not around, and I definitely owe them a debt of gratitude also!

I have great respect for my mom. She worked so hard but she still struggled to fulfill our basic needs. I can remember getting food given to us. To get other things I wanted, I did school contests with door-to-door sales and did a lot of bartering with friends. It was especially tough for my mom to raise me without a father-figure around. To be honest, I wasn't always the easiest kid in the world and we struggled to get along. I was constantly in and out of trouble. When I was fifteen years old, she didn't know what else to do with me, so she kicked me out. I was on my own.

Shortly after leaving my mother's house, I was living on my own. I had a job and I went to high school. It didn't take long, with the daily grind of school and working as a cold calling telemarketer, for me to decide that maybe things would be easier if I just dropped out and focused on what was important – earning a living. So, I dropped out of high school.

About that time, I traveled to New Mexico to live with my long-absent father. He was an Army Vet and meant well but was more like a drill sergeant than an easy-going father. I was only able to stay at his house a few months before I moved out. Once again, on my own, I found a place to live and worked, all while being back in high school. He did pass away a few years ago and is missed despite the past, and he was loved dearly. Never forget to tell your friends and family you love them because you never know when it is their time.

By the time I graduated from high school, I'd already committed myself to join the Navy and I shipped out to boot camp. I was looking forward to an adventure and to being of service to my country and then our country experienced the 9/11 attacks. The world was relatively peaceful. Things changed quickly after the attacks and my job was now to prepare for the possibility of war which was eventually known as Operation Enduring Freedom.

The Navy was the hardest job I ever had and was not my favorite time in life, but it did show me how to work insanely hard with little or no sleep. The great thing about the Navy was that I got to see many different countries around the world. I loved experiencing the new cultures, learning more about the world, other languages, and meeting many new people. I went to Japan, Australia, East Timor, Dubai, South Korea, Thailand, Philippines, Guam, Singapore and a few other amazing places along the way. I will forever be grateful for my experience in the Navy that gave me those opportunities and disciplines.

After 4 years in the Navy, I went to college at the University of New Mexico and studied management information systems. I started to find mentors in the things I was reading. I started learning from and looking up to successful men like Brian Tracy, Darren Hardy, Zig Ziglar, Tony Robbins, and Jim Rohn. Today I consider Brian Tracy and Darren Hardy to be the biggest influences in my life and my favorite mentors in the world. From these men, I learned that to be successful I need to focus on my personal development.

After College, I worked selling cars for a few years. I realized how fulfilling it was working with and helping people with their goals in life. Next I found my way into a job working with the Boys and Girls Club of Central Wyoming. The job was incredibly fulfilling and I loved helping out and teaching the kids. I felt that way especially because so many of them reminded me of myself when I was a child, and it was really such a positive place to be. It was definitely a highlight of my life. Unfortunately, they couldn't pay very much for wages.

I knew things needed to change about the time I decided that I wanted to start settling into adulthood and buy a house. When I started the process, I was told that my salary simply wasn't large enough to afford a house and that my credit was too low. Never one to back down from a challenge, I took on a second job. I worked really hard to make money, but I felt like I was always tired and still had no money.

My real estate expert and now one of my mentors and best friends in life, was a woman named Michele Trost-Hall. At one point, she and I sat down and had a conversation about my goals and what I wanted to do with my life. At the end of that conversation, she offered me a job selling real estate with her. This was the break I'd been waiting for and a fantastic match for my skills!

Since that conversation with Michele in 2010, I've been selling real estate and sold 55 properties in 2013, thanks to her amazing training and mentorship! Fortunately for me, she is one of the top real estate agents in the nation! I am so appreciative of the opportunity she gave me and where this career has taken me so far. Because she was so generous with me, I want to pay it forward and pass on what I've learned on my wild journey here with the hope that it might help someone like me find success! If I can do it by 32 years of age, I know it is possible for anyone at any age if only they have the right knowledge!

My goal in life is to help as many people as I can become *Super Amazing* themselves – as fast as possible – and without having to go through as many hardships as I did. If you're someone who had a rocky start but wants to find financial security and make six figures or more or at least change your life for the best, here are the top seven steps to help you meet those goals:

1. **Look for people in the world who are where you want to be and learn from them.** You might know these people or have them in your community. Reach out to them. They say you will be the average of the five people you hang out with or learn from the most – so choose wisely. If there isn't anyone nearby, think big! What successful business people do you know of in the world? Take some time to search the Internet for successful people in the field you want to be successful in. Websites like YouTube often have a wide variety of free videos from motivational speakers to success mentors and coaches. Focus on the people who have the life you would like to live! Learn from other peoples mistakes and copy the successful habits that they exhibit to get where they are.

2. **Seek out learning opportunities.** If there are conferences and seminars in your area, go to them. Look for the chance to hear the people you look up to speak live and in person. Read as much as you can on the topics that are important to your personal development (at least 30-60 minutes per day). Listen to audio books while you're driving or exercising.

3. **Get a coach...or a mentor!** Look for coaches, mentors and people in your life who will want to mentor you on toward success. The most successful people in the world have the best coaches, so get a coach whose expertise is in the field that you want to dominate. Find mentors who are successful at whatever your passion is and learn how they got there and do what they did. And if all else fails, be your own coach. Take time for self-reflection and make changes

where and when needed. The best athletes track everything and adjust to get better and you should too!

4. **Delegate.** There are many tasks we do every day and every week that would be better delegated or hired out. Stop and ask yourself what your time is worth and then decide what you can have someone else do. An easy calculation is to take whatever you make a year and divide it by 2000. This is your value per hour. If you do not like to do it, or it takes you longer than it might someone else, delegate it. Ask yourself if it worth your time to run errands and do the grocery shopping or is that something you should be paying someone else to do for you? Let's say you make $25 an hour and can pay someone $10 an hour to do something for you, you are saving $15 an hour having someone else do it for you! Make sense? Your time is valuable and it should be spent doing the things that are valuable to you. Don't skip spending time with your family, making time to read and learn, or time to relax and energize yourself for your career.

5. **Stop watching TV and reading news altogether and manage your time.** Television is a huge waste of your time and does not help you become more successful. The majority of the things reported on by major news outlets are negative. Don't feed your mind with negativity because it will become a drain on your energy. If you must watch some then at least less than an hour a day or even better less than an hour a week. Time management is the best way to get the most done in the least amount of time! Get Google calendars or something similar and you have your schedule in the cloud anywhere you have your smart phone, tablet or computer. Have no white space in your schedule so you are using your time wisely and not wasting any. Time is the most valuable resource in life because you cannot buy more of it. The more you discipline yourself with your time management, the more you get done in less time – which will increase your income. Then eventually you will have enough money to trade it for more time by paying people to do simple things you used to have to do. This will give you more free time to spend with family or do the things you love doing!

6. **Feed your mind with positive things as often as you can.** Consider the use of affirmations to remind yourself that you are capable of being *Super Amazing*. I write in a gratitude journal each

night. I add three things that I'm grateful for to the journal just before I go to bed. It soaks into my brain while I sleep and I wake up on a good note, refreshed and happy to greet the day. Gratitude helps you see the abundance you already have, so you can focus on helping others more and stay in a positive mindset. Set three yearly, quarterly, monthly, weekly and daily goals. Every day have three 45-90 minute time blocks on your daily schedule that will help you reach your weekly goals, and track and adjust to make sure your weekly goals are helping you reach your monthly goals, which in turn will help you reach your quarterly and yearly goals! Make great things that you do or that happen daily a habit – so you do them on autopilot.

7. **Most importantly is your health and wellness.** Your body is your vehicle through life, but you only get one. Think of it like a Lamborghini and you should only put the best fuel there is in it. The same goes with you. Eat as healthy as possible, drink lots of water and exercise a minimum of 30 minutes a day, four-plus days a week. Also, you need seven or more hours of sleep every night to stay at the top of your game throughout the day. Do these things and you should be healthy the majority of the time, have less sickness than most people experience, which in turn will make you happier and more successful.

These are the things I use in my own life and I truly believe they have helped me become *Super Amazing*. When I was a kid, I wished that someone along the way would have told me that I could be successful and helped show me the way. I wish they'd told me that a bad start in life doesn't have to mean a bad finish. Now I have plenty of money to travel and enjoy life. I don't have to cook, clean, shop, run errands, or do laundry! It is like a dream! I do what I love and love what I do!

That's why I'm making it a point to tell you that you can be *Super Amazing*. Start adopting successful habits and that will help you find success. Keep yourself motivated and constantly work to improve yourself physically and mentally. You can be *Super Amazing* and have success beyond your wildest imagination. You just have to believe it is possible and do the steps it takes to get the things you've always wanted. Do a few things to constantly improve yourself over a long enough time period (they say it takes 10,000 hours to master something) and success in life is *INEVITABLE!*

About Diego

Diego Nicholas helps people fulfill their lifelong dream of home ownership, and helps people become successful in life, financially-free and their own boss. Coming from an extremely poor family, he worked his way up to now making a six-figure income at only 32. At the young age of nine years old, Diego started his sales career selling magazines door-to-door. He was also on his own since he was 15 years old where he learned the world of telemarketing, cold-calling prospects, selling items from cell phones to credit cards or cable television for survival. After graduating High School, he went straight into the U.S. Navy Active Duty for four years and was shipped overseas where he fought in the War –Operation Enduring Freedom. When he got out of the military, he went to college at the University of New Mexico.

After college he moved back to his hometown Casper, WY and started selling cars. It was then that Diego realized his love for sales. Wanting to help the community, he worked for the Boys & Girls Clubs of Central Wyoming. Not being able to make enough money to even purchase a small home, and while working two jobs, he decided to become a real estate salesman. In three years, he climbed his way to the top of residential sales for the Michele Trost-Hall Real Estate Team and personally made 58 sales for 2014. Now Diego focuses most of his time selling referral-based real estate, and helps network marketers be successful as an Independent Usana sales associate. Diego also does personal success coaching, and coaching in multi-level marketing/network marketing. He is also the CEO of Diego Nicholas International – which is a worldwide personal success coaching company.

Diego went to the University of New Mexico and studied business information systems. He is an Expert Advisor with the National Association of Expert Advisors®, A Certified Home Selling Advisor, and Certified Home Buying Advisor, as well as a member of the National Association of Realtors®. He was also selected as one of America's PremierExperts™ in 2013. He was the President of the Young Professionals Network's Local Chapter, and Co-Chair for the YPN's State Chapter in 2013-2014. Diego has been featured on the front page of the *Casper Star-Tribune Newspaper*, as well as on NBC and ABC television affiliates speaking on buying and selling Real Estate in today's market numerous times. He is also currently on the steering committee for the Alumni and Friends Association for the Boys & Girls Clubs of Central Wyoming. He has done numerous radio interviews with his expertise in Real Estate. Diego was also coached by Tony Robbins Coaching. He is also coached by Kinder Reece Coaching for Real Estate. His top success mentors that have had the biggest affect on his success are Brian Tracy and Darren Hardy, Zig Ziglar, Michele Trost-Hall and Jay Kinder.

You can connect with Diego at:
DiegoNicholas@Gmail.com
www.HowToBeSuperAmazing.com
www.DiegoNicholas.com
www.TheDreamHomePro.com
www.twitter.com/DiegoNicholas
www.facebook.com/DiegoNicholasInternational

CHAPTER 36

HEALTH AND WELLBEING: THE ULTIMATE SECRET

BY WILL SHANNON

I want to share with you the ultimate secret. The simplest secret. Like most people, you suffer tiredness, exhaustion, fatigue, and overwhelm, right?

Well I'm not here to solve your emotional challenges – but I can tell you one thing, unequivocally:

Devoting a percentage of your time to ensuring that you are healthy is **<u>one of the most important decisions you'll ever make.</u>** And let me tell you succinctly, it impacts everything!

We cannot be complete without optimal health. So let me share the ultimate secret with you in the next few paragraphs.

My parents were both Naturopath's, and my father, in particular, was very well known for it, having done several hundred thousand consultations. Probably the busiest natural health practitioner in the history of our country of Australia. His passion for his career was obvious and, as a result, I became passionate about natural treatments for better health, as well. So let me distill the most complex natural health lessons into one master lesson. The biggest lesson that you need to realize is: **Your body must be free of its own waste.**

Your cells are bathed in something called lymphatic fluid. Don't know what that is? Don't worry. This is the soluble fluid that puts the nutrients into the cell and carries the waste away. What pumps it? Breathing.

But where does the lymph go once it cleans the cells, or rather where does the waste go once the cell excrements it's waste? Back into the blood. Then into the liver. Then into the gall bladder. Then into the top of the bowel.

So what is the ultimate secret? To keep the body free of its own waste you MUST find the exits. . . and there are only four:

1. The Bowel
2. The Kidneys
3. The Respiratory System and
4. The Skin.

We have been traditionally taught in natural medicine that a human being should have three bowel movements a day. Not just one, as previously indicated. What does this mean? You are thousands of bowel movements short over your life time. And where is this waste? STILL INSIDE YOU.

That's right. Still in your gall bladder. Your liver. Your blood. Your lymph. And your cells. So what do you do? You clean your bowels with plants. Clean the liver, gall bladder, blood and lymph. Learn to breathe correctly and minimize animal products. Your health, your freedom is your ultimate goal. And I intend to give you that gift now. So what do you think?

Go ahead, for 10 days give up animal products, including fish, ideally. Minimize grains. Focus on fruits and vegetables. Raw food. Mainly juices. What will happen? Your energy will explode.

Learn to breathe. Inhale through the mouth, and out through the nose. Hold it at the peak of the breath. Don't raise your shoulders while you breathe. Oxygen, water, and movement are the ultimate human resources for health. Even cancer grows in a low oxygen environment. We can thank Dr. Otto Warburg for discovering that in 1932. And his Nobel Prize was deserved.

So what can I tell you? Don't stop. Do something. Now. Learn to breathe. Don't raise your shoulders. Put your belly out. Have juices with vegetables, preferably leafy greens, and low sugar fruit such as lemon, lime, and grapefruit.

Go and get a bowel cleansing product with herbs. The future of your family depends on it. At Pinnacle Health Clinic, where I practice in Australia, thousands of people from all over the world get attended to every year. What do we practice? Without discrimination, people are taught how to breathe, how to stand, move, how to drink water. How to eat. We aim to repair the family. Give people the gift of LOVE. I believe it is one of the ultimate human needs.

This is the quick overview, but it comes from the heart, and is meant to give you more out of life. Now, let's talk about…

YOUR BOWEL – A DIRTY SUBJECT

Your colon is nearly thirty feet from one end to the other and most of us treat it like an entertainment area. We shove dead cows, pigs, kangaroos, or fried food into it, and we wonder why we wake up sick. The chemicals inside you will kill you eventually. Sure, George Burns lived to be 100, but he was the exception, not the rule.

This cell pool becomes like a dirty garbage bin. You're like a sewer. Your brain is cells. Eyeballs, you name it. An attractive woman or man – has learned to harness this inherent force to make herself/himself look healthier, cleaner, richer in oxygen, and hence more attractive. And obviously there is a life cycle to this.

The problems with enemas and colonics

The best way to clean the bowel is from top to bottom. Not from the bottom. Cleaning it from the bottom only cleans the large intestine, not the small intestine. The one way valve, the ileocecal valve between the small and large intestine, blocks upwards progress.

Take out toxins. Increase oxygen. Timeless principles never go out of fashion. The greats in our industry, and I mean the legends. Dr. John Christopher – the father of American herbalism; Dr. Richard Schulze – his main student; Dr. Bernard Jensen – the father of American Iridology; and, Eli Shannon – my father, all taught the importance of bowel care

– the root system in the body. . . the primary system in Iridology. Your clients' bodies must be free of their own cellular waste. These transport systems must be working.

I once saw an interview with Mr. Giorgio Armani. If you don't know who he is, he is the greatest fashion designer out of Italy – one of the most famous in history. They asked, "Mr. Armani, what is the secret to producing a quality garment year after year, decade after decade, and staying ahead of the trend?" He replied, "The secret is there is no trend. Timeless principles never go out of style. Timeless must be adapted to the environment. This is called trend. The study of context." A brilliant man.

God, nature, the ultimate force, whatever you want to call it, changes slowly over millions of years. Notwithstanding a radical change in evolution, humans and our planet will not need less oxygen or water anytime soon. And both these substances, oxygen and water, can be IMPRINTED or shaped. I am going to give you insight on how to imprint solid, liquid, or gas matter for your health. It will give you the edge over other people. People who don't understand movement through breathing.

Your conscious mind is one of the greatest forces in the universe. It's inherent power in conjunction with your subconscious, is much more powerful. Most of us are living an unconscious life we setup at a young age. We never consciously sat down and thought out our beliefs, values, response to stress, key decisions. Most people are living a life enslaved to who they were – years before. You and I are guilty of this at times.

Some of the most important substances for your body are healthy fats such as olive oil, liquids, and greens. Animal foods, red meat, and chicken are high in cholesterol and contain no fiber to push them along. They also contain chemicals, hormones, and other additives. It is the ultimate waste.

I encourage you to passionately search knowledge that will change your life. You must detox at least once per season. That is moving your bowel more than three times per day. Not just once. The ultimate advantage is to eat less. Use food, rather than it use you. Being at the mercy of food is being at the mercy of the one thing causing you more problems than anything. And the odds are stacked against you. Because God loved us, he created taste. Taste is problematic. It's this craving for diversity, emotions, that screws with us all.

Now you don't take into your body the ultimate nutrition, and fast moving food. You take in what tastes good. What tastes good? Chemicals. The natural chemicals in food give it taste, but artificial chemicals are added to food to trick your taste buds and affect you even more in some cases.

If you love your family, if you want to avoid doctors' visits, clean up your dinner plate. Teach your children. Convenience creates long-term consequences. Doing things the easy way is problematic. Begin with the end in mind. Tomorrow is never promised. But if you don't have a plan or rough guide for where you will be in 30 or 40 years your body will arrive – and you with it. NOW is the power to change. NOW is the moment you have to harness. I encourage you to seize it.

It's this ability to influence that has made me and my practice the envy of many. We succinctly hold your hand until you change. When you change, your family changes. And guess what? People do more for the people they love than they'll ever do for themselves. Your children are for you to train – not enslave.

There are many other tools we offer in our clinic such as protection against Electro Magnetic Fields (EMF's and other things). I could name over a dozen things that would explode your energy straight away. Dairy, sugar, wheat/white pastries are all foods natural therapists have traditionally thought of as poison. There are consequences of animal food. Hey, it can be scary. I understand too well.

Your health is not just your ultimate emotion. Your legacy will be what you do with now. I encourage you to make it. Charles Darwin is known for his work on human evolution. He is hated by creationists. Did you know that his main work was emotion? This is paraphrasing, but he said: emotion is in the muscles. That's right, the way you move, breathe, and your facial expression. You can radically change your emotion now just through your muscles in your face.

Moving, breathing, eliminating animal products and moving your face differently, how quick could you change your life? In a moment. A week of loving your family differently, and your whole life could be different. You have the ability to harness your life at any moment with a choice.

It's where your body, mind, spirit and language are aligned.

You know when you stop eating rubbish what you'll feel? Incredibly bored. You'll need some new passions. We use food as a drug to change the way we feel. We use it as a tool against our empty lives, maybe our empty peer group sometimes. We use it to cope with stress, as a tool to redirect our mind. We've had years of practice.

If you do nothing else, move, breathe, love, empty your bowels, move your face differently. Be conscious of how others breathe. I could spend the chapter discussing this, but this is a good start. Notice how their changing breathing patterns effects their moods. You can predict their emotional states just through respiration.

I encourage you to become one of the hundreds of thousands of people who have benefitted through our clinic, Pinnacle Health Clinic in Australia. We have qualified people who can get you off anything. But the choice is with you. Make each moment count. Remind the people you love that you love them, and show it every day. Treat strangers with care. You never know when you might be on the receiving end. Everyone is facing their own battle. Your upsets are disowned parts of yourself.

Smoking, drinking and drugs are three of the leading preventable causes of death in the world. As is your own thought process, and the way you move and use your physical body – your emotions and thoughts. The great thing is that God gave you control over all of them. What didn't he give you control over? Your environment – not always – which is why flexibility is important. You can't be all things to all people, but you can be most. Not everyone has multiple personalities, but it is true we all have multiple selves. We all have the ability. Movement is the ultimate gift. Your mind, body, emotions and so on.

You've been exposed to over 200,000 chemicals since World War II, and most haven't been tested. What is the takeaway from this chapter? Go home and tell your spouse you love them. You are changing. You are committing. You are choosing to live better. You want to eat better for one week, and see how it changes. You want to walk with them. You want to hear about their day. You want to be a better example. You want to be inspiration for change. You want to value life. You want to change.

The odds are stacked against you currently. According to the World Health Organization, 15% of the planet is infertile. They can't bear children. Humans are overloaded with hormones like never before in human history. We've become races of mutants. Mutating from the hormones coming out of our paints, and plastics, and knowingly into our food. Your meat is probably treated with carbon monoxide to make it look pink so you can't see its real color.

If you're a health care professional. STOP. Don't just flood your clients with nutrition. Eliminate toxicity too. Don't put further toxins into an unhealthy body. All change starts with healing the spirit. But this spirit is in physical form. We aren't just spirit, we are a physical body. They must be clean. Dr. Alexis Carrell found he could keep chicken embryo cells alive indefinitely by keeping them free of their own waste.

Your choices are infinite. Make your dreams and your goals come true.

About Will

Will Shannon is one of the world's leading authorities on natural medicine, the science of Iridology, Herbalism, and how to overcome incurable illness. He is the president of the Australian Complementary Medicine Association. His expertise has been called on by individuals from around the globe – having personally consulted tens of thousands of people from over 140 countries.

Will Shannon has served as an advisor to leaders from all walks of life, including global celebrities, actors, media and entertainment figures. In the sporting arena, he has advised national and international athletes. In the area of politics, his clients have included government departments and individuals, including current and former heads of state. He has also served as a consultant for the legal community.

Will Shannon is a second generation practitioner of natural medicine whose father Eli Shannon started the Pinnacle brand of health clinics, and products. He is the founder of BioMediK Companies, which offer health care, medical service, and education to individuals globally, including those who might not otherwise have access to medical care.

He is a recognized catalyst in personal and social change, and has been lauded for his training in understanding and protecting the access of medical care to minority groups. He is committed to change in social systems and is trained in the Eriksonian approaches, direct and indirect negotiation, brief and family therapy, conflict resolution, life cycle theory, the third side, and human-needs intervention. Having trained both Western and Natural Physicians worldwide, his innovative work in Iridiology, and teaching materials have been utilized by a variety of educational institutions around the world.

His work through the World Health Care Council has assisted people in the Second and Third World obtain access to life-saving care. The WHCC offers framework, guidelines and training programs for government and private sector for development and implementation of health care systems.

The clinic he heads, Pinnacle Health Clinic, offers treatment to all individuals regardless of race, origin, political or religious view, creed or any other circumstance and is based in Sydney, Australia.

You may contact Will Shannon at: 0404 891 784 if you are in Australia, or internationally at: +61 404 891 784.

His website is: www.willshannon.com.

CHAPTER 37

OPPORTUNITIES EXIST IN ALL ECONOMIES — SIX STEPS TO TAKE ADVANTAGE OF THEM

BY ROGER O. HUDSPETH

Nothing in this world can take the place of Persistence. Talent will not; nothing is more common than unsuccessful men with talent. Genius will not; unrewarded genius is almost a proverb. Education will not; the world is full of educated derelicts. Persistence and determination alone are omnipotent. The slogan 'Press On' has solved and always will solve the problems of the human race.
~ President Calvin Coolidge

'Press on' has been a touchstone phrase my entire adult life. I was first introduced to the phrase as a college freshman as I pledged Phi Gamma Delta. The Persistence quote was one we were encouraged to learn as President Coolidge was a Phi Gam as well. The quote resonated so strongly with me. I had witnessed it in action throughout my life. I had seen as a child the dogged determination of my mother, Diane, as she raised four boys, worked multiple jobs, all while pursuing her dream of owning her own business. It was her refusal for my brothers and I to never do without even though we were not wealthy, that has led to the success of all four of us. Three are entrepreneurs and the other is an executive for a Fortune 500 company.

She taught us that anything worth having is worth the effort you have to put into it. Without that effort, you will never appreciate what you have. And most importantly, if you want it badly enough you will find a way to get it. I realized that when you own a business, much like a parent, you don't get a day off. You must always be thinking of your next move. And unfortunately failure really isn't an option. For some reason the bank does not accept "I tried" as an answer when the mortgage is due each month.

This philosophy has been put to the test as my Partner, Daryl Bank and I have built and expanded our firm. While many firms contracted, and laid off employees, we expanded, added new services and began taking our message nationally. This Persistence has led us to having financial managers in nearly every state and a nationally-syndicated radio show. We have never lost sight of our goal – to assist as many as possible in a more personable way.

I have seen how Persistence can lead to success in life, health and wealth by following a few fundamentals:

1) Understanding and belief in why anyone would want to do business with you.

As much as your company may like you to think otherwise - it's not the company - It is you! People want to develop a relationship with you, because of you and not some product or company. They do business with you because they know you, like you and trust you. No matter where you go, if they believe in you, you will have a relationship for life.

I have spent my career developing those relationships. When we created and ran the investment divisions of some large banks, the CEO's often referred to our investment clients as bank customers. And when our contract ended and we became an independent firm, the banks believed that those investment clients would want to remain with them as they were larger, better known and believed that they offered more products. They underestimated the power of relationships. The clients didn't have a valued relationship with the bank. They had one with me! I knew their personal situations and to me they were not just accounts. Think of others in terms of an extension of your own family. How would you want someone to work with your parents or grandparents? With that approach you will always put their needs above your own. And you will have a relationship for life.

2) Approach your goals one small bite at a time.

When I want to accomplish something, it is not enough for me to just set a goal. I break it into smaller bites that are easily tracked, providing quicker gratification and higher motivation. I take what I want to accomplish and determine the lowest constant which will tell me what my smaller focused goal should be. For example, the goal is to sell $1,000,000 in real estate and an average home sells for $250,000. The goal should be to sell 4 new homes ($1,000,000 / $250,000 = 4). You can then focus efforts on how to sell 4 homes, not selling $1,000,000 of real estate. Regardless of what the ultimate goal is, break it into the smallest amounts possible. It is far easier to focus on a smaller goal than a more daunting, larger goal. This will make efforts far more effective. It is then faster to establish what is working and what is not.

3) Never be the smartest person in the room... that is not enough.

You can never be the master of all things. All aspects of life require you to have a knowledge and understanding of various things. Although you should never stop educating yourself, there comes a point where it makes sense for you to not be the expert in an area. Surround yourself with talent you trust that have the knowledge and can see and believe in your vision. I suggest building a team of experts. I have always been a believer that 1+1 must equal 3 or 4. As we have expanded our firm, we realized that it is more cost effective to bring in new team members to enhance what we are doing. Anyone who joins our team must have the same drive and determination to accomplish our vision. It is not something that is taught. It is something that can become infectious and makes everyone in the organization better.

4) Don't be afraid to step outside your comfort zone.

This can be very difficult and often the easiest to dismiss. I have always gravitated to areas in business I felt most comfortable. Like many, I rarely ventured into uncharted areas. In an effort to expand our business,

Daryl asked me to begin working with him on a series of educational events and a new radio show. My role was to be one of support and to introduce the speaker. The more of these events we did, the larger the role and the amount of speaking he wanted me to do. It wasn't too long before I was on the stage alone. What I did not know at the time was that was his intention all along. Although I always believed that I was uncomfortable in front of large crowds, Daryl could see something that I could not. I have a way of speaking the audience's language. Unknown to me, I was able to connect with the audience in a more personable way. Due to Daryl's foresight, I am going in a direction I never thought would be possible. I am now giving speeches monthly in six cities in multiple states, I have received requests to be on various professional and university boards, and I am now training others in how to give an effective presentation.

5) Always keep an eye on the ends; the means can and will change.

In our industry, like many others, just when we find something that works we usually change it or it is changed for us. Therefore you must maintain the ability to adapt and remain flexible. No matter the task, there will always be something in the way. At some point or another what you are using will no longer be in favor. Be flexible enough to adapt your strategy in order to accomplish the end goal. At various times the investment world has been turned on its head. When that has happened, many in the industry did not survive. In life as in business, you must be able and ready to take advantage of the opportunities that present themselves.

Trends change and what is in today is no longer desired or appropriate tomorrow. For us, if we had relied only on the traditional markets we would have been forced to slow and possibly reduce what we were doing instead of expanding. Each step of the way we added additional products and services. No matter which direction became appropriate for our clients, we have been able to provide them with what they needed. When the market is booming we could offer them an active approach to increase their return. When the market crashed we had already begun taking a more defensive position, and moved in directions that our peers hadn't realized. It is not cliché to make sure that you are not a one-trick pony. There will come a day when what you offer will not be in favor. Make sure that you are ahead of them when that day comes.

6) Maintain an air of confidence even when in doubt.

When asked what one change has made the most impact on my success, I state it was when I began speaking with confidence and direction. Instead of asking my clients what they should do in this crazy economy, I began to explain where they were and what that meant for their family in the simplest of terms, and I advised them on what they could do about it. I have never gone to a doctor and had them ask me what medicine or procedure I thought I should take. Instead, I was told my options and led to the one that was best for me.

A prospective client once came to me in the midst of the 2008 economic downturn to ask if I had any suggestions. She had been trying to reach her broker and when she finally got him on the phone the broker asked what she would like to do. This left her with an uneasy feeling. I took the time to get to know her situation, looking forward to what her long term direction would be and I, very matter of fact, gave her advice. I explained that we are all adults and we should be able to have adult-like discussions. The days of riding out the storm and that "you will be fine" are over. I commended her broker on what they had accomplished so far, but I also explained what steps must be taken to maintain it. She appreciated that I did not just tell her everything would be ok. I let her know that it would not be easy. And that she may not be able to do some of the things she had wanted to do, at least not as soon as she would have liked. This straight forward discussion lead her to move her assets to me and for her to being an advocate of our firm.

As I look back over the years of triumphs and pitfalls, each of these have been fundamental to my success. I am so grateful not just for the triumphs that have happened in my life, but even more so for the pitfalls. At the time they seemed to be terrifying, but looking back they were only speed bumps on the way to success. Without them I may have continued down the path I was going and would never have arrived where I am today. Change one decision, one instance and my life would be different, and not for the better. Those mistakes, trials and tribulations have molded me into who I am. My mother taught me it was OK to make mistakes; it's what you learn and take away from them that help you grow as a person, a parent, and ultimately shape you into who you should be.

As an Investment Advisor, I take a very personal approach with my clients. I am confident that opportunities exist in all economies. For my clients, it's not about stocks, bonds or mutual funds. There is so much more riding on their investments – their retirement income, a down payment or child's education; so I take pride in being an advisor that is as passionate about their wellbeing as they are. I have maintained my persistence and have been able to keep an eye on what my clients need to accomplish – even when they cannot see how it is possible.

About Roger

Roger O. Hudspeth is a Managing Partner of Dominion Investment Group. For over fifteen years, Roger has served his clients financial interests with a more individualistic and objective approach; assisting his clients in the fulfillment of their hopes and dreams. It is this commitment to developing lifetime relationships that drives his pursuit of excellence in service and knowledge within the industry.

Raised in Portsmouth, VA, Roger has lived in South-Hampton Roads all his life. After graduating from Churchland High School, he graduated with a degree in Political Science and Law from Old Dominion University. Roger began his financial career at Mutual Federal Savings and Loan as a teller while paying his way through college. Roger was a founding partner of True North Financial Group. In January 2003, he joined the investment division of Resource Bank and managed their Chesapeake office up to the Fulton Financial acquisition of Resource Bank. From 2005 to 2008, he helped form the investment and wealth management divisions for other community banks and managed their retail advisors until March of 2008.

Recognized in America's Premier Experts® featured in *The Wall Street Journal* as one of the "Financial Trendsetters" along with other leading experts across a wide array of industries, Roger continues to provide a personal approach for his clients.

Roger is a frequent expert on the syndicated radio show, *Getting Your Financial House in Order*. He is an advisor of Project Life Saver International and helped develop its "Secure Their Future," assisting special needs families. Roger is on American Equity's Gold Eagle Program, the Pacific Advisory Council, and Nationwide Circle of Excellence. He also spent time on the Board of Trustees and finance committee of Lyric Opera Virginia. He is a member of Phi Gamma Delta and lives in Chesapeake, VA with his daughter, Lauren.

Contact info. for Roger O. Hudspeth:
Tel: (757) 226-9440
Email: roger@dominv.com